D1594650

The Al Qaeda Connection

The Al Qaeda Connection

Terror in Pakistan's Tribal Areas

IMTIAZ GUL

PENGUIN
VIKING

VIKING
Published by the Penguin Group
Penguin Books India Pvt. Ltd, 11 Community Centre, Panchsheel Park,
New Delhi 110 017, India
Penguin Group (USA) Inc., 375 Hudson Street, New York, New York 10014, USA
Penguin Group (Canada), 90 Eglinton Avenue East, Suite 700, Toronto, Ontario,
M4P 2Y3, Canada (a division of Pearson Penguin Canada Inc.)
Penguin Books Ltd, 80 Strand, London WC2R 0RL, England
Penguin Ireland, 25 St Stephen's Green, Dublin 2, Ireland (a division of Penguin
Books Ltd)
Penguin Group (Australia), 250 Camberwell Road, Camberwell, Victoria 3124,
Australia (a division of Pearson Australia Group Pty Ltd)
Penguin Group (NZ), 67 Apollo Drive, Rosedale, North Shore 0632,
New Zealand (a division of Pearson New Zealand Ltd)
Penguin Group (South Africa) (Pty) Ltd, 24 Sturdee Avenue, Rosebank,
Johannesburg 2196, South Africa

Penguin Books Ltd, Registered Offices: 80 Strand, London WC2R 0RL, England

First published in Viking by Penguin Books India 2009

Copyright © Imtiaz Gul 2009

All rights reserved

10 9 8 7 6 5 4 3 2 1

The views and opinions expressed in this book are the author's own and the facts are
as reported by him which have been verified to the extent possible, and the publishers
are not in any way liable for the same.

ISBN 9780670082926

Typeset in GillSans by Eleven Arts, New Delhi
Printed at Replika Press Pvt. Ltd, Sonipat

This book is sold subject to the condition that it shall not, by way of trade or otherwise,
be lent, resold, hired out, or otherwise circulated without the publisher's prior written
consent in any form of binding or cover other than that in which it is published and
without a similar condition including this condition being imposed on the subsequent
purchaser and without limiting the rights under copyright reserved above, no part of
this publication may be reproduced, stored in or introduced into a retrieval system,
or transmitted in any form or by any means (electronic, mechanical, photocopying,
recording or otherwise), without the prior written permission of both the copyright
owner and the above-mentioned publisher of this book.

To my parents
and Sameena, my extremely caring better half
and my sons, Faraz and Saad

Contents

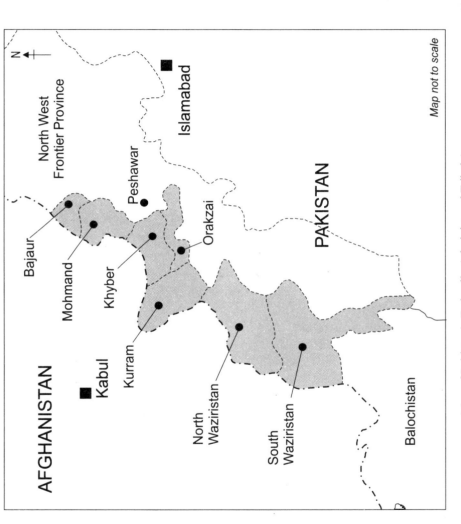

Map of Pakistan's Federally Administered Tribal Areas

Prologue

'Tahir Jan is dead'

In the early hours of 16 March 2004 this news reached the village of Landi Dok in Kaloosha district. Kaloosha, some ten kilometres west of Wana in South Waziristan, is one of Pakistan's tribal agencies. The men of the Zillikhel tribe were outraged. They poured out of their homes and by the afternoon had surrounded the few hundred South Waziristan Scouts who were laying siege to the house of Noorul Islam—one of five wanted Al Qaeda backers. The Scouts believed that Tahir Yuldashev or 'Tahir Jan' as he was known locally, the charismatic leader of the Islamic Movement of Uzbekistan (IMU), was hiding there along with at least twenty-five of his followers.

This area was under the control of five Islamist militants—Nek Mohammad, Noorul Islam, Mohammad Sharif, Maulvi Abbas and Maulvi Abdul Aziz. The Scouts suspected that these men were allowing foreign terrorists from the Afghan Taliban, as well as Arab, Chechen and Uzbek militants, to shelter in the region. The IMU leader and his army, however, reacted to the Scouts' call for surrender by unleashing a massive barrage of gunfire on the Scouts and their commander, Colonel Khalid Usman Khattak.

Over a month later locals in Wana and the nearby village of Sheen Warsak told me that rumours of Tahir's death provoked a strong local reaction and resulted in armed tribesmen surrounding the Scouts as Tahir Jan was a well-known figure in the region, held in high esteem for his chivalry and love for Islam.

Though wounded, Tahir Jan managed to escape in the ensuing frenzy, but what followed was bloody and messy. Crossfire brought down at least eighty Scouts and other soldiers; the army claims it lost forty-six people. Scores of vehicles belonging to the Scouts and to the army were rocketed and torched by the angry tribesmen. Even today, burnt and charred vehicles lie on the road between Azam Warsak and Kaloosha and the walls of the neighbouring apple orchards are riddled with bullet marks. When the army regrouped and moved back in full force, it bulldozed about eighty houses, overrunning decades-old irrigation channels called karez, levelled wells and tube-wells, arrested over 200 locals and, according to one of them, killed scores of people as well. Dozens of Scouts who had been hiding in mosques and houses were rescued by soldiers from Wana, disguised in civilian clothes. Even Colonel Khattak, the Scouts commander, could only come out of a shelter alive after a few tribal maliks (leaders) and reporters who belonged to the local ethnic group and had relatives in the area managed to escort him to safety.

This series of bloody and dramatic events left its trail of grievances and allegations. During the extended operation in the third week of March 2004, locals alleged, the army and the Scouts plundered not only the demolished houses but also those hastily evacuated as their owners feared retribution. 'Several families have lost jewellery, antique utensils and what not,' said Abdullah Khan Wazir, a resident of Kaloosha. He also questioned claims by Major General Shaukat Sultan, head of the Pakistan army's public relations department, Inter-Services Public Relations (ISPR), that several foreigners—non-Pakistani nationals—had been arrested during the operation. '[Since] they did not spare even local young students,' Abdullah Wazir argued, 'if they had killed or captured a foreigner, why didn't they parade him?' A teacher from a local private school described the fate of one of his students—a boy of ten. 'They shot him in the head, breaking the skull in two while looking for Al Qaeda people; they even humiliated our women,' he said, his voice shaking. He described how on 18 April dozens of families from the Kaloosha and Azam Warsak area evacuated ahead of the 20 April deadline that the army had given for the surrender of the five wanted men—Nek Mohammad, Mohammad Sharif, Noorul Islam, Maulvi Abdul Aziz and Maulvi Abbas.

The first four men belong to the Yargulkhel clan of the Zillikhel sub-tribe known for their fierce independence. Mohammad Sharif, also known as Haji Sharif, is the brother of Noorul Islam. The fifth man, Maulvi Abbas, reportedly taking care of his ailing father somewhere in the North West Frontier Province, is from the Kakakhel sub-tribe. Nek Mohammad was killed in a missile fired from a drone in June that year, while most of the others are hiding in North Waziristan.

'Those were really terrible days,' recalled Noor Mohammad, the elder brother of my friend Allah Noor (Noor is a common name in this area—it means enlightenment or spirituality). It was April and we were having dinner in the courtyard of their fortress-like house and he described how foreigners, mostly Arabs and Uzbeks, were frantically moving from one shelter to another to escape arrest. As he spoke, we heard several thuds, constant reminders of artillery fire coming from inside the Military Camp near the airfield. Allah Noor explained that this had become routine ever since March. He recalled a chilling encounter which happened during the March operation. A tall stranger, clearly an Arab, knocked at their door, in the middle of the night. 'It must have been about two o' clock when we heard the knock,' he said. Alarmed, his brothers and he picked up their guns, drew near the door and asked who it was.

'A Muslim brother, a friend of your brother Noor Ahmed,' the stranger replied in broken Pashto. 'I need to spend the night here.'

The Noor family, following a brief consultation, let the stranger in, offered him some food and a bed, without asking any questions. Everybody went to sleep but when they got up the stranger was gone.

'We didn't ask him what he was up to because it is not in our tradition,' Noor Mohammad said.

Two days later, the stranger returned in the middle of the night, again looking for shelter.

He got shelter. I was not told whether the guest paid for the shelter or not.

The Kaloosha Operation: The Catalyst for FATA's Al Qaedaization

The Kaloosha operation, undertaken jointly by the Scouts and the army to flush out foreign militants from the area, concentrated on a fifty-square-kilometre area near Wana, South Waziristan around the villages of Sheen Warsak, Daza Gundai, Kaloosha, Ghwakha and Kari Kot. The operation was a spectacular failure as local and foreign militants ambushed the troops, inflicting heavy losses and taking several civilian officials and army men hostage.

As subsequent events demonstrated, the Kaloosha operation also sowed the seeds of dissent among many locals, created a feeling of hatred for the army and laid the ground for the concentration of militants in Waziristan under the leadership of the Taliban and Al Qaeda. Locals viewed the operation as a betrayal because even while the political administration was negotiating with locals on the fate of foreigners, the army deployed troops in the Angoor Adda, Azam Warsak, Kaloosha and Shakai areas which foreign militants were known to use as transit points to cross into or out of Afghanistan.

'We were stabbed in the back,' said an Ahmedzai Wazir tribal elder. 'We were promised dialogue and development funds, but all the time plans for military operations against our tribes were well under way.'

Affluence Returns to Waziristan

Soon after the defeat of the Taliban and the retreat of Al Qaeda from Afghanistan to Pakistani tribal areas in December 2001, the

Waziristan region in particular was flushed with money. This new-found affluence of dozens of tribal elders also became very obvious.[1] The Afghan administration led by President Hamid Karzai resumed the payment of stipends to these ethnic tribal elders. These stipends were paid by Afghan rulers to select local tribal elders as 'goodwill' gestures which, effectively, prevented them from making trouble in Afghanistan. However, after the April 1978 Saur Revolution by Afghan socialists, Kabul stopped paying them.

The resumption of stipends prevented the Taliban and Al Qaeda from establishing sanctuaries in the tribal areas. But many of the recipients (and this is confirmed by locals) managed to collect money from Kabul, as well as from the Taliban and Al Qaeda.

Khan Malik Bakhan, seventy-one, an influential local leader, was known to be one of Al Qaeda's hosts. When I met him at his home in Wana in April 2004 he firmly refuted my suggestion that he might be sheltering foreigners. 'I have given my commitment to the government not to allow any foreigners here and will honour it,' Bakhan told me, clearly taking offence that I should question his loyalty to the government.

But equally clearly, commitment to the government sometimes did succumb to the temptation of making money off foreign guests. Close friends who accompanied me into Bakhan's compound in Wana told me afterwards that even while the elderly malik bragged about his 'uprightness and loyalty to the authorities', just a ten-foot-high wall separated us from about a dozen Uzbek and Arab militants who had put their trust in him for their stay in Wana.

One of my friends, Malik Inayat Abdullah, a tribal elder and resident of Wana, was, in fact, upset that the area was hosting Uzbeks and not the Arabs. Abdullah's frustration stemmed from the fact that Malik Bakhan reportedly hosted both Arabs and Uzbeks. 'Uzbeks are short of funds but Arabs have plenty of money and they are generous too,' Malik Inayat Abdullah told me. Initially he would not acknowledge the presence of foreign guests at his second home nearby, but later reluctantly admitted, 'We have just one Uzbek as a guest and we are not demanding much [money] of him.' He promised to show me the compound, but later backed out.

These were times when all the big families in and around Wana were hosting at least one foreigner, some of whom had even brought their families along.

Waziristan Sinks in Terror

Another trip to Wana and its northern and southern outskirts in June 2004 confirmed that, despite government claims of 'damage control', the region was gradually turning into a battlefield between the security forces and the militants; led by Arabs and Pakistani Taliban militants, Al Qaeda injected new spirit into its cadres that comprised Chechens and Uzbeks. They became increasingly determined to go down fighting.

The way the army and the paramilitary forces came under attack on and after 9 June in the Shakai region, some forty-five kilometres north of Wana, made the militants' resolve abundantly clear. A Waziri friend recalled that on that day a Pakistan army captain posted at the Torwaam check post in the Shakai hills grew suspicious when he spotted a bearded man carrying a shovel walking up to the post. When the captain demanded to know what he was doing, the man replied he was a local farmer and was looking for rotting wood and bush (used locally as fuel for cooking stoves). The captain, however, told his men to stay alert and spread out around the post. Hours later, a dozen people clad in Scouts' and army commando fatigues conducted a swift surprise attack on the post, killing five and injuring another six.

The man with the shovel was actually an Al Qaeda fighter disguised as a farmer on a pre-attack reconnaissance mission. The Torwaam check post was not the only one attacked: several hours later in the early hours of 10 June, the militants struck at the Narai Ubba militia post some ten kilometres north of Wana, killing nine army personnel.[2]

The incident triggered a massive response from the Pakistan army and the militia, who embarked on retaliatory action that left over seventy alleged Al Qaeda and Taliban militants dead and destroyed at least three hideouts in different parts of the mountainous valleys.

'We saw the bodies of three foreigners brought to the Frontier Constabulary camp in Wana,' said a Waziri friend who gave up a steady job with the Tochi militia, a local police force, because of his ideological differences over the army's hunt for Al Qaeda militants. 'They were wearing commando and Scouts' uniforms. One local, also among the dead, was wearing the same uniform,' he said.

This was a new tactic that the militants adopted from early June onward—to approach the security posts dressed in militia uniform or military fatigues; another was to lob rockets from a distance at the forces. This impelled the Pakistan army and the paramilitary forces to move into the Shakai area in large numbers, pounding suspected hideouts with helicopter gunships and fighter aircraft.

On 10 June 2004 the army captured the Mandatta area, fifty-five kilometres from Wana, in a blitzkrieg operation. To their surprise they discovered a massive cave under the tree-covered mountains. It was a big living complex inhabited by Arabs, Europeans, Uzbeks and Chechens 'speaking all languages . . . from different countries,' a local, Abdullah Wazir, a former member of Al Qaeda told me, while sipping tea in a mud fort at the Kaloosha village. He had trained with them for about a week and said some Indian and British Muslims were also among the trainees.

The presence of the cave complex high in the mountains exemplified the engineering skills of Al Qaeda operatives. They had used empty rocket shells as ventilation pipes which pierced the thick rock of the big cave, allowing fresh air to come in. The army recovered small mobile welding machines, apparently used for joining the rocket hulls to make long ventilation pipes. The stocky Waziri added that to treat their wounded, '[Al Qaeda] used an ointment that instantly numbed the affected body part to help the person reach the sanctuary in time for treatment.' One Al Qaeda fighter who survived the Mandatta military operation told this former Al Qaeda fighter at the Wana Hospital that the area also served as the training camp for Al Qaeda fighters.

Abdullah recalled that his injured friend was admitted to the hospital only after Abdullah introduced him as a Waziri tribesman. 'The paramilitary doctors on duty there were not sure whether to attend to my friend. They asked how and where he had received the bullet wounds. I told them my friend was caught in the crossfire between the military and the militants during the Mandatta operation. Once they heard this, the doctors immediately treated his wounds,' Adbullah Wazir told me during an extended chat over dinner.

Al Qaeda chose the Shakai and Mandatta region because its rough and remote terrain offered the perfect environment to shelter as well as train its cadres. 'They gave us sixty- to seventy-kilo sandbags to carry as we climbed up and down the mountains,' a Kalashnikov-totting militant told me in Azam Warsak. The objective was to train fighters in survival tactics and for the retrieval of wounded companions.

During the course of the discussion, Abdullah Noor promised to take me to his home in the Sheen Warsak hamlet some day. Though I persisted for several days, Abdullah dithered.

'You have a guest at home, I presume,' I eventually asked him point blank.

Surprised by the direct question, Abdullah denied it.

'But your reluctance in taking me home indicates something fishy,' I said, smiling to take the sting away from my words.

Abdullah was clearly uncomfortable with this. He assured me, 'There is no one at my place. Your suspicion is misplaced.' Sensing his discomfort, I stopped smiling and we changed the subject as we ate our raisin rice and yogurt, but my conviction that several

Ahmedzai Waziris were hosting 'nice paying guests' at that time remained unshaken. Not surprisingly, another friend who had made a similar promise for a meeting with his guests also backed out at the last minute, citing 'family reasons'.

During those months of April and May, Wana residents— including maliks, shopkeepers and local Taliban—treated the government claim to have killed dozens of foreigners with derision. 'In Saudi Arabia, the government killed one terrorist and paraded his body before the media, but here all we have seen are just a few dead bodies,' an influential local malik, Abdul Jalil, said scornfully. 'Where are those arrested foreigners that the government is chest-thumping about?' he asked.

Militants Turn 'Pakistan into Kashmir'

'Pakistan created the Kashmir insurgency for India, we will turn South Waziristan into Kashmir for Pakistan,' said a local Al Qaeda militant, who identified himself as a follower of Nek Mohammad and was staying in Ghwakha, a small village on the periphery of Wana. We will avenge Nek Mohammad's brutal murder, said another. They had all congregated to condole the killing on 9 June of Nek Mohammad in a drone attack. Also sitting by them was Haji Mohammad Omar, Nek Mohammad's successor and brother of Noorul Islam and Haji Sharif. It was a sombre occasion. The moment the condolence prayers for Nek Mohammad's departed soul were over, his uncle said firmly, 'Thank you gentlemen, you may leave now.' We found out later the gathering was meant to nominate Omar to succeed Nek Mohammad, and they did not want strangers around. As we drove out of the isolated, walled compound—surrounded by the demolished houses of many alleged Al Qaeda supporters—we came across several gun-totting Pakistani Taliban. They warned us threateningly to shut down the camera. They told us that it is still a no-go area for non-locals. This was the very place where the Uzbek leader Tahir Yuldashev had been cornered in mid March.

A series of meetings between the authorities and elders of the Ahmedzai Wazir tribes following Yuldashev's escape led to the demolition of the houses of Noorul Islam, Mohammad Sharif, Maulvi Abdul Aziz and Maulvi Abbas.

Under the existing laws, the political agent can order the demolition or confiscation of a person's property or banish that person from the area if found guilty of a crime (see Appendix 1). The authorities invoked that law to punish these men for sheltering Yuldashev and killing scores of paramilitary soldiers.

We encountered similar situations in Azam Warsak and on the way to Bagar, where the army had recently conducted operations against terrorists. Anti-army sentiment was quite strong in the area, and again we were asked to leave as soon as possible.

In various encounters with locals and purported Al Qaeda activists at different locations, almost everyone denied having any links whatsoever with the radicals nor would they admit to have hosted foreigners. Surprisingly, though, most of them were open in their defence of Al Qaeda and the Taliban. 'If the rulers bring upon their own Muslim people the misery that the Israelis and Americans have imposed on innocent Palestinians and Iraqis, no God-fearing Muslim would hesitate in picking up the gun,' said the Waziri tribesman Abdullah Noor Wazir.

Another man from the Shakai area, who introduced himself as Commander Zarar Khan, minced no words in the praise of his comrades: 'Al Qaeda and Taliban are one—their mission is common and that is to put down the Americans and their allies, be it Musharraf or anybody else.' Khan claimed he had been part of the Shakai operation against the army in early June.

Ameer Rehman, an educated lower-middle-class political activist and member of the Pasthoon nationalist Awami National Party (ANP), had this to say when asked about foreigners the government believes are hiding in the area: 'I have never seen foreigners here, some may be there. But how can you connect them with every act of violence without any proof?' He did, however, blame the wave of militant Islamization of the region on what he called the Mulla, Military and Malik Alliance. This clique, an alliance of the clergy, the army and the landowners, is determined to maintain the status quo, that is, the century-old administration system for the tribal areas that was devised by the British. And on the other hand, Rehman believes the clique had strongly endorsed the support given to the Afghan mujahideen and subsequently to the Taliban.

Effectively, almost everybody in Waziristan lived in a state of denial until it dawned on them within a couple of years of the March 2004 Kaloosha operation that the short-term gains from hosting 'foreign guests' had brought upon them prolonged misery; in other words, their hospitality, tolerance and denial of foreigners' presence permitted Al Qaeda to organize and consolidate itself in the region. Because of this, the entire region fell under the unprecedented electronic surveillance of American satellites and the network of informers that the FBI unleashed in the entire region.

The economic blockade that the authorities imposed in Wana on 2 May 2004 to punish its residents for helping militants were crippling, yet of little consequence as locals failed to eject foreigners. Only non-locals—people from surrounding areas— could bring in or take out the agricultural produce and the daily commodities, which meant that most of the vegetables and fruits were rotting as the Wana bazaar comprising at least 5600 shops remained shuttered through 2004 to the turbulent summer of 2005. Ripe and rotting apples and apricots hung from the trees in the orchards. The farmers did not bother to pluck them as they knew there were no buyers.

Clearly, for many residents of the region there were alternative sources of livelihood. So despite the outcry over the blockade, a good number of locals did not incur financial losses, and remained undeterred as far as allowing foreigners to live in their homes and under their protection was concerned. The ethic of the tribe is that, come what may, Waziris surrender their guests only over their dead bodies. This was the sense one got from conversations with locals, though nobody actually admitted to hosting 'guests'.

Based on what I saw and heard during my visits to the region, it was not difficult to draw certain conclusions: the situation then provided ample evidence and multiple reasons to presume that the hide-and-seek between the Al Qaeda militants and the security forces would end very soon. Although the majority of Ahmedzai Wazir and Mehsud tribesmen as well as others in Bajaur and Mohmand agencies deny the presence of foreign Al Qaeda cadres, privately they relish the resistance that the Arab, Chechen, Uzbek and Uigur Muslims and foreign-origin Americans are putting up. Radical Muslims, both local and foreign, as well as their hosts are simply oblivious to threats and persuasion.

Until 2006, the year the militants came out in the open, ambushing army convoys, rocketing military and government installations and abducting as well as executing government civilian and army personnel, most people in the Federally Administered Tribal Areas (FATA) were convinced that the Pakistani government was a partner in their oppression which was aimed at forcing them to betray the Al Qaeda and Taliban militants in their region. Standing up to army oppression seemed to be the only option to them. Even if they only bluffed about turning 'Waziristan into Kashmir for Pakistan', they appeared ready to lay down their lives for the cause—social norms, religious dogmas and financial benefits had all combined to nudge FATA tribesmen into taking a position against the state's authority. Beyond doubt, they also gained financially from the presence of foreign militants. Equally significant was the climate of fear created by the militants, who spared no one they considered close to the government or to the United States. Betrayal was rewarded with physical elimination. Government servants—both civilian and military—were scoffed at and considered American agents, while political opponents were looked upon as infidels. This was the attitude which resulted in thousands of target killings.

Target Killings: The Al Qaeda Way?

'We don't know who Al Qaeda is, we only know Afghan refugees. That is it.' (Statement by locals in the Shakai valley in South Waziristan)

A flying visit to the sprawling Shakai valley north of Wana in May 2005 confirmed the conclusions I had drawn during earlier visits to Waziristan. Less than a year ago, the area was infested with foreign and local militants, engaging the army and the paramilitary troops in fierce battles from their hideouts in the hills and from inside the village houses. Now the area was open and buzzing with life, a couple of schools had reopened and several road-construction and water-well projects were under way.

The army, operating in a socially hostile environment, was running medical camps to save people an arduous journey through rough, mountainous terrain to the Wana hospital.

All this looked impressive if weighed against the fact that until March 2004 the army's presence even in the South Waziristan headquarters, Wana, was minimal; but by June, the military and the Scouts had extended their reach to strategic landmarks and hilltops.

As it turned out, it was not as normal as it looked. Our meetings with Ahmedzai Wazir tribesmen in the heart of Shakai betrayed different realities underlying the expressions of contentment over the army-led development work that was taking place. People at large *sounded* happy that the school enrolment had gone up, that water supply schemes were materializing and that roads were coming up. The locals were also apparently pleased that the situation was peaceful—the army had incurred more than 250 casualties in fifty-one minor and major operations which had resulted in the killing of 306 militants, including over a hundred alleged foreigners. Many of those dubbed as foreign militants were local tribesmen.

'We have eliminated the miscreants [the Pakistan army's term for Al Qaeda and Taliban militants] from the area,' Major General Niaz Mohammad Khattak said triumphantly while addressing elders drawn from areas around Shakai. 'Ask the people; they will tell you how they lived in fear until our arrival here,' Khattak bragged.

Away from gatherings where officials were bragging about their successes, the atmosphere was altogether different; I interviewed several people in two different locations to elicit their views on the situation. 'It is very good now, we are very happy,' they assured me, echoing what the army officials and political leaders had just told us.

But why and how was it bad, I asked.

'We didn't know it was bad,' responded an elderly Wazir.

But we are told there were Al Qaeda people here, I quipped.

'We don't know who Al Qaeda is, we only know Afghan refugees whom the government had itself allowed into these areas,' said one of them.

'By the way, how would you tell someone from Al Qaeda or Taliban apart from a local—they all look like us, they are all refugees,' said another orange-turbanned elderly Wazir. Another was equally voluble in refuting my suggestion that the militants had held them hostage.

'No, we have been free, and moving around. All we need is peace, medical facilities, water and roads,' said Bazim Khan Wazir.

But weren't there any mujahideen and Taliban here? 'No we don't know, we never heard of these people, nor did we see them,' came the response from a well-built young man with long locks, a big moustache and a white cap.

But the gruesome murder the next day of the former legislator and tribal chief Malik Faridullah Khan, near Jandola, the border between South Waziristan and the town of Tank, appeared to be a direct reaction to the chest-thumping of General Khattak and Faridullah Khan. During a meeting with elders, both had boasted of their 'strength which enabled them to break the militant hold over Shakai'. Khan had just crossed the border from the Jandola check post, when unknown armed assailants rained Kalashnikov fire on him, killing him on the spot. It was several hours before his blood-soaked body was discovered.

In fact, Faridullah Khan had been instrumental in facilitating the army's entry into Shakai. In the presence of visiting journalists, his speech in the national language, Urdu, to his tribesmen sounded odd because Khan was a Pashtoon from the area who would have more naturally spoken to his fellow tribesmen in their common tongue. General Niaz Khattak acted more intelligently and delivered his speech in his native Pashto language. Khan's appearance also perhaps annoyed many locals. He was distinctly attired differently from the rest of the tribesmen. Most of his words thus fell on deaf ears.

'Everything is fine,' Khan told me after his speech. 'We hope things will improve further,' he said, unaware that it was his last hurrah in the long-drawn-out battle against militants, who do not forgive those who betray them or hurt their interests.

A day later locals stumbled upon two bodies in the Sheenpond mountain range around twenty kilometres north of the town of Mirali in North Waziristan. A note in Urdu was placed beside the bodies of Jalat Khan and Fazal Noor, saying the two were killed for spying for the US and warning other US agents of the same fate. Jalat Khan from the Janikhel Wazir sub-tribe of Bakkakhels was said to be leader of a criminal gang.

If locals are to be believed, more than 300 alleged informers had been eliminated this way since March 2004, when the army and the militia met with unexpectedly strong resistance from the Uzbek leader Tahir Yuldashev and the locals who harboured him in Sheen Warsak outside Wana.

Locals believe that all these people, both locals and foreigners, were killed by Al Qaeda and the Taliban in retaliation for the fast depleting safe havens afforded these militants in the North and South Waziristan agencies. It has been a double-edged sword for the militants. On the one hand, for security reasons, they became extremely careful about selecting shelter; on the other hand, local tribesmen also became increasingly cautious in offering them accommodation for fear of inviting missiles fired from CIA-operated drones.

The cold-blooded murders of Faridullah Khan and several others in North Waziristan probably also explained the 'ignorance' that the tribals in Shakai expressed about Al Qaeda and the Taliban. The common people fear revenge killings and are not prepared to risk their lives by admitting to the presence of the militants in their ranks, let alone acknowledge publicly the harassment and fear the

Al Qaeda and Taliban militants put them through until the army moved into the area in June 2004.

Journalists who visited an emerging Taliban leader, Hakeemullah Mehsud, in late November 2008 in the mountains of the Orakzai agency, also brought back several tales of such harassment and high-handedness. 'We were put up with various local people for the night. They served us plain bread and tea in the morning, with helplessness writ large on their faces,' one of the journalists based in Peshawar told me. 'People in these areas stuff you with food but in our case, the treatment was shabby. This made it quite clear that people out there were living both in fear as well as poverty, and hence the cold-shoulder they gave us,' the journalist said, requesting his name not be published.

The government would like the world to believe that all the people of FATA require are peace and basic amenities—water, roads and medical facilities. But it did not realize it was dealing with ultra-conservative and secretive tribesmen with an overwhelmingly strong sense of pride and honour. Therefore the authorities as well as the army were self-congratulatory when they should have been self-effacing and supportive of a culture where even a single word can cause lifelong offence.

Taliban and Al Qaeda: On the Run but Omnipresent

Though on the run, the militants changed their response to the army operation by carrying out target killings, that is, eliminating government employees and security personnel, thus triggering a wave of fear among tribesmen as well as government employees. 'Anyone opposing us openly must face consequences' was the loud and clear militant message.

The strategy yielded remarkable results: hardly anyone would openly speak up against Al Qaeda or the Taliban. 'A single word against the militants or in support of the government can result in a person's death,' said one local elder.

Against this backdrop, the authorities resorted to putting their point across to the local people through pamphlets dropped from military helicopters in different parts of South Waziristan in June 2006. These pamphlets contained critical questions about the 'designs of the foreign militants' hiding in South Waziristan. Titled 'Is This the Reward for Hospitality?', the pamphlets provided details of an incident on 1 October 2005 in which four school boys—Shah Hussain, Ahmad and two brothers, Nizamuddin and Khan Mohammad—from the Shamankhel Mahsud tribe were killed by a toy-bomb planted by foreign militants at Bangashwala on the Jandola–Wana road.

The pamphlet, in Urdu and Pashto, pointed out that after the boys' funerals the Shamankhel tribesmen killed one of the suspected militants, an Uzbek, arrested his Tajik accomplice, Khalid, and chased away a third. It said this was proof of the presence of foreign terrorists in South Waziristan. 'Is it jihad or return for your hospitality?' asked the pamphlet, published by 'A well-wisher of Pakistan Army'. The pamphlet praised the tribesmen for taking on the foreign terrorists, expressed support for the military operations in the area, and declared that terrorists who target children should be denied sanctuary and forced to leave the area.

But such endeavours proved futile to contain the cancer from spreading to other areas. By 2008 militants—whoever they are— had eliminated over a thousand civilian and military officials across all the tribal agencies, including alleged intelligence operatives and those whom they dubbed 'US spies'. More than 400 maliks also lost their lives because the militants viewed them as 'government collaborators', and by December they were knocking at the doors of Peshawar, the provincial capital, which is surrounded on three sides by the tribal areas.

Why Pakistan's Tribal
Areas Fell to Al Qaeda

Pakistan's history since its formation in 1947 has not been a
happy one. I do not believe that extremism and terrorism are
part of our DNA. When I look back down the years, I believe the
turning point was in the mid 1970s when the then civilian
government of Zulfiqar Ali Bhutto decided to recruit dissident
Afghans as assets to deploy against a new government in Kabul
that was leaning alarmingly towards the godless Soviet Union. It
was then that Pakistan's semi-autonomous tribal areas bordering
Afghanistan became the springboard and the training ground for
the Afghan dissidents.

A quarter century later, in 2001, the 9/11 terror attacks in
the United States were followed by Operation Enduring Freedom
in Afghanistan. The subsequent vicious and bloody military
campaign in Pakistan's tribal border regions known as the
Federally Administered Tribal Areas (FATA) brought the region,
particularly the Waziristan, Mohmand and Bajaur agencies, to
international attention.

Until the launch in the early 1980s of the anti-Soviet Russian
jihad, sponsored by America's Central Intelligence Agency (CIA)
and the Saudi Arabian General Intelligence Directorate (GID),
and executed by Pakistan's powerful Inter-Services Intelligence
(ISI) agency, most of the tribal lands—governed by the Frontier
Crimes Regulation (FCR), a legacy of British colonial rule—

had largely been ignored, under-funded and devoid of basic infrastructure; therefore the writ of the government in Islamabad was both minimal and rather compromised. This combination of factors offered a fertile environment for many illegal activities— drugs, gun-running, smuggling goods imported under the Afghan Transit Trade Agreement via Karachi port on the Arabian Sea, as well as space for criminal gangs to shelter fugitives from Pakistani law. Government functionaries benefited, doing little or nothing to stop them. The federal government too turned a blind eye to these activities in return for loyalty from the tribesmen, whom the military establishment considered the first line of defence on the western border.

Soviet Invasion of Afghanistan

Soon after the Soviet army invaded and occupied Afghanistan on Christmas Eve 1979, the United States enthusiastically adopted the idea that the Russian presence could be thwarted with the help of Afghan opposition forces, which the Pakistani establishment had groomed as proxies since the mid 1970s. They included Gulbudin Hekmetyar, Maulvi Yunus Khalis, Professor Burhanuddin Rabbani, Professor Abdurrab Rasool Sayyaf, Nabi Mohammedi, Sibghatullah Mujadeddi and scores of others.

Major General Naseerullah Babar was then the inspector general of the Frontier Corps (FC) in the North West Frontier Province (NWFP) capital of Peshawar (he was later Pakistan's interior minister under Benazir Bhutto from 1993 to 1996). Babar initiated a process that was to influence more than two decades of the country's Afghan policy. The FC is stationed in the NWFP and Balochistan province and is under the interior ministry, not the army. Its primary task is to help local law enforcement agencies maintain law and order when called upon to do so. Border patrol and anti-smuggling operations are also delegated to the FC.

Babar had earlier tasked Brigadier Aslam Bodla and Aftab Sherpao (the latter was then a captain in the Pakistan army—he subsequently became NWFP chief minister twice and was Pakistan's home minister between October 2002 and November 2007), and a few Pashtoon police officers including Syed Fida Younus to enlist Afghans to aid Pakistan's push into Afghanistan.

By October 1973 the chosen Afghans started visiting Pakistan regularly for briefings. Most were put on the payroll of the Frontier Constabulary, the police force deployed in the Frontier Regions (FR) situated between FATA and the southern districts of the NWFP. In early 1974 Pakistan's embassy in Kabul received a list of 1331 Afghan nationals and their families from a colonel with the Inter-Services Intelligence, with instructions for monthly payments to be made to the Afghans. The document, of course, was coded for fear of interception. I was given this information by a former official who had served at the embassy for several years.

Younger Afghans in the group, including Hekmetyar, were then selected for commando training at Cherat, a mountainous area some eighty kilometres south-east of Peshawar where the Pakistan army's Special Services' Group (SSG) commandos train. These Afghans later formed their own mujahideen groups. They not only received training in guerrilla warfare, but also ample funds to mould public opinion in favour of Pakistan and against the pro-Moscow parties. Through the FC, Pakistan began earmarking small arms and modest funds for its proxies in Afghanistan—less than USD 200,000. Everything went through the FC, where Babar created an inspection team to look after its 'boys'. Typewriters, duplicating machines and stationery were provided to develop, print and distribute propaganda material inside Afghanistan.

At that time almost the entire Afghan group formed the Hezb-e-Islami, but from 1977 onward the Pakistan army chief General Zia ul-Haq divided them. During one of our meetings Babar told me he never fathomed why Zia did this.

Well before the Russians moved into Afghanistan in December 1979, Babar claimed he became the bridge between Pakistan's 'boys' and the Americans. The first contact came about in May 1978 when Babar sent Rabbani and Hekmetyar to American diplomats in Islamabad for an evaluation. 'They [Americans] asked for my assessment of these people, whom I would refer to in my phone conversations with the American diplomats [by the code names of] "mason" or "carpenter" being on his way to Islamabad.'

At that time, General Zia ul-Haq was still lukewarm to the idea of using Afghan protégés and the ISI was not yet involved in the anti-Soviet operation, which meant Pakistani financing which had begun with Bhutto was already on the wane. General Zia finally woke up when, following the Saur Revolution of April 1978, the Soviets installed a pro-Moscow government in Kabul in December 1979. General Zia eventually agreed to turn Pakistan into a conduit for funds and arms from the CIA and GID.

The Zia Years: The Rise of Religious Right

During General Zia's repressive rule, in the first three years in particular, his so-called Islamization drive gained currency and acquired legitimacy. Shortly before his ouster Bhutto had banned alcohol and declared Friday a public holiday, but General Zia, who combined religious zeal with political shrewdness, took the Islamization to new levels with military officers and civilian bureaucrats falling over one another to prove their Islamic credentials to the dictator.

The noted US author Stephen Cohen wrote in his comprehensive study of the Pakistan army, *The Idea of Pakistan*[1]: 'For Zia, a more truly Islamic Pakistan would have the moral qualities necessary to stand up to India, since its scientists, generals, and politicians would be strengthened, not weakened, by their faith. Zia also cynically used Islamic groups internally against leftist opponents, especially the PPP, though he was not above betraying them when he felt the alliance had outlived its usefulness.'

Inspired by the CIA, the University of Nebraska designed an Islamized curriculum for Afghan students. General Zia also ordered a drastic review of the curriculum at home, with a special emphasis on the virtues of the Islamic way of living which would, he had hoped, throw up a new Islamized generation. It was under General Zia that Pakistan became the battleground for the Saudi-Iranian proxy war—both countries poured in millions of dollars to sponsor parties that propagated their respective religious ideologies. An unchecked growth in seminaries of various schools of thought and official donations to thousands of these 'nurseries of jihadists' also became common under General Zia, who had hoped to pitch the religious parties and their affiliated seminaries against liberal political forces. The funding of religious seminaries and financial handouts to 'like-minded clerics' all over the country thrived during the Zia years, largely to the detriment of the state educational system which began its decline then, a slide which continues to this day.

ISI during the Afghan Jihad: Combining Intelligence and Operations

Pakistan's border regions became the staging posts for the jihad because of their proximity to the eastern and south-eastern Afghan provinces of Paktika, Paktia, Nangarhar, Kunar, Zabul and Kandahar. These lawless regions served as transit posts for both weapons and Islamist zealots pouring in from all over the world to join the anti-Russian jihad inside Afghanistan. They also provided the training ground and storage compounds for the ammunition the CIA was funnelling to the 'mujahideen', a term that became synonymous with the US-led challenge to the Russian invasion. Besides dozens of training camps located in the FATA regions and stretching to Balochistan in Pakistan's south-west where ISI instructors trained Afghan mujahideen, hundreds of seminaries also mushroomed in FATA, which catered not only to the tens of thousands of Afghan refugees but also served as indoctrination centres for the recruits in the war against communist forces next door.

This new role offered Pakistan an opportunity to realize its long-cherished dream of 'securing strategic depth in Afghanistan through a friendly and pliant government in Kabul'. This at least was the premise when General Zia decided to co-opt his security and intelligence apparatus into the CIA-funded war. It was a godsend to the establishment to find new friends and consolidate old alliances with Hekmetyar and others. Once victorious, it was hoped these proxies would look after the interests of Pakistan and provide a safe and secure western border thereby allowing the military to concentrate on the border with India.

Paul Todd and Jonathan Bloch, writing in *Global Intelligence: The World's Secret Services Today*, noted that the CIA funnelled almost six billion dollars, while Saudi Arabia matched the US in arms funding for the Afghan jihad, providing some five billion dollars by 1992.[2] 'A network of ISI-run training camps in both Pakistan and in Afghanistan itself had instructed over 35,000 foreign Mujahidin from throughout the Islamic world by early 1990s, a significant proportion from Saudi Arabia. They were to continue their activities, often taking would-be jihadis directly from Pakistan's 20,000 Saudi-financed madrassas. In 1989 the Makhtab al-Khidmat or services centre, the Peshawar-based Saudi-ISI headquarters coordinating the Afghan Jihad, was supplanted by a more clandestine body, the military base of Al Qaida. In some estimates, over 100,000 Islamist radicals were to emerge out of the Afghan conflict to form a loose, globally connected network.'

After 1992, Todd and Bloch said, the CIA left the scene but the ISI, which had grown tenfold to almost 20,000 operatives in the intervening years, continued to expand, 'rising to an estimated 40,000 and a $1 billion annual budget by the mid 1990s'.

Viewed against Pakistan's financial resources and its gross national product (GNP) in the 1990s, the figures on the ISI budget are probably extremely inflated, yet other facts do carry credence. The anti-Soviet jihad had helped the ISI grow into a monolithic organization whose involvement in Afghanistan centred on 'securing strategic depth in that country'.

The engagement also brought monetary affluence and material resources—ammunition and arms appropriate for guerrilla warfare—to the ISI and by extension to the army. The involvement in the Afghan jihad had in fact bestowed a double duty on the ISI:

intelligence and operations. This was bound to have consequences for domestic politics. Even after General Zia's death in an air crash in August 1988, the army continued to use the ISI infrastructure to influence and nudge government policies in the direction the army high command deemed best. It pitched right-wing politicians and religio-political parties as a counterweight to mainstream parties such as the Pakistan Peoples Party (PPP) of former premier Benazir Bhutto to pursue its India and Afghan policies.

This was not the first time the army relied on Islamic groups for its narrow political purposes. During the Bengali separatist movement in then East Pakistan (now Bangladesh) in 1970–71 the Pakistan army co-opted Jamaate Islami (JI) cadres in its crackdown against justice-seeking Bengali intellectuals, politicians and other supporters of the Bangladesh movement. With this began the sad and ill-fated trend of using Islamist parties to neutralize or eliminate political opponents, ethnic separatist leaders and those religio-political groups and persons considered to be against the army's scheme of things.

General Zia ul-Haq, having ousted Zulfiqar Ali Bhutto in a July 1977 coup, took the policy even further. He not only openly praised groups like the JI, but also sought their help in running the government. He also made sure that the JI and its Afghan associates, Hekmetyar's Hezb-e-Islami in particular, received adequate supplies of arms and money for their jihad against the Soviet forces. In Peshawar, the provincial capital, the ISI set up cells to cultivate Arab and African volunteers for the jihad.

These ties deepened in the late 1980s, when the ISI began training Kashmiri dissidents, many of whom had fled to Pakistan after the controversial Kashmir election of 1989, first under the flag of the Jammu and Kashmir Liberation Front (JKLF) and then under the Hezbul Mujahideen (who subscribed to the JI school of thought). The ISI went on to support smaller emerging groups and even helped various Pakistani based groups, such as Lashkar-e-Taiba (LeT) and Harkatul Ansar (later Harkatul Mujahideen), to operate in Kashmir.

The ISI-led military establishment pursued a path that turned out to be fraught with danger and the current situation in Pakistan is perhaps the blowback that many had feared would ensue from the support extended to the Afghan mujahideen, Kashmiri militants and the Afghan and Pakistani Taliban. Public opinion on the consequences of the establishment's policies on these struggles had been sharply divided, but by January 2009 the divisions had narrowed because of the sharp deterioration in the security situation. By early 2009 a consensus had emerged within Pakistan that the establishment's attempt to extend its influence deep into Afghanistan had backfired, but the establishment remained wedded to 'the doctrine of strategic depth'.

However, General Ashfaq Pervez Kayani, who became the chief of army staff after General Musharraf gave up the post in late November 2008, insists the issue of 'strategic depth in Afghanistan' has been universally misunderstood. During a long discussion on the FATA militancy at his Rawalpindi residence on 16 January 2009, General Kayani claimed the notion is a 'peaceful, stable and friendly Afghanistan—nothing less, nothing more. We cannot wish for Afghanistan what we don't for Pakistan.' Kayani said this in an attempt to reject allegations, largely coming from Washington, London and Kabul, that the Pakistani establishment had always dreamed of colonizing Afghanistan. 'That is not possible, nor are we oblivious to Afghan history, which tells us that this nation has never accepted foreign rule,' said Kayani, recalling the bloody nose the Russians got in Afghanistan and the resistance the US–NATO-led coalition is currently facing there.

Back in the 1980s, Osama bin Laden, America's most-wanted terrorist allegedly responsible for the current international wave of anti-American Islamist extremism, had also found sanctuaries on the fringes of Miranshah in North Waziristan, the tribal agency that borders the eastern Afghan province of Paktia. When the Soviets pulled out of Afghanistan in February 1989, the Americans also turned their back on the region. The tribal lands fell off their radar, but religious groups, business cartels and the drugs mafia continued their business as usual. This also meant little government attention was focused on the legacy of jihad and this indifference has come to haunt Pakistan as Al Qaeda-inspired insurgency sweeps through the rugged tribal territories and areas adjacent to them.

9/11

The spotlight fell on these territories again in late 2001 when, in the aftermath of the deadly 9/11 attacks on the World Trade Center, the United States cobbled together an international coalition and unleashed the questionable 'Global War on Terror'. Operation Enduring Freedom began on 7 October 2001 and within weeks swept the hosts of bin Laden, the Taliban, from power leaving thousands of Al Qaeda fighters, mostly Arabs, Africans, Uzbeks and Chinese Uigurs, no choice but to retreat into Pakistan's tribal areas.

By December that year, Pakistan had begun deploying army units in the remote mountainous region of Tirah, which overlooks Afghanistan's Tora Bora mountains, as well as in the Waziristan and Mohmand region. Lieutenant General Ali Jan Orakzai, the then corps commander responsible for the entire FATA region, told us during a briefing at his Peshawar headquarters in June 2003 that most of the border had been secured through the deployment of thousands of troops, even in areas which were hitherto considered virtual no-go pockets due to their remoteness and inhospitable nature. In the face of reports from American military and intelligence officials and allegations from the Kabul administration that thousands of foreign fighters were holed up in Waziristan, General Orakzai as well as Pakistani security officials played down these reports—essentially a state of denial.

The Kaloosha operation in March 2004—when security forces tried to evict Tahir Yuldashev from a big compound near Wana— was a turning point. Within hours of the siege, dozens of Frontier Corps soldiers found themselves trapped by IMU fighters and hundreds of Ahmedzai Waziri tribesmen. The siege ended in a bloodbath for the FC, which according to some counts lost up to 200 people, but it also turned the tide on Al Qaeda's hosts in South Waziristan. Unleashing a new cat and mouse game, the authorities and the military began forcefully asking for eviction of foreign militants. The locals—still caught between personal gains and denial of the presence of foreigners—largely remained intransigent; scores of meetings between officials and tribesmen and intra-tribal consultations—jirga—yielded little result.

Even an economic blockade of the Wana valley failed to convince or force locals to give up their foreign guests, who had meanwhile begun planning and training for attacks inside Afghanistan. It invited more US pressure—do more, so read the advice—and a major increase in the Pakistan army presence along the border with Afghanistan, taking the deployment to almost 120,000 by 2006, for which the Pentagon provided an average of 80 million dollars a month from Coalition Support Funds (CSF). These numbers remained almost unchanged until Lashkar-e-Taiba terrorists struck in Mumbai on 26 November 2008, triggering a new phase of India–Pakistan tension. The Pakistan army, responding to hostile rhetoric from the Indian leadership, moved a couple of thousands of regular troops to the eastern border. Following the ban the then President Musharraf had imposed on LeT and five other sectarian extremist groups, the LeT too had moved a number of its camps to FATA, mostly in the Waziristan and Mohmand agencies, where they lived close to the compounds of the Arab Al Qaeda, whose ideological leanings—the Sunni wahabist version of Islam—they shared.

The Mumbai carnage in November 2008 triggered yet another vicious and acrimonious exchange between India and Pakistan. Explosive rhetoric, allegations and counter-allegations—with the LeT and the ISI at the centre of the storm—flew across the border, causing world capitals like Washington and London to intervene. Indian rancour was directed at the ISI. Once the United Nations proscribed the Jamatud Dawa—the successor to LeT in Pakistan—in December, Islamabad also followed suit. Some Indian ministers and politicians, nevertheless, kept the heat up by asking Pakistan to expeditiously put people responsible for the Mumbai attacks on trial.

Waziristan: A Haven for Al Qaeda

After their retreat from Afghanistan, the majority of foreigners had settled down in the North and South Waziristan and Bajaur regions, where networks operated by Afghan war veterans Jalaluddin Haqqani and Gulbudin Hekmetyar became instrumental in securing shelter for bin Laden's surviving fighters. Haqqani and Hekmetyar also acted as the umbrella group for the reorganization of Al Qaeda, which co-opted local leaders like Abdullah Mehsud and Baitullah Mehsud, both of whom had been captured during Operation Enduring Freedom in Afghanistan, kept at the notorious Guantanamo Bay Camp X-Ray, and released after a couple of years.

The *Washington Times* reported on 16 January 2009 on the concentration of Al Qaeda stalwarts in Waziristan areas. Those it named included Abu Khabab al-Masri (Al Qaeda's most seasoned explosives expert and trainer, responsible for attempts to obtain chemical and biological weapons) and Usama al-Kini (accused of planning Islamabad's Marriott Hotel bombing and killed in a drone-fired missile strike on 1 January 2009).

Once safely ensconced, Al Qaeda top brass began reorganizing its cadres with the help of the Haqqani clan and Hekmetyar's Hezb-e-Islami. They hooked up with local Taliban, playing on the sympathies the coalition's onslaught had created for the Afghan Taliban and their one-eyed leader Mulla Omar.

The presence of the Al Qaeda hierarchy including Dr Ayman al-Zawahiri, bin Laden's deputy, provided the requisite inspiration to the ultra-conservative and religious tribesmen of Waziristan to join the ranks of Pakistani Taliban—which came to be known locally as Al Qaeda. The Arabs in particular brought with them two gifts for the FATA residents: money, which they showered on people they trusted would host them despite warnings by officials, and ideas of Muslim fraternity and Islamic ideology, which appealed to the emotional tribesmen. Al Qaeda also introduced the tribesmen to its version of jihad—suicide attacks, a technique it had mastered in Iraq.

Al Qaeda ranks soared in the green Wana valley in South Waziristan, in the high, rugged mountains and partially forested ranges in Shawal that separate South from North Waziristan, and in small towns like Miranshah and Mirali (North Waziristan). Pakistan's military and civilian authorities did not focus on these dangerous developments: their repeated attempts to prevent local influential elders from sheltering militants and the demand that they turn over wanted people—both local and foreign—simply fell on deaf ears. Al Qaeda rewarded this defiance with money and motivation. Nor did the authorities make a serious effort to dislodge Al Qaeda and its local affiliates from the region. Old ties with the likes of Haqqani and Hekmetyar and an overwhelming empathy for 'anti-American mujahideen' also worked against efforts to flush out Al Qaeda leaders and those inspired by them.

Sympathetic officials and operatives within the intelligence agencies—the ISI, the Military Intelligence (MI) and the civilian Intelligence Bureau (IB)—as well as those within the armed forces would look the other way when confronted with the challenge of arresting Al Qaeda and Taliban, or stopping their movement to or from Afghanistan.

During several visits to both North and South Waziristan, we saw foreigners openly walk or drive by in central towns and hamlets like Wana, Azam Warsak, Miranshah and Mirali. Clad in shalwar kameez, the traditional local attire, and usually sporting turbans or traditional caps, these foreigners would also frequently visit internet cafes and local restaurants. The civilian and military authorities—through their intelligence networks—were fully aware of this foreign presence but they either lacked the will to lay hands on them or did not want to touch them at all. This phenomenon was rooted in history: the ISI's long involvement with militant outfits such as those of Haqqani and Hekmetyar, who also patronized scores of Pakistani groups including those led by Baitullah Mehsud, Hafiz Saeed and Maulana Masood Azhar.

For a long time, Pakistani officials including former President Musharraf denied the alleged nexus between the intelligence agencies and the militants. 'Al Qaeda might have its bases in the tribal areas of Pakistan but no state organ is supporting it,' Musharraf said in an interview with the private television channel Geo News on 6 October 2007. He claimed terrorist elements were on the run or confined to their hideouts because of the stern action being taken against them.

Once Musharraf resigned in August 2008 his successor President Asif Ali Zardari and Prime Minister Yousuf Raza Gilani took more candid positions. Within days of the deadly bombing of the Marriott Hotel on 20 September 2008, one of their most trusted aides, Rehman Malik, suggested that the investigation into the Marriott bombing would end up pointing to Al Qaeda and Taliban militants based in FATA on the Afghan border. Earlier, the *News* of 21 July 2008 reported that Malik had tabled a report ahead of Gilani's first visit to the United States, which spoke of the presence of more than 8000 foreign fighters in the tribal areas.

But much before high-ranking Pakistani officials like Malik admitted to the reality of FATA, the US intelligence network and NATO-led military and intelligence officials based in Afghanistan had all arrived at a consensus: FATA is 'Al Qaeda Central', they had concluded.

'Next 9/11 to come from FATA,' said General David Petraeus, while he was the Commanding General, Multi-National Force–Iraq.

A US Congress commission report on the prevention of proliferation of weapons of mass destruction and terrorism titled 'World at Risk', released on 2 December 2008, issued a scary pronouncement on Pakistan, calling it 'the geographic crossroads for terrorism and weapons of mass destruction'.

In its introduction, the commission members noted: 'the border provinces of Pakistan today are a safe haven, if not the safe haven, for Al Qaeda'. The commission also quoted from a February 2008 testimony to the House Intelligence Committee by Mike McConnell, director of National Intelligence, which said: 'The FATA serves as a staging area for Al Qaeda's attacks in support of the Taliban in Afghanistan as well as a location for training new terrorist operatives for attacks in Pakistan, the Middle East, Africa, Europe, and the United States'.

The Congress commission report also noted that 'another senior intelligence official responsible for dealing with terrorism recently affirmed that Al Qaeda has strengthened its ties with Pakistani militants in the past year, replenished its mid-level lieutenants, enjoys in the FATA many of the benefits it enjoyed in Afghanistan before September 11, and remains the most serious terrorist threat to the United States'.

US intelligence outfits in particular were incensed that, despite the much-touted 120,000-strong armed forces deployment, about four peace deals in South and North Waziristan between April 2004 and February 2008 and countless rounds of talks with tribal elders, Pakistan had been unable to plug the border to Al Qaeda and Taliban, who had been piling up misery on Afghan and coalition troops inside Afghanistan, making every year bloodier than the previous one. Nor could Pakistani forces regain real control over these troubled lands. This stoked frustration and gave rise to doubts within the US and western establishments about the sincerity of the ISI and the Pakistan army in hunting down Al Qaeda and Taliban militants.

They believed the ISI, given to the notion of 'strategic depth in Afghanistan', was still playing favourites among the militant groups; while the army was seen busy going after terror networks inside FATA, US officials suspected the ISI was still maintaining contacts with Haqqani, Hekmetyar and Mulla Omar. US, Afghan and Indian intelligence openly accused the ISI of direct complicity with the Haqqani network, which carried out a deadly suicide bombing outside the Indian embassy in Kabul in July 2008.

Pakistani officials, on the other hand, peddled another conspiracy theory: Baitullah Mehsud, they said, is a US proxy, backed and funded by US and other interested countries, to keep the Pakistan army busy in FATA. They also accuse India of funding 'miscreants' based in FATA and Balochistan, the province that shares a 1360- kilometre border with Afghanistan, for terrorist activities (see Chapter 11).

Rehman Malik, the interior adviser, touched on the issue again on 21 January 2009, when he spoke of the role of external factors in FATA. 'Foreign hands are patronizing terrorists in Swat and the Federally Administered Tribal Areas but we are determined to flush out terrorists from Swat and FATA,' Malik told the media after addressing a seminar in Islamabad. Pakistan's MI and the civilian IB officials also often allude to the 'Invisible Indian hand' in Balochistan's unrest which cost 433 lives in 2008, up from 390 in 2007, accompanied by damages to gas power infrastructure worth several billion rupees.

During his 2008 election campaign, Joe Biden, the Democratic Party's vice presidential candidate, warned in his address to the Democratic Party Convention in Denver on 28 August 2008, 'The resurgence of fundamentalism in Afghanistan and Pakistan [is] the real central front against terrorism. The fact is Al Qaeda and the Taliban—the people who actually attacked us on 9/11—have regrouped in those mountains between Afghanistan and Pakistan and are plotting new attacks.'

Mullas and Al Qaeda Rule the Roost in FATA

As Pakistani and US establishments overtly exchanged mutual vows of cooperation in the anti-terror war and senior American civilian and military officials—through media leaks and in private meetings—kept conveying their reservations, casting doubts over

Pakistan's sincerity in taking on insurgents, the war on terror was already taking its toll on Pakistan. For reasons still inexplicable, this havoc wrought by the combination of the mulla and foreign Al Qaeda based in FATA has done little to remove the deep-seated perception that, somehow, the army and its intelligence agencies are conducting a fake war against the militants.

Locals also point to scores of seminaries still functional under several Taliban outfits and to the makeshift, short range FM radio stations being run by some militants for the purposes of preaching and recruitment and to inject fear in the minds of people at large.

The gradual spike in violence inside FATA as well as elsewhere in Pakistan is a telling reflection on the reach of terrorists; in 2003, for instance, Pakistan suffered a total of 189 terrorism-related fatalities. In 2004, 2005 and 2006 terrorism-related casualties were 863, 648 and 1471, respectively. In 2007 terrorism-related fatalities shot up to 3599, an average of 9.86 a day, with about fifty-seven suicide attacks, one within a second of the assassination of Benazir Bhutto, who was shot dead at an election rally at Rawalpindi. Apparently, a suicide bomber blew himself up instantly after shooting Bhutto from a close range, thereby causing the death of several others as well.

The siege of the Red Mosque in the heart of Islamabad and its bloody end on 10 July 2007 was another illustration of how radical militants had begun to project and exercise their power in the capital itself. The mosque had turned into a hub for Punjabi militant groups, their tentacles extending to the NWFP as well as FATA. Following several days of talks, accompanied by intense pressure from Washington not to negotiate peace with the chief cleric Abdul Rashid Ghazi's conditions, army commandos finally raided the mosque and the seminary adjacent to it. Rather than surrendering, the radical cleric went down fighting along with about 150 diehard students. The incident left deep scars, and galvanized the Taliban, which struck back with a massive string of suicide bombings throughout the country.

The next year, 2008, turned out to be even bloodier; almost 1000 deaths from at least sixty-one suicide strikes shook the entire country, with fatalities touching 6400. This included about 2000 militants the army claimed to have killed in the Bajaur and Swat regions alone.

All through 2008, Pakistan reeled under a medium-intensity insurgency, with the Taliban influence growing rapidly; the state virtually lost territorial control to Taliban militants not only in most of FATA, but also to a great extent in the Swat region, which is not part of FATA. Beginning from North and South Waziristan, the Taliban movement spilled over to Mohmand, Orakzai, Kurram and Bajaur agencies. In early summer, militants from the Khyber agency almost converged on Peshawar, assisted by other militants from another semi-autonomous region, Darra Adam Khel, triggering fears the provincial capital might be within the grasp of the militants.

The army responded with force, and carried out several operations in Darra Adam Khel, which connects Peshawar with the highway to Karachi—the lifeline for Pakistan's external trade—through a tunnel. The Japanese-funded tunnel remained closed for several weeks following its brief seizure by Taliban militants, who also attempted to blow it up in January. Militants and military traded heavy fire for days, until the army forced the Taliban out of the area, and reopened the strategic tunnel, which is also a vital link between the southern parts of the NWFP and capital Peshawar through the Indus Highway.

Meanwhile, American CIA-run pilotless drones kept lobbing precision missiles into Al Qaeda hideouts in Waziristan, making it a double loss for the authorities; the drone attacks amounted to a loss of sovereignty, while the virtual control of Baitullah Mehsud's men over most of FATA meant loss of territorial control to the insurgents.

In 2008 the CIA replaced Predators with Reaper—a more lethal unmanned aerial vehicle. Unlike the Predator drone, the new Reaper can fire Hellfire missiles and drop 500-pound bombs. For instance, Reaper-fired Hellfire missiles killed at least twenty people on 23 January 2009. The Associated Press news agency, quoting security officials, reported that at least five foreigners were killed in suspected Al Qaeda shelters in North and South Waziristan.

The deadly attack on Islamabad's Marriott Hotel on 20 September 2008 which killed over sixty people underscored a new reality; after hitting targets inside FATA, in Swat and Peshawar, the insurgents were now knocking at the heart of the capital. Within four hours of President Asif Ali Zardari's avowal to 'eliminate terrorists from the face of Pakistan', a suicide bomber rammed a six-wheeler dumper truck into a barrier outside the hotel. The truck was loaded with 600 kilograms of TNT, RDX explosives including mortars, artillery rounds, mines and aluminium powder—which caused a massive blast, followed by a rapidly spreading fire that reduced the entire hotel to a concrete shell.

The close-circuit video system of the hotel froze as a result of the huge impact but the shots before the explosion showed the attacker blowing himself up after the truck had become entangled in the steel barrier. As he vanished with the explosives strapped around his waist, the ensuing flames ignited the ammunition at the back within a couple of minutes.

I was in the hotel at that time, dining with two friends at one of the restaurants by the pool at the rear of the hotel. About 300 people, mostly women and children, were enjoying their dinner after breaking their Ramadan fast. As many as twenty-two foreign nationals were injured; four of them died, including the Czech ambassador to Pakistan and his Vietnamese partner. Two American soldiers assigned to the US embassy also lost their lives in the incident.

I was among the 350 or so lucky ones who escaped unhurt. Once safely out, I looked back to see the inferno spreading over the building. Hell had arrived in Islamabad, the leafy capital of Pakistan.

Thus far, the attack on the Marriott Hotel, which reopened in December 2008 following massive and speedy restoration work, was the most consequential as far as the impact was concerned;

the planners chose the high-profile hotel in an obvious attempt to scare foreigners and dent the country's image abroad. Stay off Pakistan, was the message delivered through this strike, the third on the hotel in three years. The tactic worked, with the United Nations enforcing evacuation of dozens of families, followed by dozens of diplomats and their families, who were either evacuated to their country of origin or relocated elsewhere.

For the first time, signs of a political war on Pakistan became visible. Prominent Pakistani analysts including Talat Masood, Rasul Bakhsh Raees and Dr Hassan Askari Rizvi declared the attack was on the 'symbols of a functional state'. This war knew no social values, no tribal tradition and carried no religious trappings, they suggested in various interviews to the print and electronic media. Nor were attacks on innocent locals and foreigners morally justifiable. The chickens had indeed come home to roost as the events unfolding in Pakistan for over seven years showed; religious zealots whom Pakistan's security apparatus had helped and used as proxies for missions in Afghanistan and Kashmir had turned on their erstwhile mentor.

Two months later, ten gunmen held Mumbai, India's commercial capital, in the grip of terror for almost three days, going on a killing spree that claimed 179 lives. India, backed by the US and Britain, blamed a Pakistani group for an act that sickened the world. Once again, my country was being held to account.

In 2009, two important developments took place on Pakistan's north-western front; on 16 February CIA-operated Reaper drones fired three missiles on training camps run by Baitullah Mehsud, in the Kurram agency, leaving over two dozen dead, including Uzbek and Arab trainers. This denoted a broadening of the American campaign inside Pakistan.

The same day, the NWFP government entered into an understanding with Maulana Sufi Mohammad, the elderly chief of the Tehreek-e-Nifaze Shariate Mohammadi (TNSM), to secure peace in the embattled Swat valley. After two days of talks, on 21 February, Mohammad succeeded in persuading his estranged son-in-law Maulana Fazlullah, the dreaded Taliban leader in the region, to agree to a permanent ceasefire. This became possible after the government gave in to the TNSM demand to enforce the Islamic system of jurisprudence for inexpensive and speedy justice, the sharia.

The Mohammad–Fazlullah deal was to pave the way to reopen girls' schools and allow the reconstruction of over 201 girls' schools destroyed or damaged by the militants. The deal was to also help the civilian administration resume its functions. The controversial deal evoked adverse reactions at home and from abroad but the Pakistani authorities defended it as a move to control damage and an attempt to re-establish the government's writ in the Swat region.

The following chapters are an endeavour to explain how Pakistan got here. The socio-historical context of the Pakistani tribal areas will enable the reader to understand why and how these areas turned into a hotbed of radicalism, how the Al Qaeda ideology found a foothold in the region. The tribal areas had for centuries remained a largely no-go area, where drugs and guns thrived because of laws dating back to the British era. These laws, while imposing many arbitrary restrictions, allowed certain liberties which the wily tribesmen used to their advantage. Pakistan, after emerging as an independent Muslim state, inherited the system and continued with it.

The current turmoil in FATA stems from decades of neglect, political expedience and the connivance and complacence of successive Pakistani establishments. They failed to foresee the grave consequences that would spill over from the cauldron of religious radicalism which had begun simmering immediately after the anti-Russian jihad, and which by 2009 has turned into a full-fledged and vicious challenge—insurgency—to the state of Pakistan.

FATA has become an arena for the competing interests of regional states—Russia, Iran, India, China as well as the United States—fuelling speculation that all five countries might have their fingers through their proxies in the pie that is called Afghanistan and Pakistan.

Mutually competing interests and the quest for space and resources also fuel conspiracy theories: who is funding the instability for whom and why? The search for answers to this question will most likely engage many of us in the years to come. But, quite obviously, as of February 2009, the spiralling conflict offers little cause for optimism, with insurgents firmly entrenched in the valleys and mountains that separate Afghanistan from Pakistan. That Al Qaeda and its non-Arab affiliates found a home in FATA and the border regions of Afghanistan comes as no surprise. History, ideology, conservatism and socio-political alliances have all combined to transform these border regions into Al Qaeda sanctuaries. Ironically, it was the United States, and its western and Muslim allies that originally sowed the seeds of militant Islam in the region by throwing their weight and resources behind the Afghan resistance. Pakistan was used then to raise the jihad. And in the aftermath of 9/11 the US and its allies again fell back on Pakistan for undoing the jihad—taking down the very forces they had jointly raised and groomed. The mission this time was to exorcize the jihadis.

Tribal Lands:
Cauldron of Militancy

Al Qaeda Transcends the Durand Line

The Federally Administered Tribal Areas is overrun by militants of all hues, local militants, Pakistan and Afghan Taliban and Arab, Uzbek and other foreign elements pitched against the US-led international coalition against terrorism. Not only have these pro-Al Qaeda groups been fighting the US and its allies, but they often also fight one another for territorial influence and political power. Caught between the militants and the military, the common people live in fear because the Taliban virtually control vast swathes of the region.[1]

Since the launch of the anti-terror war in October 2001, the militant Islamist movement has undergone a reactive transformation. From simply being an organization, Al Qaeda became an 'ideology that transcended borders' and was able to network local extremist outfits to pursue its narrowly defined but globally consequential objectives.

Already in 2005, the German terrorism scholar Rolf Tophoven, director of the German Institute for Terrorism Research and Security Policy, had concluded that 'the US-led onslaught had forced Al Qaeda and its affiliates to form decentralized small units that were spread across the world and threatened the States more than the group did when it attacked the US on Sept 11, 2001'.[2]

According to Tophoven's assessment, there are more than 30,000 Muslim extremists in Germany, while about 10,000 active supporters and affiliates of Al Qaeda are present in the United Kingdom. Most of these people had a direct or indirect connection with Afghanistan, Tophoven said.

Jason Burke, a British journalist and one of the best sources on Al Qaeda, says that 'Al Qaeda has metamorphosed from an organization to a movement that can be called "Al Qaedaism".' The term denotes Al Qaeda's transformation from an organization with specific linkages with its affiliates into a movement that has become influential in inspiring radicals into attacking in the name of Al Qaeda. This transformation has allowed Al Qaeda to transcend the physical limits imposed by its isolation in the remote border areas of an obscure part of the world to an organization of global infamy. Al Qaeda may no longer provide operational leadership, but its 'central command' is now providing inspirational leadership, encouraging others to attack.

Muhammad Amir Rana, a Pakistani terrorism and militancy expert, says that the January 2002 ban on various Pakistani militant organizations had forced them into restructuring for the sake of survival. The logic behind the restructuring was that jihad organizations would no longer use the words jihad, lashkar, jaish or mujahideen (as prefix or suffix) to appear more political than militant.[3] Rana and other analysts agree that the complex situation— the continuous hunt by the Americans and the ban by the Pakistan government—prompted them to join Al Qaeda's underground groups and start operations on Pakistani soil. This also instilled fear into the government machinery as well as people at large.

For instance, the Pakistani newspaper *Daily Times* reported in January 2007 that 'Tribal chieftains are wary of getting on board because speaking openly against Al Qaeda can invite serious problems from the militants.'[4] It is difficult to take on Al Qaeda since the organization shows no mercy to people working against it and for the government. Three jirgas (assemblies of local elders) have been called since the Damadola incident (where a US missile strike on 13 January left at least eighty-three seminary students dead) but most tribal elders stayed away for fear that Al Qaeda-linked militants may target them, the paper quoted a tribal elder, who wished not to be named for fear of reprisals from the administration and Al Qaeda, as saying.

In the new structure, movers and shakers of the Muttahida Jihad Council (established in 1991 but extensively used as an umbrella organization for the anti-India jihad in Kashmir) co-opted five Pakistan-based organizations: Lashkar-e-Taiba, Jaish-e-Mohammad, Brigade 313, Al-Badr Mujahideen and Jamaatul Furqan. All leaders agreed that no organization would issue any press statements nor disclose their activities and operations. These five outfits—all headquartered in Pakistan's most populous province of Punjab—drew inspiration from Hezb-e-Islami of Gulbudin Hekmetyar, Jalaluddin Haqqani, Mulla Omar and Maulvi Nabi Mohammedi.[5]

However, Markaz-al-Daawatul Ershad, essentially Lashkar-e-Taiba's parent organization, which is ideologically close to the pro-Saudi Arab–Afghan war veteran Professor Abdurrab Rasool Sayyaf, was an exception. It had realized the gravity of the situation just after the shift in Pakistan's pro-jihad policy and renamed itself as Jamatud Dawa, dissolved LeT's Pakistan chapter and shifted its offices to or in Pakistan-administered Kashmir.

Jaish-e-Mohammad (JM) converted into Tehreeke Khudamul Islam (Movement of Servants of Islam), Harkatul Mujahideen into Jamiatul Ansar (Party of Hosts) and Sipahe Sahaba became Millat-e-Islamia. From December 2001 to August 2002 these organizations remained silent, but in time they resumed their activities. They also work through certain affiliated charity organizations; Jaish-e-Mohammad, for instance, carries out its charity work through Al-Rehmat Trust, which in fact represents the non-militant face of the JM and also raises funds for the organization. Al-Ershad Trust performs similar functions for the Harkatul Jihad-e-Islami and Al-Asar Trust works more or less the same way for the Harkatul Mujahideen in Pakistan.

The Pakistani Punjabi Factor

The ideological nexus between groups based in and outside FATA is underscored by the presence of Punjabi Taliban—activists of the Punjab-based organizations mentioned above—scattered all over FATA, attached either to Baitullah Mehsud, Mulla Nazir (South Waziristan), Mulla Faqir (Bajaur) or Tehreek-e-Nifaze Shariate Mohammadi (which operates in Malakand, Swat).

Soon after then president Pervez Musharraf proscribed most sectarian organizations including the Jaish-e-Mohammad, Sipahe Sahaba Pakistan (SSP), Sipahe Mohammad (SM), Lashkar-e-Taiba (LeT) and Harkatul Mujahideen (HM) in a nationally televised speech on 12 January 2002, their leadership either went underground or was apprehended. Over 2000 zealots associated with these outfits were arrested, only to be released a few months later. Most of their workers melted into the population for the time being. Gradually they sought sanctuary in FATA, where they created alliances with various pro-Al Qaeda Taliban outfits.

A number of these organizations, except for the Shia Sipahe Mohammad, had their roots in the anti-Soviet Russian jihad, and had moved to Kashmir after the February 1989 Russian pullout from Afghanistan. But their contacts with the mujahideen-turned-Taliban remained, with the Jaish-e-Mohammad, Lashkar-e-Taiba and Harktul Mujahideen running several training camps in Afghanistan in the 1990s. Not only did they help out the Taliban in their fight against the Afghan Northern Alliance, but they also trained people for the jihad in Kashmir.

Muhammad Amir Rana and Mubasher Bukhari in *A to Z of Jihadi Organizations in Pakistan* and Amir Mir in *The True Face of Jehadis* say among the over 450 terrorists captured by Pakistan until late 2003, as many as 200 were Yemenis and Saudis. At that time as many as two-thirds of the prisoners at Guantanamo Bay were from Pakistan, all of them captured inside Afghanistan. About fourteen of Harkatul Mujahideen, seven of Jaish-e-Mohammad and eleven of Harkatul Jihad militants of Pakistani origin were also among the Guantanamo Bay inmates.[6] This underscored the presence of hard-core Punjabi jihadis within the militant ranks—both Taliban and Al Qaeda. Punjabi militants also filled and supplemented the ranks of Kashmiri militants, who have been battling the Indian forces since 1989 for what they call 'independence from India'.

When a dispute arose in a Mohmand agency village in August 2007 over the control of the shrine of the Pashtoon freedom fighter Haji Sahib Turangzai and the mosque adjacent to it, it came to light that around 300 masked Urdu-speaking Taliban members were among the 3500 militants who had occupied the site. Most of them were actually ethnic Punjabis and members of the SSP, Lashkar-e-Jhangvi and Harkatul Mujahideen. 'No one recognizes the Punjabi/Urdu speakers guarding the shrine. I talked to an Urdu-speaking Talib who belonged to Punjab and could not speak Pushto,' a man asking not to be named told the *Daily Times*.[7]

'Some Taliban have a good command over English, Urdu, Arabic and Pashto and are issuing statements in several languages to the national and international media,' the paper quoted the source as saying. The militants also went on to rename the mosque after Islamabad's Red Mosque, in support of Abdul Rashid Ghazi, the cleric who was killed during the bloody army siege in the capital on 10 July 2007.

Commander Maulvi Iqbal and several of his fighters who fell during skirmishes with US-led coalition forces in the Paktika province, which borders South Waziristan, in March 2008, were later identified as close Punjabi associates of Mulla Nazir, the Taliban chieftain in Wana. Hence, the dozen or so bodies were transported from Paktika and buried in Wana.[8]

An elderly Pakistani, called Chacha Akhtar, from the Punjab province used to be in charge of the Pakistani Taliban contingent at the Rishkore camp south of Kabul. Wanted on criminal charges, Akhtar had shifted his family to this camp in early 2001.

In its 5 June 2008 issue the *News* also confirmed the presence of Pakistani Punjabi Taliban. 'Maulvi Iqbal was killed along with many other militants including many Pakistanis from the Punjab province.'

Most of the Punjabi Taliban are associated with groups like

Harkatul Mujahideen, Jaish-e-Mohammad, Lashkar-e-Jhangvi, Sipahe Sahaba Pakistan and Al-Badr. One of their leaders is Owais Qadri, who comes from Jhang, a big town in central Punjab, riven with Shia–Sunni acrimony. Sipahe Sahaba Pakistan's Qari Hussain Mehsud is blamed for stirring anti-Shia sentiment in Kurram agency and is accused of killing a former political agent of the Khyber agency along with thirteen others—members of his family and guests, in a telling demonstration of the weakness of the government's writ in the region. Hussain had studied and grew up in the central Pakistani towns of Faisalabad and Jhang, before returning to Waziristan and becoming one of the Taliban's most important leaders.[9]

According to sources in Kabul, most trainers of recruits from the Middle East, African and Central Asian countries were also predominantly Pakistani Punjabis.[10]

Scores of activists and fighters of these Pakistani jihadi organizations were based in Afghanistan when the anti-terror war began. They lost important commanders and hundreds of warriors to the US bombings. Harkatul Jihad-e-Islami lost as many as 340, Harkatul Mujahideen lost seventy-nine, Jaish-e-Mohammad thirty-six and Lashkar-e-Jhangvi twenty-seven militants in the coalition attacks.

Profiles of Agencies

Administratively, FATA is divided into seven agencies and six additional small pockets of tribal areas known as Frontier Regions (FR). The agencies are North Waziristan, South Waziristan, Khyber, Kurram, Bajaur, Mohmand and Orakzai.

The Frontier Regions are Peshawar, Kohat, Bannu, Lakki, Tank and Dera Ismail Khan. The FRs are essentially transition areas between FATA and the adjoining settled districts of the NWFP. They are jointly administered by the NWFP and the tribal agencies.[11]

North Waziristan: The second largest agency in terms of area, North Waziristan hosts about 375,000 people, mostly belonging to the Wazir and Dawar tribes. The Waziristan region was a chronic headache for the British; even after the creation of Pakistan, Waziris continued to support Pakhtoonistan/Pashtunistan (the joining of all Pashtun areas to create a new state) and hence maintained good relations with Afghanistan. Since the 1970s, however, Waziris joined the ranks of the Pakistani armed forces in considerable numbers as compared to members of other tribes. The transport business in the region is their monopoly. It is the kidnapping-for-ransom business, however, that they are most notorious for. Waziris are also fond of music and dancing, and despite the Taliban's influence they continue to cherish these activities.

Pakistani military operations in this agency began in 2002 and have led to a full-fledged military confrontation with Waziris. Many important Al Qaeda leaders, including Abu Zubayda and Khalid Sheikh Mohammad transited through North Waziristan on their way to the Pakistani cities of Faisalabad and Rawalpindi, where they were captured in 2002 and 2003 respectively.

Several militant tribal leaders have become legendary figures. Turning in their comrades to government authorities, as demanded by the army, amounted to treachery to them and that explains why none of the tribesmen ever handed over any significant Taliban or Al Qaeda operatives to the authorities. Interestingly, soon after the 5 September 2006 peace accord between Pakistan and the tribal elders of the agency, the Taliban reopened its offices in three important cities to 'control law and order'.

South Waziristan: The largest agency in the area, South Waziristan is home to around 425,000 tribesmen from the Mehsud and Wazir tribes. Ahmedzai Wazirs boast dozens of sub-tribes and clans; for instance, the Zillikhel Wazirs are divided into three clans, Yargulkhel, Kakakhel and Ishmankhel.

Mehsuds are as valiant as they are ferocious, and believe in protecting a refugee even at the cost of their lives. The tribe has been notorious for murders, abductions for ransom and, of late, for waylaying Pakistan army and government officials. Notable members are the Afghan war veterans Abdullah Mehsud (killed in an encounter) and Baitullah Mehsud, currently the head of the Tehreek-e-Taliban Pakistan (TTP), an umbrella for like-minded extremist pro-Al Qaeda and Taliban groups operating in the entire FATA region.

The Mehsud and Wazir tribes are proud of their formidable reputation as warriors and are known for their frequent blood feuds. Almost half a century ago the historian Sir Olaf Caroe had said Mehsuds, the majority tribe, would never consider submitting to a foreign power that has entered their land. The insurgency led by Baitullah Mehsud suggests that Caroe was quite prophetic in his assessment of the Mehsud tribes. They are reputed to be good marksmen and the most independent of all the tribes. While they have produced many senior civil and military officers, the overall political leadership of South Waziristan is dominated by conservative mullas. The two National Assembly (Pakistani Parliament) members from this agency are clergymen affiliated with the Muttahida Majlis-e-Amal (MMA), Pakistan's foremost Islamic political party. Militants from Central Asia, especially those associated with the Islamic Movement of Uzbekistan, were also based in this area. In 2004 they created a stir when they launched rockets at Peshawar, targeting official and military buildings. Nek Mohammad was an Ahmedzai Waziri from this agency.

Khyber Agency: Khyber agency derives its name from the world-famous Khyber Pass which provides the most vital link between Pakistan and Afghanistan. With a population of around half a million, it is inhabited by two important tribes—Afridi and Shinwari. Afridis are widely known for being courageous, although British historians remember them as a rebellious and treacherous tribe.

Although short-tempered, the Afridis are known to be good fighters who are pragmatic in choosing their battles and making alliances. They respect Sufis (mystics) and their shrines, which intellectually aligns them with Barelvi Sunnis, the antithesis of conservative and pro-Taliban Deobandi groups. Interestingly, the Afridi tribe has also produced great works of literature. Shinwaris, the second largest tribe of this agency, are also influential, but its members mostly inhabit the Ningarhar province of Afghanistan. They are largely involved in business activities. In recent years, particularly after 9/11, Khyber agency has turned into a troubled area, known for hosting criminal gangs, warring religious factions and dozens of illegal radio stations. These groups are promoting their brand of Islam, playing up the prevailing socio-economic injustices and exploiting the absence of a legal justice system in the tribal areas. Individual groups run their own parallel systems of governance and dispense justice through Islamic sharia courts.

Kurram Agency: With a population of about 450,000, Kurram agency is home to two tribes—Turi and Bangash. Parachinar is the administrative headquarters of the agency. The agency has been a hotbed of Shia–Sunni strife in recent years. Turis are followers of the Shia sect of Islam. The Bangashs, on the other hand, are divided into Shia and Sunni sects. The presence of radical Sunni Taliban militants in the agency precipitated the sectarian tensions in recent years, leading to months of bloody clashes, almost paralysing life in the entire agency and forcing tens of thousands to flee for safety.

Bajaur Agency: The smallest of the seven tribal agencies, Bajaur is largely inaccessible due to its hilly terrain. Khaar is the administrative headquarters of the agency. It borders Afghanistan's Kunar province, which is a hotbed for Taliban forces. With a population of about 600,000, its prominent tribes are Tarkani and Utman Khel. The alliance of religious political parties—namely the MMA—has great influence in this area and two MMA politicians from this agency are represented in the National Assembly and one in the Senate.

Bajaur's proximity to Kunar also keeps fuelling suspicions that Osama bin Laden and his deputy Ayman al-Zawahiri may be hiding in the area. A village in Bajaur came under an aerial attack, reportedly executed by the CIA targeting Ayman al-Zawahiri, on 13 January 2006, killing eighteen people. Al-Zawahiri was not found among the dead and the incident led to severe outrage in the area. Interestingly, Abu Faraj al-Libbi, a senior member of Al Qaeda who was involved in an assassination attempt on President Pervez Musharraf, told interrogators after his arrest in May 2005 that he had lived in Bajaur for some time.

Mohmand Agency: The agency takes its name from the Mohmand tribe which resides there, numbering approximately 350,000. Ghalanai is the administrative headquarters of the agency. Mohmands are a very powerful and influential tribe and are known to be natural guerrilla fighters. One of the important mythic themes among Mohmands is the description and details of the wars in which they have fought. Indeed, they are widely known to have given more trouble to the British than any other tribe. Another distinguishing mark is the importance that they give to their clerics and divine leaders—they fought most of their wars under the leadership of their mullas. More recently, Mohmand tribal leaders challenged the idea of the joining of Pakistani and US forces to comb the area in 2003; later the provincial government led by the MMA supported this move. Trouble erupted after US and Afghan troops intruded into an area that Pakistani authorities claimed was their territory. The exchange of fire between the Pakistani and Afghan border security forces in June 2003 enforced a US intervention, which paved the way for the Pakistan army units to conduct search operations in the area.

It is pertinent to mention that al-Zawahiri is reportedly married to a woman from the Mohmand tribe who lives with her father in the border area between Bajaur and Mohmand agencies.

Orakzai Agency: A small agency with a population of about 240,000, Orakzai is primarily inhabited by the Orakzai tribe. The other important tribe in the area is Daulatzai. Unlike in most agencies, Shias and Sunnis live side by side in Orakzai, although seldom in peace. Regular sectarian clashes have diminished the effectiveness and influence of the Orakzai tribe. This is the only agency that does not share a border with Afghanistan. The present governor of the NWFP and former corps commander in the region, Lieutenant General (Retired) Ali Mohammad Jan Orakzai, belongs to this tribe. Some senior bureaucrats in the civil services of Pakistan also hail from this tribe, giving them influence in the corridors of power in Pakistan. Despite a comparatively higher literacy rate, the agency was the first one where Taliban militants banned non-governmental organizations (NGOs) from operating, declaring them anti-Islamic. Taliban militants in general loathe the word NGO because they consider them as extensions of the 'decadent western culture'. The possession of televisions has also been declared a crime here under the influence of the local Taliban.

Al Qaeda's Extensions in FATA: South and North Waziristan

As the Taliban movement in the two agencies of South and North Waziristan took hold, it split along tribal lines. Baitullah Mehsud formed the Tehreek-e-Taliban Pakistan (TTP) with its stronghold in the Mehsud Wazir area, while his former associate Mulla Nazir continued his activities under Tehreek-e-Taliban in the Ahmedzai Wazir region. Among the reasons for the split were differences over the activities of foreign militants, particularly the Uzbeks who were opposed to the Pakistan army, attacking it wherever possible. At the same time, both Mehsud and Nazir pursued campaigns committed to the 'jihad against foreign troops in Afghanistan' and the Afghan war veteran Jalaluddin Haqqani served as the patriarch for both factions. Haji Gul Bahdur in North Waziristan also enjoyed Haqqani's patronage. All of them provided shelter and sanctuary not only to Arab and Uzbek militants, but also to several Pakistani radical groups who fled to Waziristan and other FATA areas after Pervez Musharraf's 12 January 2002 ban on all religio-political groups.

Tehreek-e-Taliban Pakistan

Tehreek-e-Taliban Pakistan emerged as an entity in the context of a series of military operations—US-led missile strikes on the one hand and the abduction of over 250 soldiers in the Mehsud area of South Waziristan on 30 August 2007. Until then, most of its component groups were loosely organized with ties to the Afghan Taliban. The TTP started to professionally organize itself when Abdullah Mehsud of the Afghan Taliban returned to Waziristan from the Guantanamo Bay camp. He briefly led the Taliban in Waziristan before blowing himself up in Pishin, Balochistan, during a siege by Pakistani security forces in 2006. After Abdullah Mehsud's death, Baitullah Mehsud, a leading member of the Afghan Taliban, organized all the groups operating in the FATA region that professed similar ideologies and successfully knit them into what is now known as TTP. The surrender of as many as 250 Pakistani troops to the militants shocked the country and it was widely regarded as the worst humiliation suffered by the Pakistan army on its own national territory since it became an active ally in the US-led anti-terror war. Most of the captured soldiers were released in the first week of November in exchange for twenty-five Taliban prisoners.

Qari Hussain Mehsud, one of Baitullah Mehsud's close associates, had earlier been part of the rabidly anti-Shia Sunni outfit Sipahe Sahaba Pakistan (SSP) and had moved into Waziristan after Musharraf's January 2002 ban. Qari Hussain Mehsud called some of his friends in the media on Friday, 14 December 2007 to announce the formation of the TTP, an organization that would be guided by a forty-member central shura (assembly), comprising representatives from all the seven FATA agencies. Even today TTP leaders from these regions meet regularly but avoid large meetings for reasons of security. Baitullah Mehsud's TTP was in fact the revival of an older organization of the same name founded in 1998 in the Orakzai agency. As Rana wrote, 'Led by Mohammad Rahim, a former Afghan war veteran, the TTP made its appearance on the national horizon on 13 December 1998, when it sentenced and publicly executed Khial Ghaffar, a local suspected of multiple murders in the Orakzai agency.'[1]

The organization banned television, videocassette recorders and music in the Orakzai agency. Rahim had denied contacts with the Afghan Taliban, and claimed he was setting up his own organization 'to cleanse the society of crime'—an idea common to many smaller Taliban factions on Pakistani territory.[2]

Baitullah Mehsud's TTP employs modern, more lethal techniques and operates across all seven tribal agencies and has the allegiance of a very large number of Taliban groups, most of them wedded to anti-Americanism and determined to enforce sharia. The TTP's creation in December 2007 marked a new and more threatening development, arising out of a realization among most local and foreign militants that they needed a central command figure who could transcend tribal regions. In Baitullah Mehsud they found a unifying force. Individual Taliban groups in areas other than Waziristan also looked to Baitullah Mehsud for guidance but such is the secrecy in which they operate that, few acknowledge the links openly. Thus when Haji Gul Bahadur, the Taliban supremo in North Waziristan, told the BBC in May 2008 that his group had nothing to do with the TTP of Baitullah Mehsud, most observers felt it was a tactic meant to confuse the authorities, rather than the actual reality. Inspired by Osama bin Laden's Al Qaeda, most militant groups in FATA share a common ideology against the international coalition against terrorism. They have morphed into the TTP because they pursue the same goal—to drive foreign forces away from Afghanistan and enforce sharia wherever possible.[3]

Mehsud's interview with journalists in May 2008 reconfirmed his resolve to fight on until the eviction of foreign troops from Afghanistan. Other TTP leaders, including Maulvi Faqir of Bajaur and Maulvi Fazlullah of Swat (who is also the Taliban chief administrator), Mulla Nazir of South Waziristan and Mangal Bagh Afridi of the Khyber agency, share more or less the same objectives: foreign troops must leave Afghanistan, Pakistan must end its cooperation with the US and NATO forces based in Afghanistan, and sharia must replace the existing legal system, which these militants condemn as 'corrupt and repressive'.

As of November 2008, investigators found the footprints of

Baitullah Mehsud's TTP everywhere; from Khyber agency to North Waziristan almost all incidents of abductions, killings of officials, attacks on military convoys, or on government infrastructure bore the hallmarks of the TTP. 'Baitullah is the prime suspect for links with foreign instigators. His people have been all around—killing government and non-government officials as well as abducting and executing innocent people and also fighting battles inside Afghanistan,' a senior intelligence official told me in Peshawar.

Proof of Baitullah Mehsud's involvement in Afghanistan—and of the close association between the Afghan Taliban and the Pakistani TTP—came in early June 2008 when about eighteen militants belonging to his group fell to air strikes by coalition forces on militant positions in Afghanistan's Helmand province. All eighteen belonged to Makeen village in Waziristan agency. One of Baitullah's senior commanders informed a newspaper that after hectic efforts four bodies were brought back to Makeen in South Waziristan through unfrequented routes. He said dozens of Mehsud's tribal militants, led by Commander Khan Ghafoor, had gone to Afghanistan to fight against the US-led forces there. Around two dozen militants had been sent to retrieve the remaining bodies.

A journalist belonging to one of the FATA tribes, whom TTP activists regularly call upon to disseminate their views, says the organization is growing in influence among young and jobless youth in Waziristan and money seems to be no problem with them.[4] He said the TTP is using Islamic sharia (as espoused by Mulla Omar of the Afghan Taliban) to promote its political agenda. 'The TTP successfully converted their defensive war into an offensive and proactive campaign by taking on the Pakistani military and the government through rocket and suicide attacks on army housing colonies, cantonments and installations such as the Pakistan Ordnance Factory near Islamabad in June 2008,' he said. 'They have a strong political agenda and conviction backed by their own interpretation of religious beliefs that justifies killing for the sake of God and Islam, regardless of whether the target is a Muslim or non-Muslim.' Ruthless attacks on Pakistani military and government targets, says this journalist, offer ample evidence that while publicly the TTP wants to counter US hegemony, it may also want to keep Pakistani forces on tenterhooks.[5] This point of view has generated numerous conspiracy theories on the role of militants in the tribal areas. It is a widely held belief in Pakistan that the American, Afghan and Indian intelligence apparatuses are sponsoring people like Baitullah Mehsud to weaken the Pakistan army and keep it pinned down on the western front.

That as many as 300 high-profile Pakistanis, including Pervez Musharraf, several of his ministers and army commanders, were on Baitullah Mehsud's hit list underscores the transborder agenda of the TTP. Intelligence officials believe the leadership of the Pakistan Peoples Party (PPP), Muttahida Qaumi Movement (MQM), a politico-ethnic party based in Karachi, the Awami National Party, which stands for ethnic Pashtoons' rights, along with several anti-Taliban Shias and senior officials of intelligence and law enforcement agencies could be TTP targets. The TTP's aim is to wipe out rival political outfits in the area. With dozens of commanders in its fold and thousands of common fighters, TTP has become a major force in Waziristan, Bajaur and Mohmand agencies, and its numbers are multiplying in the Khyber, Kurram and Orakzai agencies.[6]

Baitullah Mehsud has amassed dozens of diehard commanders who are ever ready to take on the security forces in case of major offensive. The *Nation* quoted a senior official as saying, 'The intelligence reports from the tribal areas suggest that it is not only the threat of Baitullah Mehsud that we have to cope with but there is a large group of little known, yet equally overzealous militant commanders belonging to small non-TTP extremist groups with sectarian trappings in mainland Pakistan who could unleash terror on security forces whenever they deem it necessary for the survival and success of the Taliban ideology.' He added that while most people have heard of Maulvi Faqir Muhammad, Baitullah's deputy in Bajaur, Fazlullah in Swat and Omar Khalid in Mohmand, there are, in fact, many others like them who could come up in case of need. These commanders are the second tier of the TTP in Pakistan, ready to emerge if any of the top leaders—Baitullah Mehsud included—is removed from the scene. He refused to reveal the identities of the second tier saying it would not serve the cause of the country.[7]

The TTP's organizational structure is led by a forty-member shura that Baitullah Mehsud heads and it comprises representatives from all seven agencies. The heads of TTP in the agencies are called deputy ameer to Baitullah Mehsud and they meet when necessary. Thus the TTP essentially is a conglomerate of about two dozen individual commanders, who carry two titles, that is deputy ameer as well as head of the TTP in the respective agency. Maulvi Omar, whose real name is said to be Saeedullah, is the spokesman for the organization and he often interacts with the media via various landlines and mobile phones. He is from the Bajaur agency. TTP activists usually maintain only one-way contact with the media and with sympathizers to their cause. They mostly make the calls themselves whenever they have something to convey.

TTP components in each of the seven FATA agencies draw inspiration and strategic guidance from Baitullah Mehsud but operate independently. At the operational level, they run their own intelligence operations. Militant activities are divided into different and non-intersecting operational groups that meet only at the leadership level for scrutiny and review.

Journalists familiar with the TTP and its affiliates say that the militants spend substantial sums on vehicles, fuel and other communication equipment. They are also well-equipped for casualties; injured militants are provided quick and effective treatment in the mountains.

Tehreek-e-Taliban (Mulla Nazir)

Mulla Nazir Ahmed, the ameer of his faction of Taliban in South Waziristan, split with the loosely knit Taliban movement led by Baitullah Mehsud in early 2007, largely over the role of Uzbek militants hiding in the region. Mulla Nazir had turned against the Uzbeks once they began taking army and government officials hostage, torturing them brutally and even killing many of them. It was widely felt in South Waziristan that the Uzbeks ignored and undermined one of the strongest traditions of the region, which is to show respect to the tribal elders. Alien to the land and culture, the Uzbeks relied solely on the power of their guns and wallets. In the complex sociology of the tribal culture where questions of honour and respect are deeply ingrained and observed, this behaviour was unacceptable. Apparently prompted by the Pakistan army, Mulla Nazir stood up to preserve his militant fiefdom and restore the command of the tribal leaders. Moreover, his region had become a repeated target for army operations because of the presence of foreign militants, particularly Uzbeks and Arabs. So he resolved to push the Uzbeks out. In March 2007, Nazir, who reportedly holds dual Afghan and Pakistani nationality, put together a tribal lashkar—an army of local tribesmen—and mounted a vicious campaign against foreign militants who were predominantly of Uzbek origin, living in the hamlets of Sheen Warsak, Azam Warsak and Kaloosha, west of Wana, the administrative headquarters of South Waziristan. The Ahmedzai Wazir tribe dominates the western parts of South Waziristan, and as such controls the economically lucrative border trade routes between Afghanistan and Pakistan. Mulla Nazir, an Ahmedzai Wazir himself, found little difficulty in forging alliances with influential local leaders and commanders who, along with the embedded army commandos, became the mainstay for his anti-Uzbek campaign.

In the 18 February 2008 national elections, Ghalib Wazir defeated the former MP Maulana Abdul Malik from one of the two South Waziristan constituencies to the National Assembly. Those familiar with the dynamics of politics in the Waziristan region maintained that Ghalib Wazir owed his success to local Taliban commanders, including aides to Mulla Nazir, who went all out to help him win the election because of the mulla's close tribal affinity and long association with Ghalib and his family.

Objections by Mulla Nazir and local tribal elders to Uzbek attacks on army and government targets led to several weeks of pitched battles and skirmishes between Nazir's army and the Uzbek militants. The Pakistan army tactically supported Mulla Nazir and his militants by embedding sharp-shooters and tacticians in the tribal forces. In early March 2008, Pakistan army officials began to insist the tribesmen had turned the tables on foreign militants; the commander of Pakistani troops in the tribal areas, Major General Gul Muhammad, claimed the tribal army eliminated up to 200 foreign militants.[8] Nevertheless, he would not admit the army involvement in the operations. In fact, the army provided vital intelligence about the movement of the Uzbeks, cut down their supply routes, deployed heavy artillery, shelled their positions and embedded well-trained and seasoned army personnel from the local area in Nazir's militant outfit, all of which contributed significantly to Mulla Nazir's success. Military officials played up Mulla Nazir's achievements but conceded later (in private conversations with the author) that logistic support was provided to the tribal chief because 'he had asked for it'.

'We did provide support to Mulla Nazir, there was no way around it,' said Major General Shaukat Sultan, the then head of the Inter Services Public Relations (ISPR) department.[9] Sultan admitted that army sharp-shooters and strategists were part of the lashkar that swept across the tribal areas and forced the Uzbek militants to flee the region. Officials claimed as many as 250 Uzbeks were eliminated during the operation. Under the tribal tradition, locals can always call in the army or paramilitary for support. To pre-empt suspicion, Mulla Nazir invoked this tradition and told his people that all elders had asked the army for 'logistic support'. Local journalists recall that a Pakistan army officer—disguised as Taliban—supervised the entire operation against Uzbek fighters. Even the media management was in the hands of the army.

The then president Pervez Musharraf proved true to his reputation and was most indiscreet. 'They got support from the Pakistan Army, they asked for support,' he said, in a first public admission. 'Troops were involved in the offensive.'[10] These statements instantly turned the armed forces and their institutions into prime targets of both the Uzbek and hardcore Al Qaeda elements.

Nazir–Uzbek Fallout

Nazir had in fact fallen out with the rest of the Taliban after residents started complaining of their militant activities, which were directly affecting their lives. Whenever the Uzbeks carried out an anti-army attack, the military would turn its guns on the suspected areas. Intelligence reports would mostly lead them to where the Uzbeks were sheltering. This situation caused widespread resentment among the locals, who thought they were being unnecessarily sandwiched between the militants and the military—turning them into an automatic target of reprisals by either party.

Events of the latter half of 2006 help us understand why the Uzbeks turned against Pakistan. A tribal journalist belonging to the Bhittani tribe, who had closely monitored developments in South Waziristan between 2004 and 2007, provided a plausible account of how the Uzbeks grew wary of Pakistan. 'Scores of Arab militants have also been present in the area but Tahir Yuldashev believed that Pakistan inflicted the most damage on Al Qaeda by capturing and delivering many of its leaders to the Americans.'

Yuldashev became even more alarmed when thousands of Punjabi Taliban began pouring into Wana in the last quarter of 2006 from central and southern Pakistan. Eventually, they all vowed allegiance to Mulla Nazir at the house of a local spiritual leader, Peer Adil, in the Musa Qilla hamlet, South Waziristan. Following the oath of allegiance, all those present vowed to continue their jihad against foreign troops in Afghanistan. 'They also undertook not to harm Pakistani interests,' recalled this journalist, who monitored all these developments from his base in Wana. Mulla

Nazir also entrusted the Punjabi Taliban with the task of looking after Arab Al Qaeda militants—those 'comrades' who were retreating from Afghanistan into Waziristan for shelter. There was no mention of IMU (Uzbek) militants in that meeting, which annoyed Tahir Yuldashev further.

The Musa Qilla meeting brought Mulla Nazir closer to the local Pakistan army commanders, which Yuldashev construed as an alliance being mounted against him, in conjunction with those Arabs who were still sympathetic towards Pakistan. This inevitably deepened the already existing animosity between the Nazir-led forces and the Central Asian dissidents. With the new battle lines drawn, the IMU embarked on a lethal offensive against the rest of the forces, carrying out target killings and ambushing Pakistan army convoys and installations, thereby triggering clashes between Nazir and the Uzbeks in November 2006.

A senior intelligence official recalled that Nazir did make several attempts to patch up with Yuldashev, telling him their prime target was the foreign troops in Afghanistan and he should refrain from targeting Pakistani tribal elders, government officials and military personnel as well as strategic installations.[11] But these attempts helped little and the differences between the two groups grew. Sensing the brewing conflict, both the military and intelligence agencies leapt to exploit the growing differences between locals and foreign militants, and got Mulla Nazir on board for a crackdown against the Uzbek fighters. They eventually engineered the lashkar which became the face for the army's renewed assault on Uzbeks, neutralizing the Uzbek threat to a great extent and thereby bringing relative calm to the area.

Officials dealing with the tribal areas at the General Headquarter (GHQ) in Rawalpindi, south of Islamabad, said the lashkar operation was part of a new strategy comprising three elements, coercive deployment, political engagement and socio-economic development, to 'win over the hearts and minds of the people'.[12] This new strategy, however, appeared to be a result of the intense pressure that the United States and NATO members had been exerting on Pakistan for a stronger and more sincere effort to contain the spreading lawlessness of its tribal areas from which Pakistani, Afghan and foreign militants waged an expanding insurgency across the border in Afghanistan.

Officials and tribal journalists familiar with the situation did confirm that the Waziristan region had turned into a Taliban state after the September 2006 peace deal between local authorities, tribesmen and militants in North Waziristan. As a result, the Pakistani military abandoned broad-scale military operations in favour of negotiated peace deals with locals as well as the representatives of the militant groups. In fact, these deals were the result of peace efforts at various levels, wherein tribal elders appealed to the government to cease the military operation against the local militants and go for talks.

Mulla Nazir's tacit alliance with the authorities, and the active support of disguised Pakistan army commandos, mostly from the central Pakistani province of Punjab, drove a wedge between Mulla Nazir and the brothers Haji Sharif, Noorul Islam and Haji Omar; this family had been a staunch ally and supporter of Yuldashev and therefore opposed Mulla Nazir's actions against Uzbek militants. The Uzbeks viewed Pakistan and its military as active combatants in the US-led war on terror and therefore considered targeting them as legitimate. The brothers thus sided with Yuldashev in the conflict after Mulla Nazir's spokesman Mulla Owais Hanafi condemned Uzbek militants for their 'criminality and the failure to participate in the jihad in Afghanistan for the past four years'. Eventually they had to abandon their ancestral homes in Azam Warsak, Kaloosha and Sheen Warsak hamlets. They reportedly took refuge in discrete locations inside North Waziristan.

'They [Uzbeks] have no link with the Islamic Movement of Taliban or Al Qaeda . . . their behaviour had been earning a bad name for these pious people [Taliban],' Hanafi had maintained while defending the crackdown on Yuldashev's men.

Underlying all such condemnations, however, was the fact that the Central Asians were not the only foreigners Nazir wanted to fight. 'We will continue our jihad [in Afghanistan] if that is against America, the Russians, British or India, as long as we have souls in our bodies,' one of Nazir's aides told Pakistani reporters in Wana.[13] Outsiders also questioned whether the Nazir-led operation was directed at Uzbeks only. 'There is also no sign the offensive has targeted Arabs associated with Al Qaeda, still thought to shelter in South Waziristan,' observed an Associated Press report after Pakistan's army ferried journalists by helicopter to show them how they had regained control of the region. 'The government says that foreigners are being hunted by local tribesmen, but reports from Wana suggested that only the Uzbeks were the target of Mulla Nazir's fighters. The real Al Qaeda—the Arabs—found no mention in either official or unofficial reports from Wana.'[14]

One of the tribal journalists, now settled in Peshawar for safety, offered another interesting story about why Mulla Nazir and Yuldashev fell out; he spoke of 'a couple of thousand Punjabi Taliban belonging to Jaish-e-Mohammad, Harkatul Mujahideen, Lashkar-e-Jhangvi, Sipahe Sahaba Pakistan arriving in Wana in late 2006. They "occupied" some of the houses close to where Uzbeks were living. Becoming suspicious, most Uzbeks moved to the main town of Wana.'[15]

This was the time when Mulla Nazir agreed with the authorities including the army and its intelligence apparatus to deal separately with the Arabs, who had a history of fighting against the USSR under the auspices of Pakistani military, and the Uzbeks who, reportedly, are much more vicious and staunch as far as their loyalty to the Al Qaeda ideology is concerned. Al Qaeda Arabs were also more sympathetic towards Pakistan because of the decades-old relations between Pakistan and most Arab countries.

Mulla Nazir, possibly guided by the Pakistani intelligence community, decided to allow Arabs to stay on in his area of influence. Pakistani officials helped in creating this alliance between

Mulla Nazir and Arab fighters, hoping the Arabs could be helpful in gathering information on Afghanistan from their comrades, particularly those who retreated into Waziristan after accomplishing missions against the US and NATO forces.

Tahir Yuldashev got wind of the impending operation and began to put together a counterstrategy. The murder of a widely respected Saudi, Sheikh Asadullah, the operational commander of Al Qaeda, on 13 March 2007, served as the real tipping point in Yuldashev's relations with Mulla Nazir. Asadullah, said to be in his mid fifties, had a flowing red beard and was also known as 'Mr Money Bags' for his wealth. He had succeeded Ahmad Saeed Abdur Rehman Khaddar Al-Canadi, the Egyptian-born Canadian citizen killed in a military action in Baghar near Angoor Adda near the Afghanistan border in October 2004. Asadullah was known for being a conduit for finances to Al Qaeda affiliates and was on his way to hand over some money to the widow of an unidentified foreign militant allegedly killed by the Uzbeks, when he was ambushed and executed by Tahir Jan's men.

Following government claims of control over South Waziristan, and the relative calm thereafter, Mulla Nazir automatically came under suspicion as collaborating with the Pakistani authorities. Covert support from the Pakistani military and Musharraf's public admission of this earned him the ire of his rivals, including Baitullah Mehsud. Nazir reportedly received millions of rupees from the authorities as reward—mostly in the form of stipends and funds for development schemes in his area.

Two assassination attempts on Mulla Nazir, therefore, came as no surprise; one of the would-be assassins, a youngster from Bajaur armed with an explosive-laden belt, was intercepted just a few yards from Mulla Nazir in June. The boy told his interrogators that the Uzbek militant Saiful Asad had given him the task of 'blowing up Mulla Nazir'. He is an agent of the infidels, the boy said. That the boy had travelled all the way from Bajaur agency to carry out the mission underscored another fact—militants of different schools of Islamic thought were spread out over most of the tribal areas, particularly Waziristan, Bajaur and Mohmand agencies. Bajaur, for instance, hosted a number of Arab Muslims who looked to Saudi Arabia for spiritual guidance—the Salafi school of theology—to which Osama bin Laden and his deputy Ayman al-Zawahiri belong.

During 2008 Wana and the surrounding hamlets remained firmly in Mulla Nazir's control, and an unwritten understanding with the authorities enabled the army and government officials to move in and out of the area easily. Local residents say after the mop-up operations were concluded in some parts of South Waziristan, more Arabs returned to the area and were moving around freely. A journalist with good access to Taliban ranks said hundreds of Arabs are also hiding in Mirali, a small town a few kilometres away from Miranshah, where they have occupied the houses left behind by Mehsud tribesmen who had fled the area during the December 2007–January 2008 military operation. Unlike the Uzbeks, who are despised by the local Taliban and tribesmen, the Arabs have good relations with both.[16] The Arabs are divided into two groups: the Egyptians and the Libyans. Dr Ayman al-Zawahiri led the Egyptians while Abu Lait el Libi had led the Libyans until his death in a drone-fired missile attack in early 2008. Yahya Libbi, who had escaped from the Bagram jail in 2005, reportedly leads this group. Reports by US and Afghan intelligence sources also corroborate the increased presence of Arabs, mostly from Iraq, in Waziristan. Tribal sources, who feed satellite networks like CNN and Al Jazeera from the region, also privately confirm that Arabs are using the Waziristan region as their sanctuary.

North Waziristan

North Waziristan is the second most important outpost, a transit point as well as a refuge for all Afghan and non-Afghan radical Islamists. In September 2006, the government had facilitated a peace deal here, which it claimed was with local tribesmen and elders, to ensure peace and stop cross-border movement of

Pakistani and Afghan militants. Over 300 locals had signed it. Though there was no direct mention of local or Afghan Taliban, the agreement came into being with the full support of people like the Afghan war veteran Jalaluddin Haqqani, his son, as well as Haji Gul Bahadur. Bahadur holds considerable sway over militant forces in North Waziristan and coordinates closely with the Haqqani clan as far as operations inside Afghanistan are concerned. All these forces were represented by people of their choice when the 5 September 2006 peace deal was brokered, but none was mentioned by name. The only reference to them was the phrase 'mujahideen of the area', which actually denoted Haqqani and Bahadur Taliban parties.

Local Taliban—the TTP as well as others—suspended the deal in May 2007, alleging violations by the authorities. But the deal came to life again on 17 February 2008, weeks after the new governor Owais Ahmed Ghani took charge, and both sides agreed to respect each other's existence. 'After eight and a half years, the governor, that is me, was able to spend the night in Miranshah, meet with the people, talk to the tribal elders . . . that is a huge advantage [of negotiating with the locals],' Ghani told me at the Governor's House in Peshawar in late September 2008. Ghani shed some light on intriguing developments in North Waziristan: despite relentless US pressure to hunt down Al Qaeda and their supporters, the Pakistani intelligence apparatus apparently maintained contacts with Afghan Taliban (the Haqqani clan) and the Pakistani militants led by Haji Gul Bahadur in North Waziristan. The latter, after a long silence, resurfaced in the media in early July 2008 after a meeting with Mulla Nazir from South Waziristan. This led to the creation of a new alliance called the Taliban Ittehad.

The ostensible purpose of the alliance was to isolate Baitullah Mehsud, to unite all the Taliban including possibly those led by Baitullah Mehsud and to keep up their anti-US campaign. In this context, Bahadur and one of Haqqani's sons met Mehsud once but Bahadur skipped the next two meetings, triggering speculation that he and his allies might have acted to facilitate the government's desire to isolate Baitullah Mehsud in the Mehsud region. This was of course a trade-off; these Taliban would not harm government interests in North Waziristan and in return the authorities would not go after them. 'We understand Bahadur and Haqqani plan to raise a parallel organization from Waziristan to Bajaur to contain Baitullah Mehsud's influence,' said a senior intelligence official dealing with FATA affairs.[17] This explains why tribal sources close to the militants played down some of the intimidating statements by Bahadur and allies as 'insignificant', or perhaps a 'fixed match', as a FATA friend dubbed it. Despite their mutual accommodation, both the Taliban forces and the government keep trading charges to dispel the impression of collaboration. For instance, on 6 August 2008, Bahadur's alliance claimed responsibility for the missile attacks and bomb blasts in South Waziristan the previous day. Rival Taliban suspected of links with Uzbek militants and with Baitullah Mehsud appeared to be the targets. The Taliban Ittehad spokesman, Ahmadullah Ahmadi, said they fired missiles on three locations and vowed the group would retaliate against any attack by the government.[18] One of Bahadur's allies, Abdul Khaliq Haqqani, also issued a statement the same day, claiming he had prepared a group of suicide bombers to be used against the government.

Tribal sources—officials and journalists—interpreted these statements as fake posturing because, they argued, the Taliban Ittehad comprising Bahadur and Mulla Nazir, as well as the Afghan Haqqani clan, had a good rapport with the authorities, based on the understanding that these militants would refrain from targeting the Pakistan army or government interests. Under the peace deal, they had also pledged not to shelter foreigners. Yet, the ground reality betrayed this undertaking; the Haqqanis in particular continue to serve as the patrons of all foreign Taliban/Al Qaeda forces present in the region. Although the Haqqanis are friends with the anti-Uzbek Mulla Nazir, they reportedly continue to provide shelter to the Central Asian IMU fighters after the latter were forced to leave South Waziristan in March 2007.

An intelligence official explained the context: after Mulla Nazir threw the IMU Uzbek militants out of Wana and its vicinity, the Arabs living there had promised to guard against intelligence leaks. But on 28 July 2008 a US missile strike reportedly took out the top Al Qaeda chemical and biological weapons expert of Egyptian origin, Midhat Mursi al-Sayid Umar, also known as Abu Khabab al-Masri, along with five others. This gave rise to the suspicion that an intelligence agent from among the Arabs living in Wana might have spied on Masri and reported on him to the US forces.

'Probably that is why Al Qaeda activists and sympathizers in North Waziristan including Bahadur and Haqqani felt betrayed and lobbed rockets at possible suspects,' the official conjectured. They suspected that US and Afghan informers had infiltrated the ranks of Mulla Nazir and his Arab guests, which led to the missile attacks. These suspicions grew as US drones kept raining missiles on suspected hideouts. Between 28 July and late October 2008, MQ-9 Reaper aircraft carried out almost twenty missile strikes in the entire Waziristan region. The CIA operates these medium-to-high altitude, long-endurance unmanned aircraft in Afghanistan. The MQ-9, primarily a hunter–killer, acts as an intelligence, surveillance and reconnaissance asset, employing sensors to provide real-time data to commanders and intelligence specialists at all levels.

At a meeting of the Taliban Ittehad in late July, Bahadur accused Prime Minister Yousuf Raza Gilani and the government of killing innocent tribesmen to please the 'Americans'. He condemned the US missile attack on Zyara Leeta village of South Waziristan that killed Masri and called it 'a gift of the Pakistani prime minister for the Americans during his visit to the US'. Viewed closely, Bahadur's was only a political statement as the prime minister would not personally order or monitor such activities in the presence of military and intelligence apparatus. That Bahadur took on the premier also underscored realpolitik; the potential interlocutors of many militant groups are the military or its intelligence outfits, and not the civilian government. So the Taliban leaders can afford to hurl taunts at civilian leaders, which raises their esteem in the eyes of their followers.

Haqqani Factor in North Waziristan

Khalifa Sirajuddin Haqqani, Jalaluddin Haqqani's son, and Maulana Bakhta Jan (Khost)—both Afghans—loom large over North Waziristan, which borders Afghanistan's Khost province. They also call themselves Taliban. Both Siraj Haqqani and Maulana Bakhta Jan were part of the talks that led to the September 2006 peace deal in the area and they continue to dominate the political landscape in the Waziristan region, providing spiritual and militant guidance to the Afghan and Pakistani Taliban movement in North Waziristan as well as across the Durand Line, largely in the eastern Afghan provinces of Kunar, Paktia and Paktika.

On 21 June 2006, as talks for the peace deal were still under way, Sirajuddin Haqqani had issued a decree that it was no longer the Taliban policy to fight the Pakistan army. This marked the end of significant fighting in South Waziristan. However, the Taliban intentionally did not circulate the decree in North Waziristan, thereby keeping up the pressure on the government as the terms for a comprehensive accord were being worked out. Paradoxically, despite their commitment not to target Pakistan government and military, Haqqani and his colleagues continue to shelter IMU fugitives because of their ideological affinity. The connections with other Taliban commanders pressed them into providing necessary shelter and protection to the Uzbeks as well as their supporters from South Waziristan including the brothers Sharif and Noorul Islam. Haqqani and his Pakistani partners were also involved in the controversial September 2006 peace deal brokered between the Taliban and local tribesmen.

In July 2007 Maulvi Abdul Khaliq Haqqani, another son of Jalaluddin Haqqani, issued a press statement saying that the deaths of Lal Masjid and Jamia Hafsa students would be avenged.

'The target of our suicide attacks are and will be security officials. Those who don't understand our viewpoint will also be targeted,' he said.[19] The Lal Masjid episode demonstrated the widespread hold of Islamic orthodoxy. The mosque, situated in the heart of Islamabad, and the seminary Jamia Hafsa, built illegally on state land, shot into world headlines when female students of the Hafsa seminary occupied a public library adjacent to the seminary in January 2008 and began demanding the enforcement of sharia. Fully supported by their male comrades, many of whom were trained militants and experts in handling weapons and martial arts from training camps in tribal areas, these girl students—wrapped in black head-to-toe veils—consistently challenged the writ of the state by kidnapping alleged sex workers, taking policemen hostage, raiding massage parlours and pressing shopkeepers to burn CDs and DVDs. Despite warnings from the authorities to vacate the public library, and several rounds of talks, the students stood their ground under the guidance of their mentors—Maulana Abdul Aziz and his younger brother Abdur Rasheed Ghazi. The standoff made headlines and eventually culminated in a military operation on the complex in July 2007, during which Ghazi, his mother and dozens of others were killed. More than a dozen Pakistan army soldiers and officers also fell to the bullets fired from inside the complex. For several weeks, this blatant challenge to state authority played out in the heart of Islamabad, revealing the confidence with which the zealots felt they could enforce their brand of sharia in the capital.

The government later discovered interconnected corridors in the basement of the Jamia Hafsa which were expertly used as connecting routes from where the militants would fire on the law enforcement officers and then run away. They also used the female students and children as safety shields.

Earlier in May, the Haqqani-led Taliban shura had imposed a stringent ban on the sale of CDs and cassettes, and music in buses and passenger coaches in North Waziristan. The shura also ordered owners of music and video shops in Miranshah to wind up their businesses immediately.[20] Armed volunteers raided music centres and CD shops in the town and asked people to stop playing music in shops, buses and homes. The shura also threatened violators with 'consequences'. This decree underscored the Taliban strength and influence in Waziristan, which eventually rendered the local administration helpless and also became a source of great intimidation to the Pakistan army, forcing it to go for negotiated peaceful coexistence, as enunciated by the September peace deal.

Sirajuddin Haqqani who practically heads the Amaraat-e-Islami Afghanistan's (AIA) military operations, and Bakhta Jan, continue to influence the talks with the authorities and are closely linked with Al Qaeda leadership on both sides of the border. Dozens of Pakistani militants belonging to the Jamiatul Mujahideen, Jaish-e-Mohammad and Lashkar-e-Jhangvi, live in the area under their protection, and all have been playing host to fleeing Al Qaeda leaders and operatives. For instance Khalid Sheikh Mohammad, arrested in March 2003, and Abu Zubaida, arrested from Faisalabad a few months earlier, had transited through North Waziristan, and enjoyed Haqqanis' hospitality. 'The combination of sanctuary in Pakistan, deep links on both sides of the border and steady support from Arab and other jihadist networks has made Maulvi [Jalaluddin Haqqani] a formidable threat to the stability of Afghanistan,' observed a *New York Times* report.[21]

The Haqqani network is suspected of being behind four large-vehicle suicide bombings in eastern Afghanistan in 2008, including the attack mounted on the Indian embassy in Kabul in July 2008. The *New York Times* wrote that according to Afghan security officials one of Haqqani's senior lieutenants masterminded a multi pronged attack on the Serena Hotel in Kabul that killed seven people in January 2008, as well as the assassination attempt on President Karzai in April of the same year.

A raid on the Mumba-e-Uloom seminary in North Waziristan, on 29 July 2008 was based on the information that the Haqqani network was working overtime to prepare and send insurgents into Afghanistan. The seminary belongs to Jalaluddin Haqqani and has been almost deserted following several similar raids by Pakistani and US forces. It is located in Danday Drapa Khel, half a kilometre north of Miranshah. The AIA exercises considerable influence over local politics as well; local residents attribute the success of the 18 February 2008 elections of Kamran Wazir from North Waziristan to Pakistan's national legislature to Haqqani's influence and Kamran's close relations with Al Qaeda figures. Kamran Wazir defeated his own party (JUI-F) colleague Maulana Nek Zaman in the election, promoting locals to suggest that close ideological affinity with Taliban and Al Qaeda could well have ensured his victory over Zaman. Kamran's father runs a hospital, Zakeem, in Miranshah, which reportedly provides treatment to Al Qaeda and Taliban fighters. A black American Al Qaeda operative was treated here during the January 2008 operation before being arrested in the town of Bannu.

Khyber and Bajaur Agencies

The Khyber Pass is an extremely important artery that connects Peshawar with Kabul and is crucial for US–NATO food and fuel supplies. The Khyber and Bajaur agencies have experienced a surge in Talibanization and an increase in criminal activities—attacks on US or NATO supply trucks and plunder of their goods as well as kidnapping for ransom. The Bajaur agency is a hotbed of militancy, which began during the anti-Soviet Russian jihad in the 1980s. It borders the eastern Afghan province of Kunar and is thus ideal for groups with cross-border linkages. Bajaur, adjacent to Malakand and Swat, was virtually the birthplace of the Pakistani Taliban movement by Maulana Sufi Mohammad, most of which has now morphed into Tehreek-e-Taliban Pakistan, and is led in the region by Maulvi Faqir Mohammad and Mulla Fazlullah (Sufi Mohammad's estranged son-in-law and the TTP representative for the Swat region). Both Khyber and Bajaur witnessed numerous military operations targeting both militants and criminals. Bajaur in particular has been a tough test case for the Pakistani government. As of February 2009, the military and paramilitary forces remained locked in fierce battles all over Bajaur, resulting in the displacement of close to 300,000 people.

Taliban of Khyber Agency

The Talibanization of Khyber agency is relatively recent and differs from the evolution of these movements in other agencies. Currently, three groups loom large over the agency: the Lashkar-e-Islam, founded by Mufti Munir Shakir and currently led by Mangal Bagh Afridi; the Ansarul Islam, founded by Pir Saifurehman and at present headed by Mehbub ul Haq; and Amar bil Maroof wa Nahi Analmunkir—which translates as the Promotion of Virtue and Prevention of Vice (PVPV)—founded by Haji Naamdar, who was assassinated in August 2008.

Ideologically, most groups in the area are Sunni outfits with minor ideological deviations, mostly affiliated to the Deoband school of theology. Deoband is a city in India where, in the nineteenth century, the revival and purification movement of Islam began. Calling for a 'return to the basics', the concept underlying the movement was the belief that Muslims were drifting from the tenets of the Sunnah and Quran, into the realm of Sufism, which the Deobandis perceived as being a Hindu conspiracy to introduce Hindu rituals into Islam. Some observers believe that Deobandis, instead of focusing on the message of the Quran and Sunnah, focus more on the literal meaning of the Quranic verses. These groups have been at loggerheads, particularly those led by Afridi and Mehbub ul Haq since 2005. The Lashkar-e-Islam represents the hardline Deobandi school of thought, also akin to the Lashkar-e-Taiba and Jamiatul Mujahideen, rooted in the Bajaur agency thinking, which justifies the use of force for religious ends. They are quite puritanical and believe in following the Quran in letter and spirit, as practised in ultraconservative Saudi Arabia. They reject visits to shrines and tombs of saints as un-Islamic.

Ansarul Islam, on the other hand, follows the Quran and Sunnah in a way that most in Pakistan describe as Barelvi school of thought; the followers of this brand of Islam take a relatively liberal view of the religion, including Sufism, and see no problem in praying at tombs and shrines of saints who are seen as intermediaries between man and God. This branch of Sunni

Islam, founded in the north Indian city of Bareilly, is implacably opposed by the Deobandis as being unfaithful to the basic tenets of Islam. Peace, tolerance, harmony and acceptance of other faiths and sects have remained at the core of the Barelvi interpretation of the Sunni faith.

The PVPV identifies closely with the Afghan Taliban, and represents a fairly rigid version of Islam in which women practically do not have any role. They also believe in direct contact between God and man and can be categorized as followers of the Salafi school of theology.

Besides their ideological differences, the groups in Khyber also vie for territorial authority; the Khyber agency is strategic for exports and US–NATO supplies to Afghanistan. It is also a conduit for the huge volume of smuggled goods that cross both sides of the Durand Line along with drugs and weapons. Essentially, political power, territorial authority, protection money (that these groups make off transporters and goods movers) combined with various versions of militant Islam are all at play in the strategically important Khyber agency.

In June and July 2008 Lashkar-e-Islam and Ansarul Islam fought fierce battles not only in the Jamrud and Bara regions of the Khyber agency but also in the remote and mountainous Tirah valley. These skirmishes left over a hundred activists dead. The Pakistan army also took out several of their camps and facilities in the agency when it launched the Sirat-e-Mustaqeem (literally, the Straight Path that Allah shows) operation in late June that year, prompted by rumours that Mangal Bagh Afridi was getting ready to seize strategic locations in Peshawar.

The Khyber agency is important due to its strategic location. Bara and Landikotal are two sub-districts within the agency. Most of the area hosts markets for foreign smuggled goods and has a thriving industry in fake products manufactured or packaged in small industrial units. Historically, several armies transited through the Khyber Pass, fighting and bribing the Afridi tribes while at the same time entering into deals of convenience with them. The bulk of Afghans, forced out by the Soviet-Russian occupation of Afghanistan in 1979, also used the Khyber Pass to find shelter elsewhere in Pakistan.

Khyber is also a hotbed for criminal gangs which operate under the cover of the Taliban. Pilferage or hijacking of food trucks is quite frequent. Border officials told me at Torkham that at least 10,000 cargo trucks transit every month through this international crossing point. An official of a private freight company in Kabul spoke of more or less the same number of trucks that cross Torkham, the last Pakistani post on the Peshawar–Jalalabad route. The gangs usually target containers and trucks carrying fuel and food supplies for the US and coalition troops based in Afghanistan. In late March 2008, for instance, these gangs torched about a hundred oil tankers parked near Torkham. The extent of the ensuing fire and flames suggested the tankers were set on fire after much of the oil had been stolen. Approximately 75 per cent of the US supplies in Afghanistan, including 40 per cent of the vehicle fuel, passes through Pakistan, either on land or through the country's air space, and Pentagon officials say they are working on contingency plans to send the supplies through other countries for security reasons.[1]

On 10 November 2008 criminals waylaid as many as thirteen trucks carrying fuel and foodstuff for the US and NATO forces near the Jamrud town, about half an hour after they had entered the Khyber agency. Officials said eleven trucks contained wheat and two were carrying military vehicles. They were intercepted at four places in the Khyber Pass on the way to the Afghan border by a group of sixty masked gunmen. 'They popped up on the road suddenly and took away the trucks. Not a single shot was fired,' Reuters quoted officials as saying. A military offensive followed the hijacking, with two helicopter gunships targeting Godar, Saurkamar and Varmado Mela areas of Jamrud; finally the security forces managed to recover all the trucks after a brief gun battle. Soon after the clashes, Mustafa Kamal, a key figure of the Khyber agency Tehreek-e-Taliban Pakistan, warned that the group would attack the Peshawar airport if the military operation was not stopped. He said his group would not 'forgive' the assistant political agents of Khyber agency and Jamrud for ordering 'the killings of innocent people'. He was referring to the people killed during the truck recovery operation.

Just before the attempted truck hijackings, seven rockets had landed at the Peshawar airport. Kamal's statement could be regarded as indirect proof that the TTP actually fired those rockets into the airport area. A civilian intelligence official told me that several incidents of hijackings go unreported. 'If the incident involves [just] one or two trucks, the coalition forces prefer to keep quiet,' the official said in Peshawar, in early November 2008. Most of the clothing and food stuff stolen from these containers—flak jackets, daggers, first-aid kits, canned food, blankets, edible oil, sleeping bags—end up in the markets on the outskirts of Peshawar, called Karkhano. In March 2007, several containers went missing en route from Karachi to Afghanistan via Torkham. They were, in fact, hijacked in the Karak frontier region some seventy kilometres south of Peshawar, after which the American security apparatus adopted a different security and surveillance system, which tracks the cargo electronically all the way from Karachi to Kabul, making it easily traceable. Despite the satellite-based surveillance, pilferages or the abduction of containers remains a hazard. Security officials believe that the vehicles are burnt because that is the easiest way of eliminating evidence of thefts. After looting the trucks and silencing the drivers at gunpoint or taking the drivers on board, the gangs put the vehicles on fire.[2]

Local traders and residents say that the combination of criminal gangs and the Taliban has become a source of income for security and government officials. Together, the Taliban threat and criminal gangs are disrupting regular trade as well. The Khyber Pass is not only the vital lifeline for impoverished Afghanistan, but also for the foreign troops based there. Zia ul Haq Sarhadi, who heads an association of Pakistani customs agents helping traders move goods through the customs post at Torkham, claimed the average number of trucks has dropped to 250 a day from 500 in early 2007, before violence escalated.[3] 'Political authorities depend on the Frontier Constabulary to provide law and order in the area but FC officers receive bribes from Haji Amal Gul of the Malaka Dinkhel tribe to allow smuggling of goods through the Soorghar area,' a Khyber agency trader said.[4]

Pakistan's ambassador to Afghanistan, Tariq Azizuddin, was also abducted from there on 11 February 2008. He was on his way to Kabul when he was waylaid by unknown armed men before being handed over to Baitullah Mehsud's militants. Azizuddin (now Pakistan's ambassador to Turkey) was freed on 16 May 2008 under circumstances still shrouded in mystery; in the days preceding his release, the government had struck some deals with the Taliban in South Waziristan, resulting in a swap involving the release of about forty Taliban militants and about seventeen security forces personnel who had been in the custody primarily of Baitullah Mehsud's fighters.

In late 2003 Haji Naamdar, a local cleric, launched the Amar bil Maroof wa Nahi Analmunkir in the Khyber Agency and commissioned a fiery orator, Mufti Munir Shakir, to 'spread the word of God and also ensure justice to all'. Shakir's oratory soon galvanized locals, the majority of whom felt oppressed by the draconian FCR laws (see Appendix) which treated them as second-class citizens. Socio-economic deprivation also played a vital role in catapulting PVPV into an acceptable organization which was seen as delivering justice. By late 2004 Haji Naamdar gradually went into the background, thereby pitching Shakir, who had founded Lashkar-e-Islam, against Pir Saifurrehman of Ansarul Islam. Ironically, at least two FM radio stations were funded by Mangal Bagh Afridi and Pir Saifurrehman respectively in late 2003. Their war had to do more with the local dynamics of control and power than with religious differences. Both indulged in a vicious propaganda war against each other through these makeshift FM stations, resulting in violent clashes in 2005 among their followers. March 2006 saw some bloody feuds between rival Taliban factions in the Khyber agency resulting in more than two dozen deaths in two days—in an area that falls in FATA but is just a dozen kilometres from places where the governor, the FC inspector general, the political agent and the army corps commander's headquarters are located.

Both groups defied the writ of the government; in February 2006 a tribal jirga ordered Pir Saifurrehman to leave the area to ease tensions, and he reportedly retreated to Punjab for shelter. The expulsion, however, helped little; rival FM stations continued to spit venom against each other. Both radical clerics held their ground, making a mockery of the administration as well as of the tribal jirga, which had been asking them to shut down their radio stations.[5]

Mufti Shakir had meanwhile set up his own sharia court, which adjudicated all crimes according to his understanding and interpretation of the sharia law—mostly the Taliban way. In some areas of the Khyber agency, Lashkar-e-Islam practically established a parallel government, launching an illegal FM radio station, while its armed vigilantes punished anybody they considered in conflict with their agenda. In May 2007 Lashkar-e-Islam activists demolished ten houses after picking up all valuables from there. Local militia, media reports said, acted as silent spectators. 'Armed LI activists patrol government roads and have set up illegal check posts as well. They forced private and public girls' schools to close down and occasionally also forcibly shut down boys' schools and colleges.'[6]

Residents of Bara district have alleged that when the political authorities ordered the Frontier Corps to take action against the Lashkar-e-Islam in 2006, the paramilitary Scouts initially refused to comply. Local civilians as well as scores of government officials saw the Lashkar-e-Islam's actions as doing a service to God by keeping the area under order and purifying it from all vices. The inaction by security forces rendered the political authorities helpless. Residents also alleged that some members of the Khasadar force—local police—were aligned with the Lashkar-e-Islam. They voiced their apprehensions to several Peshawar-based newspapers, saying Peshawar was not immune to what was happening in Bara and repercussions would affect the city if the government did not put an end to this parallel government. Finally, following external pressures, the authorities cracked down on the combatants. In late 2007 the political agent invoked the Frontier Crimes Regulation 40 and consigned Mufti Shakir to indefinite detention. But he was quietly set free in the latter half of 2008, and he now lives an obscure life.

Mangal Bagh Afridi, who had replaced Mufti Shakir, continues to command authority and respect in the region. Concentrated in several pockets of the Khyber agency, Lashkar-e-Islam continues to oppose 'un-Islamic' practices: no films, no video or music CDs are allowed for open sale in the markets. Criminals, if held, are punished, as the Afghan Taliban did under Mulla Omar.

The surge in religious fundamentalism on the one hand and crime on the other prompted Haji Naamdar to revive his PVPV. In fact, the creation of Tehreek-e-Taliban Pakistan in December 2007 provided him with a reason for becoming active again.[7] Haji Naamdar had reportedly sheltered several TTP militants—both local and foreign—who had fled the military operation in South Waziristan in January 2008. This continued until a suicide attack at Naamdar's headquarters in Takya, in the town of Bara in early May 2008, which left around twenty people injured. With the abduction of the Pakistani ambassador and execution of several officials, a turning point occurred for the Khyber Taliban. A small group led by Baitullah Mehsud's deputy, Hakeemullah Mehsud had emerged and started interfering in local matters like the detention and execution of about a dozen government and security officials.[8] They also indulged in target killings of government functionaries besides dispensing vigilante justice.

A day after the attack on him, Naamdar ordered Baitullah's Taliban to leave the Khyber Agency.[9] 'All militants belonging to Baitullah Mehsud's group have been ordered to leave the Khyber Agency following the confirmation that this was ordered by Baitullah,' a close aide to Naamdar told reporters on 3 May 2008.[10] Hakeemullah defended the attack by telling Naamdar that he had 'documentary evidence that [Naamdar] was a government puppet posing as a mujahid'.[11] To justify his act, Hakeemullah presented a photograph of Naamdar published in a Peshawar-based Urdu-language daily, showing him seated next to the Frontier Corps Colonel Mujahid Hussain. 'We have ordered the attack to kill you because the picture leaves no doubt about your credibility,' Hakeemullah reportedly told Naamdar on the phone while requesting the remains of the suicide bomber.[12] Several security and intelligence officials admitted their contacts with Naamdar, saying he listens to them and does not condone crime or killing in the name of Islam. The situation in Khyber, therefore, remains tense, and the jihadis at loggerheads.

Crime, corruption and (religious) conviction keep the agency on the boil. According to an intelligence official, the authorities reached out to Haji Naamdar and his group so that the administration could counter the influence of Hakeemullah Mehsud. Although the government's overtures to Naamdar also made him suspect as a collaborator, according to people based in Khyber agency, Naamdar had only reached a verbal understanding with the authorities and undertook not to attack government interests. Naamdar never interfered in government matters, while officials kept quiet on the activities of his vigilantes, who used to travel all the way to Peshawar to fix criminals. He was therefore used as a shield against the TTP threat that looms large all over FATA.

The absence of any legal justice system and the abuse of the Frontier Crimes Regulation have all combined to turn the Khyber Agency into an explosive powder keg. The inter-tribal rifts and personal rivalries also lead to strains within the society where the rule of revenge reigns supreme.

Aversion to foreign troops and commitment to the cause of the Afghan Taliban as well as ideological affinity with Al Qaeda serve as common denominators to the militant organizations in Khyber agency where, like in other FATA agencies, the precarious law and order situation fuels the ever-increasing craving for legal and socio-economic justice.

The nexus between the smuggling mafia and the administration is too often ignored or understated under the pretext of respecting local tribal customs and traditions. In the last few years, members of the local community have been raising alarm, but the administration refused to counter the increasing influence of local Taliban elements led earlier by Haji Naamdar and now by his successor, Niaz Gul. These Taliban provide protection in the area of their influence—regardless of who pays them. Smugglers, murderers, government and non-governmental organizations usually use the Taliban cover for passage through the region, thus ensuring a good source of income for them. Naamdar, for instance, was not himself a smuggler but reportedly provided protection to them. For the sake of the short-sighted objective of maintaining peace in the area, authorities would not touch these militants. As long as they are fighting with each other without disturbing the other areas of Pakistan, the government machinery does not bother them and merely watches their actions as a silent spectator. The government, however, jumped into action when Lashkar-e-Islam zealots started kidnapping and punishing people in areas around Peshawar for their 'un-Islamic practices'.

Taking advantage of the administration's indifference and the corruption within the local police and paramilitary forces deployed in the area, the vigilante groups blatantly attempted to deliver justice even in Peshawar, the provincial capital, by picking up criminals and awarding them Islamic punishments. That is why, despite the heavy presence of the army, paramilitary troops and a huge police force—backed by the ISI, Military Intelligence, the Intelligence Bureau and several other outfits—Peshawar experienced an unusual state of uncertainty in June and early July 2008; a wave of speculation about the Taliban getting ready to march on the provincial capital created alarm among the residents who feared the Taliban arrival into the city was imminent. To quash rumours and to re-establish its writ in the Khyber agency, the government eventually mounted the Sirat-e-Mustaqeem operation, causing Mangal Bagh Afridi and others to flee into the mountains; but this was temporary. 'When the IG police told a high-level meeting in May that Taliban are knocking at the doors of the provincial metropolis and its periphery [Shabqadar, Chaarsadda, Darra Adam Khel, Mardan] everybody, including intelligence officials, appeared alarmed,' said an intelligence official.[13] 'It seemed,' recalled a senior intelligence official, 'as if a revelation had struck them all, although every informed person in the town knew how the Taliban had been preying on common people and targeting them with psychological propaganda tactics.'[14]

Dr Mazhar Durrani, a Peshawar resident, said that people like Mangal Bagh and Haji Naamdar had created an aura about themselves, as the deliverers of justice. Durrani recalled how his widowed aunt had approached Mangal Bagh for justice after her in-laws refused to surrender her share of property left behind by her husband. 'Mangal Bagh summoned the brothers, rebuked them and asked them to be fair to her.' The scared brothers agreed on the spot and promised to do the needful.

Similarly, recalled an intelligence official, Mangal Bagh and Naamdar's people created their own justice vigilantes, courts and jails. 'Mangal Bagh sent his people to one of the spots notorious for drug pedlars, and fixed them all within a few days,' said the official. The police turned a blind eye because they also got a cut in the business, which thrived mainly because of young students and workshop employees. 'If the police doesn't help, I would certainly look to Mangal Bagh to get rid of criminals and drug pushers,' said the official, who himself is wary of the corruption and indifference of the police and other government departments. He was also sceptical of the Sirat-e-Mustaqeem operation which, he said, scared people but yielded little, pointing out that, within a few weeks of the operation, people like Mangal Bagh re-emerged in Bara, Jamrud and other parts of the Khyber agency, thereby refuting government claims that these 'miscreants' would not return to the region again. 'Agreed, they are running a parallel government—

but is that a solution? Conditions that gave rise to Taliban in Afghanistan were also more or less the same,' said another government official, who once served at the FATA secretariat.

Perceptions, right or wrong, also drive peoples' fears; the most common of them revolves around the causes of the situation, which is widely believed to have been created by the US to justify direct action inside FATA as well as the NWFP against suspected terror centres. Scores of people from the intelligentsia including professors, bureaucrats and technocrats, as well as the common man, somehow believe that the US wants to establish itself in Pakistan the way it did in Saudi Arabia, Qatar and Iraq, and is therefore creating conditions for such a role.

Another perception that currently dominates public discussion in the Frontier Province and elsewhere is that of a US administration that is bent upon denuclearizing Pakistan, discrediting Islam and also cutting Pakistan to size—a plan to balkanize Pakistan for easier management.

What underlies all these perceptions, however misplaced they may be, is the absence of good governance and of swift justice. Common people, already reeling under backbreaking food inflation and a tormenting energy crisis, feel that politicians, criminals, drug traffickers and officials have ganged up against them to deprive them of an honourable living. The Taliban and like-minded religious militants on their part have successfully exploited these conditions, protesting against an inefficient and insincere government, while sowing fear in the minds of all government servants including the army and creating goodwill among the common hapless people. Providing justice on the spot, fixing criminals and ensuring fair play to the victims of injustice are effective tools which the Taliban use to make themselves look like a God-fearing, formidable force that is raring to come to the public's rescue. Little attention, however, is paid to the consequences of such advances. Often, many frustrated people—not just the conservatives—overlook the problems that arise out of the Taliban code of life. It was suppression of individual liberties in the name of a questionable puritanical brand of Islam that the Afghan and Pakistani Taliban practised, and are hoping to put into practice again at some stage. This situation obviously does not augur well for the agency or for the country. It works as a demoralizing factor for the majority of people, who find themselves at the receiving end of an overbearing but inefficient bureaucracy that is perceived as unhelpful and obstructive.

Bajaur Agency

Bajaur is surrounded by the Mohmand agency in the south and by the eastern Afghan province of Kunar in the west. It is connected through the Malakand division to the northern areas of Pakistan that border China, giving it a strategic importance. Bajaur was thus one of the most suitable places for setting up jihadi camps for the anti-Soviet Russian jihad in the 1980s. Its population of over half a million is spread over seven sub-districts: Khaar, Mamoond, Sadozai, Brung, Qazafi, Naogati and Chamarkand. Two major tribes, Utman Khel and Tarklani, dominate the population here. They are further divided into sub-tribes, Mamoond, Salarzai, Alizai, Shamozai, Mandal and Targhavi.

The agency plunged into violence and chaos in July 2008, when the Taliban led by Maulvi Faqir Mohammad came close to declaring it independent. Until late July, the civilian administration had practically lost control over Khaar, the agency headquarters, with the paramilitary Bajaur Scouts mostly restricted to their camp on the outskirts of Khaar town.

In early August, after the government gave it the go-ahead, the Bajaur Scouts, led by Major General Tariq Khan, began a search and siege operation, backed up by Cobra helicopters. One after the other, they removed barriers that had been put up by the Taliban on the road that connects Khaar with Peshawar. The Pakistan army joined in four weeks later, with F-16 combat aircraft and heavy artillery which pounded Taliban positions around Khaar, forcing the entire leadership to flee into the Mamoon and Pashat valleys near the border to Afghanistan. The army–Scouts operation became more intense by the day because the difficult topography of the area—forests, wild vegetation and hills—worked as an impregnable shield and hideout for the militants, who kept attacking army posts and convoys. As the days passed, the area turned into a virtual battlefield, forcing almost 300,000 people to escape to safety.

During a visit to Bajaur in late September, it looked like a war zone: destroyed tanks on the road, bullet-riddled walls of mud compounds and army presence all around. The thunder of heavy machine-gun fire from Cobra helicopters greeted us when we reached Tangkhatta, on the outskirts of Khaar town; the village on the Khaar–Peshawar road had served as a vantage point for the militants to ambush army and government vehicles. The army had taken this village and a big compound along the road on 11 September 2008. The compound was a typical one where small corridors connected several rooms and front yards; a hen clucked around her chicks, and over a dozen pigeons were cooing to each other, unmindful of the battle that had taken many lives on that fateful day. Yet the trail of destruction, scattered quilts and clothes bore witness to the bloody battle that took place here.

'Miscreants ambushed us thrice on that day,' recalled Colonel Javed Baloch, who had led the battle. The Taliban laid siege around them every time they attempted to retrieve the bodies of soldiers and Major Asad Akbar. 'We had to spend the entire night in the compound as we were caught between militants all around. Air support through the Cobra helicopters eventually forced the Taliban to retreat,' he said. 'The choppers kept pounding militant positions as we rummaged through the shelled compound, surrounded by maize fields all around. Most of the crop is also gone because of the hostilities that began with the 6 August FC operation.'

By November 2008, a large number of the families, men in particular, had returned but the majority still lived in camps in areas outside FATA because of the pitched battles that the security forces were fighting with the Taliban. Army officials claimed to have killed close to 1600 Taliban by end November at the cost of about 110 soldiers and officers. In a Cobra gunship raid in October, the army almost got Faqir Mohammad. Bajaur Scouts officials said several mortars hit the car carrying Faqir Mohammad. 'According to our human assets on the ground,' said the official, 'Faqir sustained injuries while at least one of his two sons was killed in the attack.'

'Despite several reversals and heavy losses, militants use everything they can to survive and attack. Security officials are surprised by the combat tactics and the stiff resistance the battle-hardened fighters are offering. They simply dissolve into local population after striking at targets,' Major General Tariq Khan explained, at the headquarters of the Bajaur Scouts, which is part of the Frontier Corps. They use residential compounds and markets as their defence mechanism, he added. Military officials interpret this as proof that Al Qaeda might be in cahoots with local Taliban, who frequently use improvised explosive devices, the suicide jackets being the most important and lethal weapon. It is not a rag-tag militia we are pitched against, they argue. 'They are fighting like an organized and well-trained army, using trenches and tunnels for vintage attacks and shelters,' Major General Khan said.

The Bajaur region also witnessed some 'reverse infiltration'; until recently, Afghan and US intelligence reports spoke of cross-border infiltration from Pakistan into Afghanistan but Pakistani intelligence officials now claim armed militants from Afghanistan are entering FATA to stoke insurgency. 'We detected close to 200 armed men crossing from Afghanistan's eastern Kunar province into Bajaur,' an FC official told me while driving through the Khaar town. He said Bajaur seemed to be attracting militants from other tribal regions, from across the border as well as perhaps from Iraq.

In light of the resistance the security forces met in Bajaur, it is difficult to predict to what extent the continuing army operation will succeed in containing Maulvi Faqir Mohammad of Tehreek-e-Taliban Pakistan and whether Maulana Fazlullah, who draws strength and support in large measure from Bajaur, can be disarmed and totally neutralized. In tandem with the military operation launched in August, the authorities encouraged the local tribesmen to resist the Taliban. The Taliban ambushed and killed three tribal elders—Malik Bakhtawar Khan, Malik Shah Zarin and religious scholar Maulvi Sher Wali—who were on their way home after a meeting with government officials in Khaar early September. They had agreed to raise a lashkar and asked the government for support, journalists in Khaar told me during one of my visits to the region. The local tribesmen held the Taliban responsible for the killings and formed the lashkar under the leadership of Fazal Karim Baro. The Salarzai tribe stepped forward and raised three lashkars comprising some 4000 tribesmen for deployment at different locations. The government has denied supporting the lashkars. Yet, given the context of the violence and bloodbath that the Taliban have been perpetrating on people they considered 'pro-government', support from the military and the civilian administration looked unavoidable. 'We are not providing any money or weapons but assured them of all possible political backing,' the army spokesman Major General Athar Abbas told me during a visit to Bajaur.

I also met a few tribal chieftains, who sounded wary of the military operation that, according to them, had displaced scores of families. But when I asked them why they had allowed the Taliban to take over, most went on the defensive. 'No doubt we allowed them to find a foothold here, we were too timid,' said Zarwali Salarzai. In fact most locals welcomed the raising of tribal lashkars in Swat, the Bajaur agency, in the semi-tribal region of Darra Adam Khel and other parts of the tribal belt. Though they remained sceptical, the move did give them some hope and many joined the tribal army to take on the militants.

Once the Taliban realized the emerging threat to their domination, they too responded with violence; the militants in

Chamarkand tehsil of Bajaur agency kidnapped eleven elders of a tribal lashkar in October 2008, of whom eight were beheaded and their bodies thrown on the main road. A suicide attack on an assembly of tribal elders of the Salarzai tribe the next month killed more than twenty tribal elders including the head of the tribal lashkar in the area, Malik Fazal Karim Baro. About a hundred tribesmen got injured in the incident. Baro, a retired Bajaur Scouts officer, had been instrumental in raising the anti-Taliban squad in Bajaur. When the jirga of hundreds of tribal elders was in progress, a tribal boy—a teenager—came to the venue in a car. Getting out of the car, he went straight to the middle of the jirga and squatted near Fazal Karim Baro before blowing himself up. The militant group Karwan-e-Nimatullah in the Salarzai area claimed responsibility for the attack.

In Buner (in the Malakand region) the local populace, largely on its own, raised an anti-Taliban lashkar in September 2008. Soon thereafter, they successfully chased and killed six militants who had attacked a police station in the Kingargali area of that district, brutally killing eight policemen on duty. After that incident the people of Buner raised a formal lashkar of volunteers to contain the activities of militants in their area. Soon, residents of Maidan area in Dir district of the Malakand region, where militants from Bajaur had taken shelter, followed suit. Following several rounds of talks, the militants had to leave the area.

However, the lashkar avoided flushing out the militants from their stronghold in Mula Said Banda and Darra areas of Salarzai tehsil. The lashkar visited both areas once but met with resistance from some Taliban splinter groups. The ensuing clash left thirteen people dead, including eight lashkar men and five Taliban.

Lashkars were formed in the Mamoond tehsil and Charmang tehsil of Bajaur tribal agency. Mamoond is considered to be the bastion of the Taliban, and the hometown of Maulvi Faqir Mohammad. It also housed the main camp of the Tehreek-e-Taliban Pakistan. The lashkars also worked as a form of social pressure on several militant groups as it became evident that the militants were losing local support. On 10 November 2008, for instance, about a dozen Taliban commanders who were on the official wanted list surrendered to the political administration at a jirga of Otmankhel tribes in Bajaur agency. Local private TV channels including Geo, Samaa and Ary quoted officials and locals as saying that the commanders had assured the jirga and the political authorities that they would not back the Taliban in future. Locals said the jirga was also held in Khaar, where tribal elders handed over the twelve wanted individuals to the political authorities. The Salarzai and Mamoond tribes also held separate anti-Taliban jirgas in Bajaur the same day, vowing to continue their drive to purge the area of militants.

During the meeting, army and civilian government officials also warned Mamoond tribesmen of full-fledged military action if they failed to take practical steps against the militants in their area. Officials vented their frustration and anger at the non-cooperation of some of the Mamoond sub-tribes, telling them they had given enough time to the tribesmen for action against militants. Journalists based in Khaar told me that the army had even halted air strikes on Taliban strongholds, hoping Mamoonds would raise a lashkar to take on the militants. Mamoond and Pashat valley close to the border with Afghanistan are hotbeds of Taliban militancy. The Tarklani tribe, of which Mamoond is a sub-tribe, is divided on both sides of the border. Locals believe that this tribe is providing support to militants, and thereby blunting all government efforts to neutralize them.

Bajaur has been under the influence of numerous extremist groups including Al Qaeda, the Taliban Islamic Movement, Hezb-e-Islami of Gulbuddin Hekmetyar, Jamaat al-Daawa ilal Quran wal Sunnah of Sheikh Jamilur Rehman, Tehreek-e-Nifaze Shariate Mohammadi, Jamiatul Mujahideen, Jamaate Islami and Jamiat Ulemae Islam. An Al Qaeda affiliate called the Takfiris (Takfir wal Hijra), led by Mustafa Al Seerat Al-Suri, also has deep roots in the area.

The presence of radical groups that share the anti-western, pan-Islamist agenda also makes it a hot target that is under continuous US satellite and human surveillance. The suspicion that Osama bin Laden, his deputy Ayman al-Zawahiri and Hekmetyar are hiding in the mountainous region keeps it under the special scrutiny of American, Afghan and Pakistani intelligence.

The *New York Times* reported on 10 November 2008 that, based on an authorization by President George W. Bush, a Navy Seal team had stopped short of raiding a suspected militants' compound in the Bajaur region of Pakistan in 2006. Quoting a former CIA official, the paper said the 2006 order was issued after the Bush administration had granted intelligence agencies sweeping power to secretly detain and interrogate terrorist suspects in overseas prisons and to bug telephone and electronic communications. (Targets in Somalia need the approval of the defence secretary, while targets in some countries, including Pakistan and Syria, require presidential clearance.)

The *New York Times* report stated: 'An operation to send a team of Navy Seals and Army Rangers into Pakistan to capture Dr. Ayman al-Zawahiri, Osama Bin Laden's top deputy, was aborted at the last minute. Zawahiri was believed by intelligence officials to be attending a meeting in Bajaur and the Pentagon's Joint Special Operations Command hastily put together a plan to capture him. There were strong disagreements inside the Pentagon and the CIA about the quality of the intelligence, however, and some in the military expressed concern that the mission was unnecessarily risky. CIA director Porter Goss urged the military to carry out the mission, and some agents in the CIA even wanted to execute it without informing Ryan C. Crocker, the then American ambassador to Pakistan. Defence Secretary Donald Rumsfeld ultimately refused to authorize the mission.'

Khaled Ahmed, an authority on Islamic movements and militancy and consulting editor of the weekly *Friday Times*, said that hardline Arabs enjoy influence in the agency, and are currently led by Abu Musab Mustafa Alsuri, a wanted international terrorist. Along with Ayman al-Zawahiri, these fundamentalists represent a philosophy that permits violence even against differing fellow-Muslims. During the Afghan jihad, thousands of Arabs came to Afghanistan. Apparently, they fought together with the Afghan jihadis but remained divided in small factions which had serious differences. The differences increased during the eighteen-year-long war, as a result of which the big groups further crumbled and started fighting with each other for land and power.[15]

Currently, Maulvi Faqir Mohammad and Maulana Sufi Mohammad share the Sunni Muslim following in the Bajaur agency. Following his futile attempt to save the Afghan Taliban from the US-led onslaught through thousands of ill-trained and ill-equipped volunteers, Sufi Mohammad was arrested at the entry point in Miranshah and put behind bars for seven years without being formally charged. The ageing cleric was released in late April 2008 in the hope of restoring peace in the neighbouring volatile Malakand/Swat region, where his son-in-law Maulana Fazlullah briefly held sway, until the army moved in in November 2007 to reclaim police stations and government offices that had been lost to Fazlullah's men.

Little did the authorities realize that with the passage of time, Sufi Mohammad had lost relevance in the face of the rising TTP influence of Faqir Mohammad in Bajaur and Fazlullah in Swat and Malakand. While Sufi Mohammad was in jail, his son-in-law had taken charge of his movement, with most of Sufi's followers vowing allegiance to him. He set up his FM station illegally, brought Taliban fighters from FATA to Swat, cooperated with the Afghan Taliban and created a following for himself. With money flooding in, he started challenging the writ of the state and is currently the Al Qaeda leader in the region.

So Sufi Mohammad's release achieved little as far as restoring peace in Swat, Malakand or Bajaur are concerned. In fact Faqir Mohammad openly scoffed at Sufi Mohammad's purported deal with the government. 'Talks with Maulana Sufi Mohammad will not help the NWFP government bring peace to Swat. The government should hold talks with Fazlullah instead of Sufi Mohammad,' Faqir Mohammad said at a press conference in Khaar.[16]

Anti-western rhetoric continues to be at the top of the list of these militants' agenda. Faqir Mohammad and colleagues remain wedded to the goal of evicting foreigners from Afghanistan. Addressing a gathering of about 5000 tribesmen who had gathered for the funeral of a local journalist in Bajaur agency, the militant leader expressed unrelenting opposition to the US-led forces in Afghanistan: 'We will not attack government positions and whoever indulges in such an attack will be treated as an enemy . . . but we are Muslims and the enemy of infidels and will continue our jihad in Afghanistan as long as the foreign allied forces are there.'[17]

The Taliban-led intimidation of the local population also continues unabated. Most music shops and hair-cutting salons here have been closed and their owners have switched to other businesses. Some of them moved out of the agency after pro-Taliban militants bombed their shops in May 2008.[18] In early May 2008, the TTP spokesman Maulvi Omar even set a two-month deadline for growing beards and warned people at large as well as barbers of strict punishment in case of non-compliance. He said shaving beards was 'against' sharia law.[19] Taliban vigilantes regularly check private and public transport vehicles searching for cassette and CD players (which they consider un-Islamic). On several occasions they seized cassettes and players from several vehicles and smashed them on the spot. Masked gunmen also warned clean-shaven commuters to grow a beard or face punishment. They also ordered passengers to remove musical ring tones from their cell phones and not to use mobile phones with built-in cameras.

Besides their contempt for non-governmental organizations for being agents of western obscenity, Faqir Mohammad's TTP also opposed anti-polio vaccination drives and the use of iodized salt. They consider them 'un-Islamic and suspect they lead to impotency', said a local resident.[20] Yet, following social pressure by local authorities, the Taliban did allow a three-day anti-polio campaign in late July 2008. Agency surgeon Dr Jehanzaib Dawar told reporters that around 593 teams had been formed to administer polio drops to children during the campaign. But the Taliban influence and propaganda proved to be a major obstruction to the vaccination against polio drive. Local health department officials said that initially the refusal rate hovered around 5000 a year ago but continued engagement helped bring down the rate to 2500 in 2008.[21]

Within one year of its creation, the TTP in Bajaur has clearly overshadowed and outpaced the TNSM. In a glaring display of their authority and their obscurantist and offensive agenda, TTP militants executed a woman after accusing her of being a spy for the US and a prostitute. The body of the unidentified woman was found dumped beside a road near the town of Khaar. According to a Reuters report of 11 June 2008 the note found by the body said, 'The woman was killed because she was an American spy and a prostitute and those found doing such activities will face the same fate.' A villager said the woman had apparently been strangled as there were rope marks on her neck. 'I didn't see any bullet or knife wounds.' It was the first execution of a woman under espionage charges. Taliban forces killed close to a hundred alleged spies since the war on terror began in late 2001.

In late July Maulvi Faqir suffered a blow within the organization when four of his influential commanders protested the 18 July killing of the rival Commander Shah and several of his comrades by TTP Commander Omar Khalid in the neighbouring Mohmand agency and resigned from the organization. 'Innocent mujahideen were killed in Mohmand. Mujahideen do not kill innocent people,' Salar Masood, a spokesman, said, in an expression of solidarity with those killed in the Mohmand agency.[22] This also underscored the fact that the Taliban movement cut across borders and regions. Masood charged the Baitullah Mehsud-led TTP with 'deviating' from the real cause of fighting the Americans inside Afghanistan. 'We took up the matter with Baitullah Mehsud but he did not take our concern seriously,' the spokesman said. 'We will form our own group—Tehreek-i-Taliban Al Jihad—to continue jihad against the United States,' Masood said on the phone from an undisclosed location in the Bajaur region. Maulvi Munir, Dr Abdul Wahab and Maulvi Abdul Hameed are the three other commanders who left the TTP to create their own faction.

Why is Bajaur a haven for militants? Bajaur is the birthplace of the banned Tehreek-e-Nifaze Shariate Mohammadi, the forerunner of the Pakistani Taliban. Sufi Mohammad had launched the TNSM in early 1990s and successfully challenged successive governments in the Malakand region by setting up illegal courts run by his own mullas. Many fighters loyal to Gulbuddin Hekmetyar are also known to have found sanctuary in Bajaur because of their ideological and ethnic affinity to local tribes. In the post-9/11 years, Bajaur first shot into limelight on 13 January 2006 with an extremely controversial US missile strike on a suspected Al Qaeda hideout. The pre-dawn strike, apparently a combination of Predators and high-flying bombers, hit three residential compounds in Damadola village. US media reports said that the attack resulted in the deaths of at least five high-level Al Qaeda figures, including Ayman al-Zawahiri.

The Associated Press quoted a Pakistani security official as saying that a dinner at which al-Zawahiri was expected had been planned for the night of 12 January.[23] A local cleric, Maulvi Liaqat, was at the dinner, but he left around midnight, unnamed Pakistani officials said. After the air strike, Liaqat was again at the scene, and he had the bodies of the Arab militants pulled from the rubble and taken away. A second cleric, Maulvi Atta Muhammad, took away the Pakistani militants, reported the *New York Times*.[24] Maulana Liaqat was among thousands of fighters who went to Afghanistan as part of Maulana Sufi Mohammad's lashkar against the US and its allies in October 2001 and stayed with Hekmetyar's party in Afghanistan's Kunar province.

The missiles were deadly accurate. Despite the pitch darkness of the night they not only located the three targeted houses on the outskirts of the village of Damadola Burkanday but squarely struck their hujra, the large rooms traditionally used by Pashtoon tribesmen to accommodate guests.[25] The destruction provided ample evidence that though the technology that guided the missiles to their targets at 3 a.m. was faultless, the intelligence that had selected those targets was not. Most accounts were conflicting as far as the presence of Al Qaeda operatives was concerned. Even as American military and intelligence sources spoke of the possible death of Ayman al-Zawahiri, the man considered to be the brains behind the militant group's strategy, Pakistani officials denied any 'foreigners' had been killed in the US missile attack. Some officials had initially said that 'preliminary investigations' suggested some foreigners were present in the area.

In Damadola itself, locals said they had never sheltered any Al Qaeda or Taliban leaders, let alone al-Zawahiri, an instantly recognizable fifty-four-year-old Egyptian-born former doctor. 'This is a big lie . . . Only our family members died in the attack,' said Shah Zaman, a jeweller who lost two sons and a daughter in the attack. 'They dropped bombs from planes and we were in no position to stop them . . . or to tell them we are innocent. I don't know [al-Zawahiri]. He was not at my home. No foreigner was at my home when the planes came and dropped bombs.' Haroon Rashid, a member of Parliament who lives in a village near Damadola, told me that he had seen a drone surveying the area hours before the attack. The dead were reported to include four children, aged between five and ten, and at least two women. According to Islamic tradition, they were buried almost immediately. One Pakistani official, speaking anonymously, told the *Observer* that hours before the strike some unidentified guests had arrived at one home and that some bodies had been removed quickly after the attack. This was denied by villagers.

US and Pakistani officials also said that the missiles were launched from American pilotless drones, which have previously been used to target senior Al Qaeda figures. A man alleged to be Al Qaeda's third-in-command had been killed in a 'stand-off' missile attack around a month ago. However, several eyewitnesses spoke of seeing planes and illuminating flares over the village, which, if true, would indicate the use of missiles from planes guided in by special forces teams on the ground rather than CIA-operated drones.

The government lodged a formal protest over the missile strikes with the American embassy in Islamabad several days later. Only a week previously, Pakistan had protested a similar attack on a suspected Al Qaeda hideout near Mirali, in North Waziristan which killed at least eight civilians. On 1 December 2006, one alleged Al Qaeda operative, Abu Hamza, or Hamza Rabia, was eliminated in a deadly missile attack from across the border, most probably fired from a CIA-operated drone.

The government had then said Abu Hamza and a few others were killed from accidental explosions inside the compound they have been living in. Public rage over these attacks was mounting and the authorities thought official protests might assuage bruised egos and thus the need to concoct the story of accident.

On 29 October 2006, Bajaur once again made international headlines, this time with the death of eighty-three alleged Taliban militants bombed while 'training' inside a compound in the Chenagai village. Once again, al-Zawahiri and Maulvi Liaqat and Maulvi Faqir Mohammed seemed to be the prime motives behind the deadly strike.[26] Religious parties and their leaders, led by MP Sahabzada Haroon Rashid and tribal Taliban members insisted that most people killed in the air strike were students of the seminary and had nothing to do with terrorism or militancy. Most religious parties blamed the attack on the US but the Pakistani government insisted its security forces carried out the operation, following intelligence reports that the seminary was the hub of militant training.

Ten days later, a cloaked suicide bomber sprang the most audacious attack yet on the Pakistan army, charging into a training ground and blowing up at least 42 soldiers limbering up for their morning drill at the army's main training centre in Dargai in the

North West Frontier Province.[27] The attack struck at the very pillar that props up the Pakistan state, the army, which is considered Pakistan's most feared and powerful institution. Security officials immediately launched a search for a second suicide bomber whose explosives apparently did not go off and who reportedly escaped on a motorcycle. No group claimed responsibility for the Dargai carnage, yet even the then interior minister, Aftab Sherpao, described it as a reaction to the strike on the Chenagai madrassa in Bajaur. The blame fell again on Baitullah Mehsud's men. He had not formed his TTP yet but many of his cohorts did operate in close coordination.

This incident also triggered widespread speculation and discussion on the Taliban spillover into urban centres and of the 'futility' of the September 2006 peace deal in North Waziristan, which also eventually fell through for non-compliance by the Taliban. Missile strikes inside FATA also added to the fury that already ran high among locals. 'This is a disaster. We all recognize the gravity of the situation. It's a nightmare to have an army being attacked on its own soil and by its own people,' Aftab Sherpao told me later. 'After the two incidents [Damadola and Chenagai] the doors to peaceful negotiated settlements are closed. I am afraid we are on a war course in the tribal areas,' a senior army intelligence official told the *Washington Post*.[28]

Mohmand, Kurram, Orakzai Agencies and Swat

Mohmand, Kurram and Orakzai agencies witnessed extreme violence in 2008. Here, too, historically, the relations between intelligence agencies and militant groups have shaped and fuelled the so-called Talibanization that has, in recent years, helped the Taliban entrench themselves, almost without any challenge from the locals. Mohmand agency, for instance, serves as a natural sanctuary for Taliban and Al Qaeda fighters, providing shelter and training, as well as a launch pad for their insurgent activities inside Afghanistan. In Mohmand, the Taliban initially launched itself by initiating a vicious crackdown against outlaws in the area, whipping, executing and imprisoning people found in violation of the sharia—as interpreted by the Taliban.

The Kurram agency is home to roughly 800,000 Muslims, about one third of them Shias. The arrival of several hardcore Sunni militants from the Middle East and Africa for the anti-Soviet jihad in Afghanistan in the early 1980s injected an element of conflict in Kurram and has since ruined the peace of the agency, turning it into a hotbed of sectarianism. The agency has witnessed some of the most barbarous mass killings—including instances of people thrown into wheat thrashers.

Like Mohmand, Kurram too offered an isolated sanctuary for the Taliban and Al Qaeda fighters. The emergence of the Taliban in Afghanistan and the war on terror precipitated sectarian tensions which had only been sporadic in the 1970s and early 1980s. It led to the most brutal extermination of rivals as well as protracted pitched battles between the Shia and Sunni population during 2008, the worst year in the agency's history.

The violence in Kurram agency has spilled over to the neighbouring Orakzai agency over the past two years. Local residents say that the Taliban are carrying out their anti-Shia campaign in a very calculated way under the command of Hakeemullah Mehsud, one of Baitullah Mehsud's leading commanders.

Mohmand Agency

On 22 October 2007, six small Taliban groups agreed to merge into Tehreek-e-Taliban (TTM) in the Mohmand agency, naming Omar Khalid, Baitullah Mehsud's deputy in Mohmand, as their leader. They also formed a sixteen-member consultative shura. The spokesman of the organization, Abu Nauman Sangari, told journalists at a location near Ghalanai, the administrative headquarters of Mohmand, that all six groups would work together for peace as members of the Tehreek-e-Taliban Mohmand Agency. Maulana Gul Muhammad was declared the deputy to Khalid. Khalid's real name is Abdul Wali Raghib and he is an ISI-trained jihadi who fought against Indian troops in Kashmir, but retreated into Mohmand following the 12 January 2002 ban on militant outfits.

The TTM follows the Afghan Taliban leader Mulla Omar's vision of sharia justice, adjudicating matters according to the group's own interpretation of Islamic laws, including punishments such as beheading of criminals, in the area under its influence. Rampant crime, injustice, abductions and an extremely inefficient and helpless administration provide the militants a conducive environment for enforcing their agenda.[1] Under Khalid's leadership, the TTM practically controls the entire agency and was involved in the abduction of ten paramilitary personnel, who were later released on the intervention of local elders in the summer of 2007. Following on the heels of the bloody Red Mosque incident in Islamabad in July 2007, TTM zealots ordered female teachers and girl students to wear the veil. Only days later a woman teacher was murdered by unknown gunmen, triggering apprehensions that TTM did it to strike fear in the hearts of the government schoolteachers; and they succeeded because the murder resulted in the closure of more than a hundred girls' schools in August. In November 2007 the Mohmand Taliban caught some criminals during a crackdown and later slaughtered them one after the other in the presence of thousands of people. It happened on the eve of Eid. The bodies were left on the spot for over twenty-four hours to 'teach other bad people a lesson'. In the last week of January 2008, they shot some eight officials dead and took hostage another eight for ransom. In late April 2008, in the Muchnai area, the Taliban killed another five criminals accused of theft. They shot one dead, whom they had caught alive, in front of hundreds of people.[2]

On 26 May 2008 TTM militants and tribal elders signed an accord pledging to maintain peace in the Mohmand agency. In return, several militants, who had been arrested on charges of terrorism and attacks on security personnel in the tribal region, were released.[3] Under the accord, the militants undertook to remain peaceful and refrain from targeting security personnel and government installations.

Prominent tribal elders Malik Muhammad Ali Haleemzai, Fazal Manan, former MPs Malik Fida Mohammad, Maulana Abdul Malik and local militant leaders Qari Shakeel, Nisar and Qari Akhtar Shah attended the jirga held at the residence of the tribal chieftain Malik Zahir Shah Qandahari in Lakaro subdivision of Mohmand agency. The militants gave their word to the jirga that they would not interfere in government activities and would not obstruct development projects.[4]

Qandahari secured the promise that girls and women teachers including all government staff would be allowed to go to schools.[5] The Taliban also assured security to government employees. The

Taliban also announced that NGOs would not be allowed to resume work in the area and accused them of 'spreading obscenity', which could not be tolerated. Taliban and pro-Taliban forces are antagonistic to NGOs and oppose them universally. They also consider the NGOs to be the agents of the west who, according to the TTP, are used to invade local culture and misguide innocent Muslims. Scores of Afghan and foreign NGO workers have either suffered imprisonment or lost their lives at the hands of Taliban, the TTP and other militant outfits. Usually, all of them accuse the NGOs of engaging in espionage for the US forces.

Qari Shakeel, Maulana Ehtisham ul Haq, Maulvi Nisar and Dr Assad, the organization's mysterious spokesman are some of TTM's zealots who have a following of at least 2000 armed militants. They also act as vigilantes against criminals. 'The killing of innocent people, kidnapping for ransom, blowing up check posts and attacks on government targets and officials are routine,' observed an Islamabad-based think tank, the Centre for Research and Security Studies, in its report based on a personal intercept of about 150 locals in Mohmand.

By July 2008 the Taliban were in complete control of the agency. Until June 2003 large swathes of Mohmand had thrived as no-go areas. The writ of the government hardly went beyond the small town of Ghalanai, the administrative headquarters of Mohmand. Its border with the eastern Afghan provinces of Ningarhar and Kunar was practically unmanned thereby giving free passage to the militants commuting between Pakistan and Afghanistan. To the west, Mohmand borders the embattled Malakand/Swat and Charsada districts as well as the provincial capital Peshawar in the south-west.

Interestingly, Charsada is the hometown of the former home minister Aftab Ahmed Khan Sherpao as well as of Asfandyar Wali Khan, the head of the Awami National Party which is now ruling the province. Sherpao survived two suicide attacks in 2007 within a space of five months, while Khan escaped unhurt when a suicide bomber blew himself up only metres away in October 2008. These attacks were clear indicators of the TTP-led violence in and outside the FATA region.

When I travelled to the Mohmand region in late 2003 and again in 2004, the military and civilian authorities seemed to have established and extended their control over most areas. They had begun some development work there as well, including creating new metalled roads or motorable tracks where none existed before. Meetings with tribal elders also yielded largely positive impressions because the region had remained unattended by the government until Afghan troops intruded into the agency area in pursuit of militants in the summer of 2003. This incursion caused a row over the border, which had never been clearly demarcated in this region. Only with the intervention of the US military command based in Kabul could the dispute be set aside for a while.

As it turned out later, there was much simmering underneath the facade of the government's writ being extended to these previously 'inaccessible areas'. Despite government and military claims, by July 2008, the Mohmand agency had almost fully fallen into the hands of the TTM led by Omar Khalid.[6] 'Omar Khalid is the strongest and most influential Taliban leader after Baitullah Mehsud and Maulvi Faqir,' residents of Ghalanai said.

The only other challenger was the Khalid Sahib Shah group, which was closely linked to Lashkar-e-Taiba. It had been formed in the early 1990s as a group focused on Kashmir militancy. Fully sponsored and backed by the Pakistani intelligence apparatus, the group was also financed by the Saudis because it follows the Salafi school of thought, also known as Ahle Hadith. Based in Muridke, near Lahore, the second largest city of Pakistan, they do not control territory the way Taliban do, but their fighters are among the most lethal, best trained and most feared. They are widely believed to be behind the 26/11 attacks in Mumbai. Both the Khalid Sahib Shah group and the TTP share a broad political agenda—opposition to the US and its allies—and hence both draw support from Al Qaeda. Yet, on the ground, occasionally they do indulge in skirmishes as was witnessed in the summer of 2008.

The rivalry between the two groups is mostly local. What distinguishes the TTP is its well-funded and organized structure, whereas the Khalid Shah group is much smaller with limited territorial authority in the Mohmand agency.

The two groups had been running separate training centres and had set up checkpoints on roadsides but the situation turned ugly when, in mid July 2008, militants of Khalid Shah ambushed local TTP commander, Qari Shakil, who was on his way back to his residence in Khwezo village, considered to be the stronghold of the Khalid Shah group. Qari Shakil, who originally belongs to Peshawar's Michni town, was injured in the attack when his double-cabin pick-up truck was destroyed. The incident enraged Omar Khalid and his fighters. They lost no time in storming Khalid Shah's shelters at Ashrafabad. Later in the afternoon, Omar Khalid's fighters attacked a big training camp of the rival group at Khwezo area where, sources said, around a hundred people were present at the time of the attack.

A spokesman for Omar Khalid later claimed to have captured Khalid Shah along with his 120 fighters, and said their shura would decide the fate of Shah and his militants. In what appeared to be a mock trial, Shah and several of his colleagues, including his deputy, were executed a couple of days later, on 18 July.

The two groups clashed for several days—unchallenged by security forces—executing and butchering each other's prisoners, forcing a mass exodus from the area. All the law-enforcement agencies acted as silent spectators and this probably also showed their helplessness, as a local resident, Amanullah, said.[7] Sources in Ghalani later told us that the fight had clearly stemmed from the suspicion in the Omar Khalid camp that the LeT associate Commander Shah had been collaborating with the authorities. Since many suspected the LeT of close links with ISI dating to the jihad in Kashmir, doubts about the credentials of its representatives were inevitable.

Since the execution of Khalid Shah and his men painted the TTP in a bad light, Baitullah Mehsud on 20 July asked Maulvi Omar Khalid for an explanation of the circumstances that killed

Shah. 'The ameer [Mehsud] has asked Omar Khalid to explain the murder of Shah sahib because Baitullah had considered him our ally,' Qari Hussain Mehsud, the TTP spokesperson, told a journalist on the phone in my presence.[8] Mehsud told Khalid that 'Shah group is our ally and his death is a big loss for all of us', the journalist quoted Hussain as saying.

'Any group not showing allegiance to the Tehreek-i-Taliban Pakistan will not be tolerated in the Mohmand Agency,' Khalid had told reporters in his first press conference after taking over the headquarters of the rival jihadi outfit.[9]

A week later, Maulana Fazlurrehman Khalil, the maverick head of the outlawed Harkatul Mujahideen, which largely comprises hard-core Punjabi militants of the Deobandi stream, reportedly prepared a draft agreement for peaceful coexistence in the agency.[10] The agreement proposed that all followers of the deceased Commander Khalid Shah would live under the guidance of the TTP. On the face of it, both sides agreed to coexist peacefully in the interest of their larger political objectives. In essence, though, their strong organizational structure and bigger manpower gave the TTP advantage enough to prevail over the Shah group.

Almost a week later, Fazlurrehman Khalil secured the release of six LeT activists, ostensibly to enable them take their examinations in a seminary in Punjab. Khalil spent several days in Mohmand to broker a peace deal with the help of his draft agreement between TTP and the Shah group.[11] This gives credence to the belief that activists of all important organizations that had fought in Kashmir and were banned by the Pakistani government in January 2002 had settled down in the tribal areas.

Before all this the TTM militants had launched their military training in Kared in Lakrot sub-district near the controversial Turangzai Sahib shrine and the mosque they had named the Red Mosque in solidarity with the embattled Red Mosque in Islamabad in August 2007.

Initially, a few dozen militants participated in the training, which focuses on learning ambush techniques, hit-and-run skills, assembling assault rifles, planting and detonating bombs along with preparing them, first aid and survival techniques. The housing in the camps are shabby but have all basic facilities. The recruits are largely from FATA, but recruits from the southern part of Punjab have also joined. The actual number of trainees varies and largely remains secret from outsiders. According to some estimates, initially about forty zealots took part in the training but this later swelled to hundreds.

In the earlier phase, militants trained in the dark after sunset, but the inaction of the administration emboldened them to brandish weapons even during the day. Citizens' complaints fell on deaf ears.[12] After about two months of intensive training, the TTM began sending out threatening letters to barbers, drug dealers and video shop owners of the area, ordering them to stop their non-Islamic businesses. In May 2008 a newspaper report said, 'Now the militants appear in a uniform wearing war-jackets and long boots. They march through the bazaars to show their strength and uniformity and have started confronting security forces, and chasing criminals. These incidents are still occurring.'[13]

This obviously is not typical of the Mohmand agency alone; Swat, Kurram, Bajaur and South Waziristan too witnessed similar scenes, but with the passage of time the open display of Taliban power has waned in the face of increased Pakistani military presence and the constant satellite-based surveillance of the Waziristan region by the Americans.

As of February 2009, the army and paramilitary forces—the Frontier Corps—occupied several prime locations in the Mohmand agency. Occasional gunfights between TTP zealots and security forces kept the situation tense and also forced several thousand families to flee the agency for safety.

Kurram Agency

Kurram's Shia population consists of two tribes, Turi and Bangash. The Sunni consists of Chamkani, Masuzai, Alisherzai,

Bangash, Zarmusht and Mengal tribes. The agency is hemmed in the west by Paktia, an eastern Afghan province, in the south by North Waziristan, in the north-east by Khyber and in the east by Orakzai agency.

The emergence of the Taliban in Afghanistan and the war on terror precipitated sectarian tensions, which began with the influx of Sunnis in the early 1980s. With Pakistani and Afghan Taliban trying to extend their tentacles into Kurram, the agency witnessed occasional pitched battles between Shia and Sunni populations. This resulted in the closure of the main roads that connect it with other agencies and main towns like Hangu, Kohat and Peshawar.

The arrival of hard-core Sunni militants, most of whom had settled down here after the government banned their radical outfits like Lashkar-e-Jhangvi, Sipahe Sahaba Pakistan and Harkatul Mujahideen, added fuel to the sectarian strife. Their presence precipitated latent Shia–Sunni tensions. The Afghan Sunni sectarian militants also inspired their 'ideological brothers' in Kurram and elsewhere in FATA and mounted a huge war effort against the Shias.

Kurram witnessed unusual violence through most of 2008, with Sunni militants threatening the minority Shia population; the Shias inhabit the valleys, while most of the Sunni population lives in the hills surrounding Kurram. Taliban militants used the local Sunni population and vantage points in the hills overlooking Shia settlements to unleash terror on the Shias. Throughout the year, the agency was cut off from the neighbouring NWFP cities of Hangu and Kohat, forcing commuters to take a long detour for their business in other Pakistani towns. Afghan provinces Paktika and Ningarhar are the alternative routes for people to travel to Pakistan.

The present conflict in Kurram started in 2007, badly affecting life in Puwara, Bara Chamkani and Masuzai sub-districts, and claiming over 200 lives in one year. In the February 2008 elections a Shia candidate for the national legislature, Riaz Hussein Shah, escaped two assassination attempts, one of them a suicide attack on his election rally, resulting in about sixty deaths. In the second attempt, Shah survived but his guards were killed.

Despite a string of peace efforts, skirmishes between the combatants have continued. Qari Hussain, the in-charge of the TTP suicide squads, has reportedly supervised the Sunni response to the Shias as well as guided actions against them. On 9 June 2008 Shia–Sunni representatives reached a ceasefire agreement, and vowed to work towards peace. Three months later, in October, a grand jirga consisting of parliamentarians, tribal elders and the political administration of Kurram agency brokered a peace deal between the warring Turi (Shia) and Bangash (Sunni). Interestingly, the jirga was finalized and signed in Islamabad, the federal capital, following several rounds of consultations. Under the agreement signed on 16 October 2008 by a fifteen-member committee from each side and twenty-three representatives from the neighbouring Hangu, the warring Shia–Sunni tribes agreed to swap prisoners as well as remove bodies of those killed during clashes and buried temporarily on 'enemy territory', local media reported. Both parties also agreed to remove roadblocks and vacate bunkers and hand them over to the Frontier Corps. They also submitted undertakings worth Rs 60 million each (USD 75,000) in case either of the parties violated the accord. This meant the onus of maintaining peace, under the existing Frontier Crimes Regulation (FCR), was the responsibility of both rival camps, who also agreed to stay in touch to ensure peace was maintained.

Following the peace deal, roads that connected Kurram with Hangu and other towns were finally opened after a year and a half. The road closure had resulted in severe food and medical crises, sending prices of basic items such as wheat, flour and sugar sky-high, forcing thousands of families to emigrate to safer towns, such as Hangu and Kohat. Although an uneasy calm prevailed in Kurram after the peace deal, such agreements rarely eliminate violence and conflict permanently; underlying sectarian tensions and simmering acrimony continue to obstruct normalization.[16]

During much of 2008, government officials and security forces remained at the receiving end as the Taliban kept targeting them every now and then. Besides human losses—as many as 1600 deaths in two years—the conflict has also caused the displacement of thousands of people who had to move to safer locations. People who could afford to shift did so, for safety or for business or even for putting their children in school. The tribal feud, wrapped in sectarian colour, sucked in teenagers as well; both sides kept recruiting fighters as young as fifteen, many of whom were reportedly asked to perform barbaric tasks such as beheading rivals or shooting them down.

Trouble in Hangu

The trouble in the southern NWFP district of Hangu, which is the last town short of the tribal area of Kurram, is also directly related to the strife in the Kurram agency, where the majority Sunni population inhabits the surrounding hamlets and hills and basically controls the entire region by virtue of their strategic location. The Taliban in particular keep shuttling between Parachinar, the administrative headquarter of the Kurram agency, and Hangu.

Hangu had been tense even before the flare-up in the Kurram agency in July 2008 because of the Shia–Sunni conflict. In early July, tensions rose when local police attempted to demonstrate its authority over the area by conducting a flag march on the Tal-Hangu road that meanders into Kurram agency. The march alarmed the TTP militants present in the outskirts of the city. They took it as intimidation and consequently ambushed a Frontier Constabulary convoy in Zargari on 12 July 2008, killing seventeen men. The police retaliated and not only killed some of the invading Taliban but also got hold of about a dozen of them, including Rafiuddin, a deputy of Baitullah Mehsud.

The same day, furious over losses, the Taliban raised a band of 400 volunteers and laid siege to a police station in one of the sub-districts, Doaaba. The Taliban continued the siege for over twenty hours during which they also blew up the transformer that supported power supply to the police station.[17] The local administration eventually called out the army for rescue. But the moment the Taliban heard of the advancing army units, they retreated. The army then launched a search and surveillance operation, removed barriers on the main roads that had been put up by the insurgents to strike terror into the hearts of locals, and helped the police regain its position all over the district. The entire district was placed under curfew for about two weeks to maximize surveillance and minimize movements of insurgents.

However, the Taliban mounted a counteroffensive and began attacking army, paramilitary and police targets. In one of the ambushes, twenty-nine FC personnel were taken hostage. The militants threatened to execute the hostages one by one if the military did not abort its operation. They also refused to allow the bodies of the FC personnel killed on 12 July to be removed. But an assembly of local tribal elders managed to secure the bodies and also delayed the feared execution of the hostages. Apparently under the pressure of locals, the army wrapped up the Hangu operation on 24 July and retreated from Hangu. Almost the same day, eight of the twenty-nine hostages were also set free, which hinted that some kind of deal had been struck with the militants. But while the tribal elders were still deliberating and negotiating with the militants, they still held at least fifty government officials and paramilitary personnel, and the brother of Hangu district mayor went missing along with three other friends. 'The operation objectives have been achieved,' said Major General Athar Abbas, the spokesman for the Pakistan army.[15] He said that areas like Zargari, Shanawari, Doaaba and Yakhkandao had been cleared of militants.

It was of course a tactical statement focusing on the present, because militants, following losses, had fanned out in different directions for regrouping. Incidents of violence, attacks on government and security forces later demonstrated that the Taliban threat was omnipresent and needed a long-term strategic response, rather than surgical strikes, which bring with them shock and awe but whose impact also vanishes soon.

The TTP also threatened retaliatory strikes against the provincial government for crackdown against the 'Taliban'. It also set a five-day deadline for the government to resign or face attacks on official targets across the province. Ameer Haider Hoti, the NWFP chief minister, however, laughed off the threats and brushed aside the TTP deadline: 'While we pursue the course of dialogue with those ready to lay down arms and work for peace, we will not be intimidated by unreasonable militants.'[16]

The provincial government also engaged local tribes to fend off the Taliban threat. As a consequence, as many as eight tribes with an overwhelming Sunni majority in the Hangu district agreed not to provide shelter to the Taliban or any other militant outfit and to cooperate with the government.[17] The decision was taken at a jirga held at the office of the Hangu district coordination officer and attended by representatives from numerous tribes. A local elder, Nazim Malik Jaleelur Rehman of the Darsamand Union Council, told the BBC all the tribes had agreed not to shelter militant outfits, and that every tribe would be responsible for maintaining law and order in its area with the help of the government if required.

Kurram and Hangu are not the only places simmering with Sunni–Shia tensions. Gilgit, a mountainous valley on the old Silk Route in the far north of Pakistan, and the towns of Jhang and Multan in central Pakistan have also witnessed this rivalry. But scant administrative machinery, the jihadi culture that cuts across the Pakistan–Afghanistan border and the tribal nature of life make places like Kurram ideal for followers of both sects to indulge in violence.

Orakzai Agency

A deadly suicide attack in the Khadezai area of Upper Orakzai agency in October 2008 on a gathering of hundreds of local tribesmen—busy discussing a strategy on how to counter Taliban militants—demonstrated the extent of violence being perpetrated by Taliban and Al Qaeda militants across FATA and elsewhere in Pakistan. A suicide bomber drove an explosive-laden Datsun pick-up truck into the crowd and blew himself up, thereby also causing the truck to explode. Earlier in the spring, terrorists had attacked a similar gathering in Darra Adam Khel near Peshawar and eliminated at least forty-two people. In summer, the TTP slaughtered twenty-two people from the Bhittani tribe in South Waziristan. The victims were part of a jirga which had been convened to negotiate peace. Instead, the TTP took them hostage, eventually executing twenty-two of them, alleging they were part of criminal gangs. This trend shows that tribal, social, religious and moral traditions and norms no longer restrain militants; they pursue their political agendas without compunction.

The suicide attack in Orakzai agency had targeted a gathering of the Ali Khel tribe, who had assembled there after the Friday prayers to discuss anti-Taliban strategy. Local television channels quoted eyewitnesses as saying at least thirty-two people died on the spot after the massive blast which left an eight-foot-deep crater in the ground. The channels aired devastating images of human body parts and personal belongings scattered all around. The tribesmen, backed by authorities, had gathered to raise more tribal militias in Orakzai to drive out the Taliban and Al Qaeda from their area. A day earlier, members of the jirga had destroyed three Taliban hideouts, including the houses of two Taliban commanders in the Dabori area and fined four Taliban members Rs 200,000 each.

Kamran Zeb, a top government official in Orakzai, told Reuters, 'The Lashkar had taken a decision to destroy militants' headquarters in the region. Shortly afterwards, this attack took place.' On 5 October, the same tribal assembly had decided not to allow 'outsiders' into the area. They said anyone found sheltering 'outsiders' would be shot dead and his house demolished, the Express News channel reported. The jirga also asked tribesmen not to brandish arms and not to cover their faces. The jirga went on to constitute a committee to destroy the Taliban training camp in the area.

Sectarian tensions and the involvement of TTP elements in the conflict in the last couple of years have infected the relatively small Orakzai agency. Though the Shia population in Orakzai agency is just 7 per cent, the conflict in the neighbouring Kurram agency does affect it, as sympathizers and supporters from there try to help their respective combatants in Orakzai. In September 2007, for instance, in a major sectarian incident spread over fifteen days, at least seventy people lost their lives.

Since early 2008, most of the Orakzai agency including Sunni-majority areas like Dabori Ghalju and Masoodzai have remained under virtual Taliban control, with government forces and political authorities having little influence there. That even people like former governor Ali Mohammad Jan Orakzai cannot visit his hometown reveals the gravity of the situation.

The Taliban initially launched themselves in the area through a vicious crackdown against outlaws and the execution of five people after convicting them. In April 2008 the Taliban arrested nine criminals and shifted them to Waziristan for punishment. To press their agenda, local Taliban issued a decree the next month banning women's education and barring NGOs from the Orakzai agency. 'From now on we will not allow girls and community schools and NGOs to operate in the Orakzai agency,' Taliban leaders told a jirga in the Dewray area of the Orakzai agency which was also attended by members of Ulema Council and elders.[18]

Media reports said the jirga took strong notice of the activities of the NGOs in the area and vowed to hand out tough punishments in case of any violations. They also warned kidnappers, robbers and other criminals to surrender before the Taliban shura or face punishment according to the sharia.

The participants of the meeting urged the government employees to resume their duties and improve their performance without fear and said they would monitor the performance of government schools and hospitals in the agency. During their drive against criminals, the Taliban also recovered two Sikh community members, who had been kidnapped, and helped them return home.

In early August 2008 tribal elders of the agency reached an agreement with the government, undertaking not to shelter or protect militants, criminals or foreign elements. The elders also promised that the agency's soil would not be used against the Pakistan army, nor would anyone be allowed to enforce a parallel government.[19]

In an environment that is politically loaded and morally devoid of respect for compromise and understanding, this agreement also collapsed. Agreements may exist on paper with several influential local chiefs abiding by them, but the real problem lies with the TTP and like-minded militants; they have exploited the historical Shia–Sunni rivalries to peddle and promote their interpretation of Islam and jihad. This helps them protect their power in and outside FATA and destabilize the region to their advantage.

Swat/Malakand (NWFP)

In the summer of 2007 two couples from Lahore, accompanied by their children, travelled up to the scenic ski resort Malam Jabba (Swat) for a peaceful weekend. After spending the day there, they came down to Mingora, the administrative centre of the Swat valley, to stay in a hotel there. At around 2 a.m., a band of about a dozen Taliban knocked at their doors and asked them to leave.

'Don't spread obscenity here, just leave the place,' one of them thundered while swinging his gun. The two frightened women took refuge in one of the bathrooms. But the Taliban ordered them to come out and even shot several times at the door. As a result, both women got a bullet each. Terrified and bleeding, they eventually opened the door. Amid the cries of their wailing, terrified children, the women bleeding from gunshot wounds, the families packed up and fled. The hotel staff were silent spectators.[20] The families had to travel for about two hours before they got treatment at a government hospital in Mardan, some sixty kilometres from Peshawar.

This is reminiscent of the early Taliban era in Afghanistan, when zealots used to drag men out of beds for not offering prayers or not sporting beards, or whip women for travelling alone. But this happened in Mingora, often compared to Switzerland for its beautiful mountainous scenery. It also offered a glimpse of what was to follow in the ensuing weeks; by mid November, the entire Swat valley, once a favourite destination for tourists, had turned into a battlefield, the local people caught between the military and the militants of the Tehreek-e-Taliban Pakistan.

In the next eighteen months as many as forty educational institutions became practically non-functional in the Swat valley. Most school buildings were either badly damaged by bombs or mortar shells. On 25 June 2008, the worst day for schools here, militants burnt or bombed ten schools in the district. A local lawyer and social activist, Shaukat Saleem, told journalists at the Peshawar Press Club that Taliban militants had even occupied several schools in the Matta sub-district of Swat. Saleem said that out of the roughly two million inhabitants of the Swat/Malakand region, up to 700,000 were of primary school going age, whereas the government enrolment of such children hovered around 528,000. Damage or destruction of female educational institutions, he said, deprived around 148,000 girls of education.

By February 2009 as many as 182 schools, predominantly girls' schools, largely stood in ruins because of Taliban attacks. Locals say that because of the insecurity and fear that Taliban had instilled in peoples' minds, schools even in safer areas had been closed down. About 400 hotels were also shut down or damaged, including the beautiful Malam Jabba Hotel situated amid picturesque hills.

Taliban militants targeted prominent educational institutions of excellence in the valley, including the missionary institution of Sangota Public School and College, which was attacked and damaged on 6 October 2008. Established in 1952, the missionary institution was a gift of the British government to the then ruler of Swat, with about a thousand pupils on its rolls. Initially boys and girls studied together but since 1998 admissions here were restricted to girls only.

Throughout 2008, the Taliban kept targeting female educational institutions, apparently to express their rejection of what they call 'western education' for girls. But, based on my experiences with the Afghan Taliban in Kandahar and elsewhere in Afghanistan, as well as going by the TTP ideology, one can assume that these Taliban are not interested in education at all. It stands low down on their list of priorities. The TTP in Swat, led by Maulana Fazlullah, offers little rational explanation when asked why they oppose the education of girls. They duck the question by saying the answers lie in the enforcement of the Islamic sharia. They themselves have little to offer when asked what sharia is. Ironically, Muslim Khan, the TTP spokesman for Swat since early 2008, denied any hand in the destruction of these schools and announced his organization would reconstruct all damaged girls' schools at their own expenditure.[21]

To go back to the events of 2007: In mid-September, within weeks of the Mingora hotel incident that struck the tourist families, militants overran vast swathes of the Swat valley, seized about a dozen police stations and declared the imposition of Islamic sharia. People watched in awe as TTP zealots checked to see whether their orders were being followed. Besides the army and government installations, TVs, VCRs, music shops, barber shops and girls' educational institutions were all under TTP attack. The Taliban also staged several public incinerations of video and music equipment to demonstrate how much they loathed these 'tools of obscenity and immorality'. They even sent leaflets to private institutions like banks barring employees from wearing jeans and trousers, described as 'symbols of the immoral west'. Buoyed by their success, Maulana Fazlullah set up several sharia courts to dispense justice to 'criminals'. In early November, one of the courts punished three alleged criminals by flogging them in public. 'After the government's indifference, we have set up our own Islamic court to dispense justice to the people and today is the beginning of the struggle for a cherished goal [enforcement of sharia],' Sirajuddin, the then spokesman for Maulana Fazlullah, told the media afterwards.

The alleged criminals were caught 'red-handed' while trying to kidnap two women from Matta tehsil the previous month. Maulana Shah Dauran, head of the private Islamic court who also does a regular programme on Fazlullah's FM radio station, read out the crime the three men had allegedly committed as well as the punishment they had been awarded, adding that the punishment was 'reformatory' and not under the penal code. Eyewitnesses said the three men had pleaded neither guilty nor innocent before they were lashed. Maulana Fazlullah's armed guards warned the media against photographing or taping the punishment.

'We are reporting these incidents to the provincial government [headed by the religio-political alliance the Muttahida Majlis-e-Amal, MMA] with the warning that the cleric in Swat could spell trouble for the entire province if left unchecked. But the provincial government simply ignored the warnings,' a senior intelligence official had told me in Peshawar in December 2006.[22] The MMA ruled the province for almost five years but did little to contain the activities of militant groups, many of which had good relations with several ministers and local leadership in these regions. Most of them were reluctant to take any action for fear of reprisals by the militants. The Taliban was in effect running a parallel administration in Swat and Malakand; their local leaders would write instructions to government officials for trade permits, postings and transfers of officials and even summon government functionaries for explanations.

As things went out of control in November 2007, the army launched the Rahe Haq operation and a cat and mouse game between the Pakistan army and the TTP militants began. One by one, the army vacated police stations, while zealots of Maulvi Fazlullah kept moving from one town to the other, leaving their footprints and then speeding away in double-cabin trucks. Small in numbers indeed, not more than 3000, according to some counts, they still managed to terrorize people and seize places at will.

These small bands gave the police and the military a difficult time, affecting general life and businesses. The government, educational institutions, banks, shops and commercial centres remained closed for months, or conducted limited businesses partially because of the uncertainty and fear of getting caught between the military and the militants.

Janikhel and Piochaar appeared to be the strongholds of Fazlullah but, strangely, the army stayed away from these valleys, surrounded by high mountains. In a briefing at the General Headquarters in Rawalpindi, General Ahmed Shuja Pasha, former director general of the military operations who became the head of the ISI in October 2008, had declared these areas as the hubs of Taliban but also explained that the formidable topography of the area—high mountain passes and narrow gorges—made it difficult for the army to operate there. Those who have flown over the 1360 kilometres that the Frontier Province shares with Afghanistan understand the barriers that the environment and terrain confront the army with. 'A nightmare for those who move through these gorges and passes and a haven for those who want to ambush,' said the general. General Pasha also complained that about twenty informal but often frequented routes between Pakistan and Afghanistan, and another 350 unfrequented passages as well as nine divided villages on the 2560-kilometre border impede efforts aimed at checking and controlling illegal cross-border movement, which is now also affecting events in Swat and Bajaur regions. Another obstacle in the way of an all-out offensive, General Pasha explained, is that the militants live among the population thereby making it extremely hard for the army to launch indiscriminate attacks.

'A very difficult and worrying situation for us,' the general told us, while explaining how the army was fanning out to clear the areas of militants. General Pasha also vented his frustration over the inaction by the MMA government, which he believed simply left the TTP unchallenged to spread its wings in the entire region.

Although General Pasha announced wrapping up the military operation in early 2008, the army had to remount its efforts on 30 July 2008, after scores of security personnel were abducted, and several government installations attacked. The army claimed to have killed close to a hundred militants, including two of their important commanders, but over two dozen civilians and fifteen soldiers also fell in the crossfire.

Maulana Fazlullah had warned that his group would carry out suicide attacks if the government relaunched a military operation in the valley.[23] Fazlullah, with his back to the cameras and most of his face covered with a white shawl, hurled the threat during a press conference in the remote mountainous Taran area of Kabal sub-district and also announced the suspension of talks over the implementation of a 21 May accord with the provincial government.

As the military was pounding militant positions at various locations in early August, Fazlullah also executed the first of his threats on the military; eight security forces personnel were killed and six others injured when a remote-controlled device blew up the van carrying them in the Hazara area of Kabal sub-district. Muslim Khan claimed responsibility for the Hazara attack and said it was a reaction to the military operation in Swat. 'We avenged the killing of innocent civilians by the security forces in unabated shelling,' Khan told the media on the phone from an undisclosed location. 'We will carry out suicide and bomb strikes in response to attacks on the Taliban,' he threatened.

Elsewhere, the militants torched six more educational institutions including the Swat Public School, a private girls' college in Mingora and a primary school in Matta on the same day, while two bridges, one at Allahabad on the Kalaam Road and the other at Khwaza Khela, were damaged by mortars. In Darmai area of Matta, militants abducted two nephews of a police official, Jamaluddin, warning him to quit his job failing which the victims would be executed. Local authorities also imposed limited curfew in and around Mingora to restrict collateral damage in the operation, thereby bringing daily life and business activities to a halt.

To further rub salt into the government's wounds, TTP's Bajaur chief Maulana Faqir Muhammad and the organization's spokesman Maulvi Umar convened a joint press conference on 5 August 2008 at Inayat Kalay near Khaar, the administrative headquarter of Bajaur, to threaten the government and military with retaliation.[24] 'We can instigate our fighters into action across the country if the government does not stop the ongoing military operation in Swat,' Umar warned at the press conference.

Both Faqir Muhammad and Umar cautioned Altaf Hussain, the self-exiled leader of the ethno-political Muttahida Qaumi Movement (MQM), 'to cease his statements against the Taliban'. In a telephonic address to his people from London, Hussain had urged his followers to rise and resist the 'Talibanization of Karachi'. He also requested foreign countries for help in fighting the Taliban. Although hollow on substance, Hussain's outburst did provoke the Taliban into equally emotional and provocative responses. 'Once we are given the go-ahead by Baitullah Mehsud, Karachi's residents and Mehsud could take control of the city whenever,' Umar said.

In a nutshell, by late 2008, Fazlullah's TTP had mounted an inassailable insurgency against the Pakistan army outside the FATA region, where the entire security apparatus—police, paramilitary forces and intelligence—had existed for decades. How could the TTP take over the entire Swat valley in the presence of this security infrastructure, for brief periods in October and November 2007 and later too? General Pasha offered few convincing answers. Nor could local residents offer a satisfying response to the question as to how a small army of vigilantes managed to terrorize an entire population. Fear of reprisals, once again, was probably a major factor.[25]

Several factors seemed to have combined to level the space for the militants. Initially, the army appeared to be hesitant to take on the militants. Secondly, the extremely poorly trained and badly paid police were never a match for the zeal of the insurgents, who were driven by the Islamist ideology. The provincial police was also deficient in numbers in most areas, with less than twenty policemen for each police station. Above everything else, despite official claims of 'relentless crackdowns on the militants', doubts on the role of some government agencies abound. Locals believe there is a nexus between intelligence agencies and the militants. Army and intelligence officials deny any linkages. 'How can we protect groups that are killing and butchering our own personnel and government functionaries?' asked General Pasha during one of our discussions. People in the affected areas, who have witnessed the rise of Taliban forces, take such claims with a big pinch of salt. Basically, the historical relations between intelligence agencies and militant groups shape and fuel the situation that also allowed the Taliban to entrench themselves, practically unchallenged by the locals.

The bitter reality facing Pakistanis is the prospect of a TTP insurgency spiralling into other areas, Peshawar, Kohat, and so on. Three incidents occurred within the space of thirty-six hours in Peshawar. These were a suicide attack outside the Qayum Stadium on 11 November 2008 that killed five during a ceremony to mark the successful completion of the regional games; the gruesome murder of Stephan D. Vance, who headed the 'Livelihoods' project of an American group working on USAID-funded schemes in FATA the following morning; and the abduction of an Iranian diplomat based in the city, also on 12 November. There was another suicide attack about thirty kilometres north of Peshawar when a suicide bomber rammed an explosives-filled bus into the gates of a school. All these were signs of the insecurity that prevailed in Peshawar and other areas of the NWFP. Many locals interpreted it as a direct consequence of the war on terror and the Pakistan army's crackdown against TTP and other militants.

ANP in the Eye of the TTP Stampede

In August 2008 the provincial assembly of the North West Frontier Province witnessed an emotional and fiery debate on the situation in Swat. And those bemoaning it were ministers of the provincial cabinet.

'Swat is burning. Innocent people are being killed,' the minister of forests, Wajid Ali Khan, said during his speech to the House. That Khan openly broke down during the assembly session was a manifestation of the toll that the constant threat of danger had taken on him and other members of Provincial Assembly (MPAs). This was an unusual scene the provincial assembly witnessed as another MPA followed Wajid Ali Khan with an emotional speech of his own. 'We cannot go to our constituencies for fear of being killed . . . whether it is mosques, women and children, or young and old, none of us is safe. The MPAs cannot return home,' said the minister for science and technology, Ayub Ashari, alleging that the government had lost its writ in Swat. As MPAs vented their anger and frustration over the alarming situation, the body of Ahmed Khan, the brother of a politician, was found in the Kabal sub-district of Swat. He had been kidnapped by the militants a few days ago and subsequently executed. The same day, the bodies of two youngsters from a political family, who had been kidnapped about a week ago, were found in Aligrama, with their throats slit.

Only a few days ago, about 200 armed Taliban besieged Swat's Shah Dheri suburb in the early hours and after a brief exchange of fire entered the compound of Iqbal Ahmed Khan, the elder brother of the ruling Awami National Party MPA. They overpowered the servants and security guards, and shot dead Iqbal Khan, two of his sons and seven servants in the courtyard of the residential compound. The entire family had locked themselves inside the house, but the Taliban broke open the locked gates. They told the women to stay inside, and led the men into the courtyard, where they were all shot dead. After the cold-blooded murder, the militants blew up the house with explosives, killing all those inside, including women and children. Waqar Ahmad Khan could not even attend the funeral ceremony of his brother and young nephews after relatives advised him to stay in Peshawar for security reasons. Later, their family hotel in Swat also came under militant fire.

One after the other, leaders of this ethnic Pashtoon nationalist ANP, the lead partner in the coalition that has been in power since

February 2008, received threats: resign from the government or else face the consequences, was the bottom line. The head of the party, Asfandyar Wali Khan, the grandson of the famous 'Frontier Gandhi', narrowly escaped death at the hands of a suicide bomber at his residence on 2 October. The TTP claimed responsibility for this as well as the 11 November suicide attack outside the Qayum Stadium in Peshawar. In the latter case, the TTP said the ANP minister Bashir Bilour was the target. The bomber in fact had blown himself up near Bilour's car, but Bilour luckily was not in it. Afzal Khan, another veteran ANP leader, also faced the wrath of the Taliban, when they shelled his home in Swat. Fortunately, the leader, who has practically retired from politics, escaped unhurt.

Such is the level of fear created by Taliban militants that all assembly members, many district mayors and most leaders affiliated to ruling political parties such as the ANP and the PPP have abandoned Swat and taken refuge in Peshawar and Islamabad. Two members of the national legislature, ANP's Muzaffar-ul-Mulk alias Kaki Khan and the PPP's Syed Allauddin, and all seven ANP-affiliated members of the provincial assembly—Wajid Ali Khan, Ayub Ashari, Jaffar Shah, Dr Haider Ali, Waqar Khan, Dr Shamsher Ali Khan and Sher Shah Khan—cannot visit their homes and constituencies due to fear of suicide bombers and target-killers tasked to eliminate them. Even if they dare, they do it in a highly clandestine way. The district mayor, Jamal Nasir, left Swat in early 2007 after surviving an attempt on his life. Civil and police officers are reluctant to serve in Swat and more than 350 policemen have given up their jobs. The Swat district government system, therefore, remains paralysed, crippled by long curfew hours.

This situation obviously is the result of a deliberate effort to create fear through violence or the threat of violence. The militants' objective behind the bombing campaign is to intimidate the ANP into resigning from their office. They also want the PPP brand of politics to be replaced at the centre by their brand of draconian Islamic sharia.

After the departure of Pervez Musharraf, the ANP as well as the PPP of Benazir Bhutto, which is currently leading the coalition at centre, also earned the wrath of the TTP and its affiliates for their policies; the militants perceive them as 'agents of the United States of America, who are out to demolish Islamist forces'.

The secularist ANP used to look up to Moscow for political guidance and had also maintained close links with Afghan governments before the Soviet-Russian invasion and occupation of Afghanistan in December 1979. The post 9/11 events, however, seemed to have influenced the ANP's outlook on the region and it opened up to Washington. The warm relationship between American diplomatic missions in Pakistan and the ANP after the February 2008 general elections, have not only raised eyebrows in the country but also alarmed the TTP for a very simple reason: the ANP leadership have been calling for the elimination of terrorist sanctuaries in FATA, and supported the military operation in the region as well as in Swat and Malakand.

The TTP and affiliates view the ANP support to the military operation against its members from Waziristan to Bajaur as an international alliance against 'Islamist forces', and hence their violent reaction to the cooperation among the ANP, PPP and the US-led coalition forces. It was probably because of these suspicions that the peace accord between Maulana Fazlullah's Swat–TTP and the ANP–PPP coalition government in NWFP signed in May 2008 also collapsed amid absurd claims and demands by the militants. The failure of the agreement also underscored that the conflict in Swat could not be resolved through conventional methods.

Officials categorize 'Talibanization' as the biggest challenge to the government, but the locals seem to differ: the biggest challenge comes from neglect, official apathy and incompetence, a corrupt police and a slow legal system that often works in favour of the haves and punishes the have-nots. The common people believe that if Islamabad and the General Headquarter wanted the Taliban would not be able to have a free run in these areas. Most suspicions fall on intelligence agencies.

During the Musharraf era, the seeming inaction of the security forces was seen by the common people as the armed forces playing a set match with the militants to convince the Unites States that the situation is dire and that Pakistan needs continuous financial support to fight it. Many people in Swat and elsewhere still believe this.

General Ashfaq Kayani, the army chief, told us during a meeting at his Rawalpindi residence in late January 2009 that he had also heard this argument over and over again. But, he asked, why would our soldiers kill their own people, why would the intelligence agencies support Taliban militants who are executing people indiscriminately? Despite Kayani's vehement denial and categorical rejection of 'forces of evil and chaos', this meeting also left us confused as to why people still believe the army, intelligence agencies and the militants are hand in glove.

What was nevertheless clear as of February 2009 was that both peaceful and military means had failed to normalize the situation in Swat, and that the continued turmoil warranted a critical review of policies. General Kayani promised to go for a new approach, that is, to clean up, secure and stay to help the civilian administration re-establish itself. This sounded like a formidable task if viewed against the battles that have been raging throughout the Swat valley even during February 2009.

Why has the security apparatus failed in changing perceptions about the alleged nexus between the forces and the militants? This perception has only benefited the militants all these years. A clearly defined approach applied with a unity of command is perhaps the only answer. This strategy will have to combine military action with political leadership and civilian administration. The army usually does the surgical operation and secures the area, but until political representatives and the civilian administration step forward, the army cannot stick its neck out for very long. If it does, people will begin viewing it as an occupation force, a perception that dents the image and intentions of the army in the long run.

Al Qaeda and Foreign Militants in FATA: Uzbeks and Arabs

As Arab and Uzbek Al Qaeda militants fleeing from Afghanistan sought shelter in North and South Waziristan, the region increasingly became a target of missile strikes undertaken by US and coalition forces based in Afghanistan. The CIA believes the militants are training there for missions against the US and coalition forces. Two deadly missile attacks fired from a CIA-operated drone on a house in the Ladha village of South Waziristan on 14 February 2009 killed over thirty people, the majority reportedly Uzbek dissidents, originally members of the Islamic Movement of Uzbekistan. This was the third Hellfire missile attack, fired off the MQ-9 Reaper (also known as Predator B) in 2009. In 2008 the pilotless aircraft conducted some sixty such strikes.

The presence of these foreign militants has led to divisions within the Taliban ranks, particularly in South Waziristan, where Mulla Nazir, heading his own faction of Tehreek-e-Taliban reportedly shelters Arab Al Qaeda militants and has driven the Uzbeks out of the Wana valley that he controls. Baitullah Mehsud, the ameer of the Tehreek-e-Taliban Pakistan, on the other hand, controls the Mehsud region, where he shelters both Uzbeks and like-minded Arabs. Since early 2007, the radical Uzbeks led by

Tahir Yuldashev, fell out with Mulla Nazir because he opposed their targeting of Pakistani security forces and government officials. Nazir's campaign against Uzbeks also won him some government sympathy.

In the early hours of 28 July 2008, several missiles, launched from low-flying drones, killed six people, including Abu Khabab al-Masri, the Egyptian chemist regarded as one of Al Qaeda's top bomb makers. The target was a small madrassa and a mosque, run by a local cleric, Maulana Jalilur Rahman, at Zyara Leeta village in the border town of Birmal, in South Waziristan. It destroyed two buildings and caused damage to a few others located in the vicinity of the madrassa. A large number of Wazir tribesmen immediately thronged the village and helped retrieve the bodies of the slain people and the injured from the rubble. Some of those who took part in the rescue operation told me that all the bodies were badly mutilated and beyond recognition.

'Nobody could recognize whether they were locals or Arabs as their bodies were split into pieces,' said Mohammad Nawab. He said five of the dead were Arabs who had just returned from Afghanistan's Paktika province and were resting at the madrassa. Pakistani security officials refused to confirm or deny this, but said Abu Khabab al-Masri might have been killed in the strike.

The fifty-five-year-old al-Masri carried a USD 5 million bounty on his head, but there have been reports of him being killed before. Spokesmen for NATO and US-led coalition forces in Afghanistan denied involvement in any cross-border strikes, but could not speak for the CIA, which also operates drones. If the intelligence-fed reports were true, then al-Masri joined the list of about ten Al Qaeda operatives killed in such attacks. This shows that the United States is primarily targeting Arab Al Qaeda leaders, who are moving into the difficult terrain between North and South Waziristan.

Coinciding with the attack in South Waziristan were reports flying in from intelligence officials in Washington as well as from within Pakistan about the 'influx of foreigners into Waziristan'.

Only days before Prime Minister Yousuf Raza Gilani was to embark on his maiden but crucial visit to the United States, he was informed by the security establishment that as many as 8000 foreigners could be hiding in the FATA region, predominantly in Waziristan. Although officially, the government of Pakistan accepts that foreign fighters are present, the unusually large number quoted in an official report set alarm bells ringing in Islamabad and possibly in other capitals as well.[1]

Interior Adviser Rehman Malik, however, did not want to reveal the source of the staggering figure of 8000, and told the *News* the number of foreign fighters would be closer to a thousand. 'According to the report presented to the PM, a majority of these foreign fighters are living in North and South Waziristan and Bajaur. Prime Minister Gilani has also been informed that some foreign intelligence agencies are pushing their agents into the Pakistani tribal areas from Afghanistan under the cover of Taliban and Al Qaeda fighters. These undercover agents are trying to instigate the local population to fight against Pakistani forces as part of a "great game" in the region,' the *News* added.

Interestingly, the beefed-up figure began emerging in late 2007 and its main source lay in Washington. American diplomats and US media representatives began dropping hints that suggested foreigners in FATA might be multiplying. This was also in sync with the claims of the US defence secretary Robert Gates and other officials that following the 'squeeze in Iraq' Al Qaeda was now pouring its resources into Afghanistan and Pakistan's border areas. American intelligence leaks through the media suggested that 'experienced and hardened Al Qaeda fighters from Iraq are entering into Afghanistan via Iran by road'.

Until late 2007, most accounts by locals in North and South Waziristan put these numbers in the hundreds and not thousands. During visits to both agencies in 2004 and 2005, I saw several Arabs and Chechens moving around in Wana, Miranshah and Mirali. But continued search and surveillance by the Pakistan army, guided by US and NATO forces based across the border, pushed foreigners into hiding or into keeping a low profile for a while. Eventually they assumed the role of planners and trainers, thus going off the scene. The biggest attraction for these young militant guests from the Middle East, Central Asia and Europe was the steady surge in the number of US troops in Afghanistan. A lot of young Muslims are coming to Afghanistan to fight the US troops who, they believe, have come to Afghanistan not to fight terrorism but to occupy more Muslim lands, including Pakistan, reported the *News* in its 21 July 2008 report.

Afghan sources say foreign fighters are present in eastern, southern and western Afghanistan as well. 'Two American-born Al Qaeda operators, Adam Gadhan alias Azzam al Amriki and Abu Ahmad alias Amir Butt, are known in the Afghan Kunar province for making travel arrangements of these young and educated Muslims from the US, UK, France, Germany, Belgium, Spain, Canada and Australia.'[2]

Some of these foreigners have married into the tribes of Kunar, Nuristan, North Waziristan and South Waziristan. The German-born Turkish fighter Saad Abu Furqan is also known in the Pakistani tribal areas for attracting young Turks to organize jihad against what he calls the 'crusaders' in Afghanistan.

Uzbek Al Qaeda Militants

Much before 2008, the year that saw considerable bloodshed and fighting between the army and militants as well as among militants, the Islamic Movement of Uzbekistan had morphed into a lethal non-Arab Al Qaeda entity. It was in the late 1990s that the Uzbeks opened their first training camp near Mazar-e-Sharif in northern Afghanistan. Following their escape to South Waziristan from the US-led Operation Anaconda in March 2002, most of the Uzbeks from the former Soviet Central Asian republics are probably now making their last stand in the Pakistani tribal areas.

Welcomed whole-heartedly and greeted with open arms in December 2001, these IMU militants led by Tahir Yuldashev faced little problem in finding support and shelter among the Ahmadzai Wazir tribesmen inhabiting the regional headquarters of Wana in South Waziristan. Yuldashev, the successor of Jumma Namangani, who was killed in a US air strike in northern Afghanistan in November 2001, in fact became a star speaker at mosques in the Sheen Warsak region near Wana.

Once well-entrenched with the local support, Yuldashev founded Mohajireen-o-Ansar.

After escaping the March 2004 Kaloosha operation and surviving the injuries he sustained during the crossfire with the Pakistan army, Tahir Yuldashev began organizing his people into Mohajireen-o-Ansar to pursue his agenda, which essentially converged with the larger objectives that Osama bin Laden's Al Qaeda had set itself. He also set up a private jail to try and punish people he thought were creating problems for the Uzbeks. The exact number of Yuldashev's followers is difficult to determine, yet various local sources spoke of up to a thousand Uzbeks being present in the region, mostly in North and South Waziristan. Usman Jan and Jafar Asad are reportedly Yuldashev's trusted aides. One of the Pakistani Punjabi fugitives, Qari Mudassir, acts as their spokesman.

Yuldashev's revered status in Waziristan took a hit when his vigilantes began targeting Pakistan army and government officials. These anti-army strikes turned the Uzbeks from revered heroes to villains, and they fell out with the pro-government Taliban commander Mulla Nazir. In early June 2008 the organization claimed responsibility for waylaying Malik Khanan Wazir, a pro-government commander, affiliated with Mulla Nazir (see Chapter 9).

Noor Islam and Qari Mudassir, who were once members of the Sipahe Sahaba Pakistan (SSP), admitted they finally got Khanan Wazir after some botched attempts to kill him. 'The other target is Mulla Nazir and we will get him too,' Mudassir told the *News*.[3]

Khanan was a commander for the hostile Shakai valley and was immediately replaced by Tensile Khan. Before Khanan, Mulla Nazir had lost another close aide, Maulvi Iqbal. He was killed along with several fighters, including many Pakistanis from the Punjab province, during skirmishes with US-led coalition forces in early 2008.[4]

Such inter-factional rivalries presented quite a challenge to Al Qaeda too; while most Pakistani militants held bin Laden's outfit in great reverence, petty political matters and the tussle for territorial authority did pitch them against one another. Local dynamics, such as attempts by Pakistani authorities to secure support from among these groups, also drove a wedge between them. Mulla Nazir's undeclared, tacit understanding with the authorities to maintain peace in the area and prevent attacks on the army also exemplified the complications that exist in Waziristan. Primarily, this understanding was directed against the Uzbek affiliates of Al Qaeda, which eventually culminated in the March 2007 operation against the Central Asian militants.

Arab Al Qaeda Militants

American defence officials estimated that in 2008 between 150 and 500 hardcore Al Qaeda fighters were operating in the tribal areas.[5] Sources in Wana claim at least 200 influential Arabs still live in the region under the protection of Mulla Nazir.

The thirty missile strikes on targets in the Waziristan region in the last four months of 2008 were all directed against Arab Al Qaeda operatives. After almost every attack, the US military authorities or CIA sources would announce the names of wanted Arabs they claimed were killed in the missile strikes. But not once was a single body paraded to back up these claims. This not only invited the militants' mockery but also raised doubts about the veracity of such claims. It also led to public outcry as the air strikes claimed the lives of countless non-combatants, largely women and children.

'Unfortunately, the leaders live among families and whenever we hit them, many women and children also fall victim,' a US intelligence official based in Islamabad told me in December 2008. 'We track them [the militants] from point A to B very precisely and therefore are able to take them out the moment they get together with other operatives after carrying out missions in Afghanistan,' said the official, leaving a big question mark as to why the US intelligence cannot pick up Baitullah Mehsud, who *Time* magazine declared the most dangerous person after Osama bin Laden.

A 16 January 2009 report in the *Washington Times* said the Al Qaeda stalwarts who had found refuge in Waziristan areas included Khalid Habib (a deputy to Al Qaeda's third-in-command Shaikh Said al-Masri), Abu Khabab al-Masri, Abu Al-Hassan al-Rimi (a leader of cross-border operations against US-led forces in Afghanistan), Abu Sulaiman al-Jaziri (a senior external operations planner and facilitator for Al Qaeda), Abu Jihad al-Masri (Al Qaeda's senior operational planner and propagandist) and Usama al-Kini (who was accused of planning the Marriott Hotel bombing in September 2008 and was killed on 1 January 2009 by a drone-fired missile strike).

During the Taliban's rule, two categories of Arabs had entered Afghanistan: those who, filled with the jihadi zeal, kept pouring in from different parts of the Arab world until the war on Taliban and bin Laden began in October 2001, and those who had moved in from Pakistan after their visas had expired and settled in the eastern parts of Afghanistan, mostly Jalalabad. Many had stayed on after the Soviets pulled out of Afghanistan in 1989.[6]

Almost all of them—several thousand—either perished in the American attacks on Kandahar and the vicinity of Jalalabad and the Tora Bora mountains, or landed in jails. Most were among the 7000 prisoners the western coalition said it held by the end of December 2001. More than 200 were caught by Pakistan's border security forces after they gave up their fight in the Tora Bora mountains.

According to a Jane's Intelligence Report (JIR) of June 2001, Arabs swelled the ranks of the Taliban fighting force, and constituted the second largest foreign contingent after Pakistani fighters. The report said the source for this information was the United Front or Northern Alliance, the predominantly non-Pashtoon Afghan opposition to Taliban headed by Ahmed Shah Massoud.

'Their numbers have grown notably over the past 18 months. There seems little doubt at least 2,000 combatants—all apparently affiliated to and financed by Osama bin Laden—are now active in support of the (Afghan) Taliban. One source monitoring the military situation estimates up to 3,000 Arab combatants may be in the field. Certainly an Arab presence, including numbers of civilians and families, is now quite open in the cities of Kabul, Jalalabad and Kandahar.'[7]

At least 200 Arab Taliban were found executed at different locations in Jalalabad and Kandahar immediately after Mulla Omar surrendered power in December 2001.

An October 1999 Jane's report said that Arab instructors and trainees were seen at Rishkor, near Kabul, which was probably the biggest training base in Afghanistan, with 1500 trainees and thirty to fifty instructors. It said, 'Courses covered basic field craft and small arms training, graduating to specialized courses in support weaponry, demolition and escape and evasion. Last June, however, following international publicity and growing diplomatic pressure, the facility was emptied. Kabul-based journalists were permitted to visit it but official denials that foreigners had ever trained there were belied by large signs on buildings in Arabic and Urdu.'[8]

The JIR stated that, generally, Arab units were deployed in an infantry role armed with nothing heavier than RPGs, PK machine guns and mortars. They were, however, widely recognized as the most aggressive and committed fighters in Taliban ranks.

Arab influence is seen as particularly strong within the ministry for the enforcement of virtue and suppression of vice, the Taliban's ubiquitous religious police, and in cities where the presence of Arab fighters is open. The Arabs were openly hostile towards western aid workers.

Chechen units and the forces of the Islamic Movement of Uzbekistan constituted the other two main foreign contingents of the foreign Taliban, JIR said. 'While organizationally separate, with distinct leaderships, links between Islamist militants from the two ex-Soviet territories are long-standing and it seems likely that Chechens are today attached to IMU combat units. Other foreigners, including Pakistanis from the SSP and Lashkar-e-Jhangvi, are also operating under the IMU's military umbrella,' the JIR report stated.

Seven years on, in 2009 circumstances turned the Uzbek-Pakistani Taliban equation upside down; until late 2001, the Pakistani Taliban enjoyed cordial relations with the Uzbeks, who were considered more pious and better Muslims for their zeal to stand by the Afghan Taliban. Moreover, their common enemy was the Masud-led Northern Alliance.

Subsequently, the US-led NATO forces and their Afghan army supporters became the common enemy. But the staunchest among the Afghan and non-Afghan Taliban treat the Pakistan army as their enemy because international obligations had forced Pakistan to take on militants, wherever they were.

The year 2008 saw the culmination of a campaign that the US intelligence agencies and military outfits had begun mounting, with a number of high-profile visits from Washington. As the voices against foreigners ensconced in FATA became louder, it was clear that the Pakistani Taliban support for IMU and Arab Al Qaeda had fragmented.

What causes concern among outsiders, including Afghans and Americans—from the Afghan President Hamid Karzai to the former US President George W. Bush—is the stated objective of all shades of militants to continue supporting jihad inside Afghanistan with the ultimate objective of evicting 'foreign occupation forces' from there. Pressure on Pakistan to go after them has mounted; the danger of this pressure translating into physical action by the US-led international community against Al Qaeda in the tribal areas is also growing.

As if to prove their point against Pakistan-based militants, US intelligence officials stated through the media on 31 July 2008 that a 'growing number of Pakistani militants who earlier operated only inside Pakistan and Kashmir are joining the intensifying insurgency against United States and NATO forces in Afghanistan'.[9] The officials claimed that the fighters included guerrillas hardened by years of combat against Indian forces and others from outside the Taliban strongholds in FATA.

'When we're talking about foreign fighters in Afghanistan, they're primarily Pakistanis,' one official said. The chief concern for US officials is Baitullah Mehsud. Mehsud was previously described as being ambitious inside Pakistan, but now he has stepped up the recruitment of fighters for Afghanistan. 'If he doesn't have to fight the Pakistan army, he's free to focus on Afghanistan,' one official remarked.

Paradoxically, the *Daily Times* had earlier quoted a US official as saying, 'Afghanistan has been drawing a fresh influx of fighters from Turkey, Central Asia, Chechnya and the Middle East; one more sign that Al Qaeda is regrouping on what is fast becoming the most active front of the war on terror groups. More foreigners are infiltrating Afghanistan because of a recruitment drive by Al Qaeda as well as a burgeoning insurgency that has made movement easier across the border from Pakistan.'[10]

The predominant American focus on Al Qaeda stems from the fear that the organization is at the heart of the current turmoil and that, while hiding in Waziristan, it might plan yet another 9/11 in the US or western Europe.

Going by the course of military action witnessed during most of 2008 in the Pakistan–Afghanistan border areas it becomes quite obvious that the US and NATO forces are chasing Al Qaeda and the Haqqani–Hekmetyar network in the region, while Pakistani forces have been tasked to hunt down Pakistani Taliban in Bajaur, Mohmand and Khyber agencies.

Al Qaeda Brings Suicide Bombings to Pakistan

S uicide bombing is a relatively new phenomenon in Pakistan that emerged a few years after the ouster of the Taliban regime in Afghanistan in late 2001. In 2006 there were only six such attacks; in 2007 the number went up to fifty-six and in 2008 at least sixty-one fanatics blew themselves up in this way. With over a suicide strike a week, these attacks and bomb blasts claimed 2116 lives, including 558 law enforcement personnel (LEP), and injured 3962, in 2007 according to a document compiled by the ministry of interior for the cabinet in January 2008. Attacks on LEP and various organs of the security establishment grew by 100 per cent with 234 personnel losing lives in about 465 attacks across the country, including some on installations and vehicles of intelligence services and one on a training and monitoring facility for special counter-terrorism Pakistani and US troops near Ghazi Barotha in the North West Frontier Province. Most of the attacks on LEP were carried out in FATA and the adjoining settled districts. North and South Waziristan have become the training ground for suicide bombers. Militants and their recruiters prey on boys as young as twelve and brainwash them on the virtues of the life 'hereafter'and this idea—essentially an Al Qaeda tactic— has snared many innocent, ordinary, disgruntled youngsters in Pakistan's tribal areas. Initially, Arab Al Qaeda zealots led the mission but this has subsequently been taken over by members of the Haqqani network as well as by close associates of Baitullah Mehsud, including Qari Hussein. Strangely, none of the mainstream religio-political leaders has ever openly condemned suicide bombing. Of the few that dared to do so, one was executed under mysterious circumstances. A conference of second-tier religious clerics in October 2008 at Lahore, however, declared suicide bombing to be un-Islamic.

In May 2008 Noor Ahmed Wazir told me in Peshawar that three of his cousins from Miranshah, North Waziristan, had already been through suicide attack training at a camp near Shawal, run jointly by TTP's Qari Hussain and Siraj Haqqani, the son of the Afghan war veteran Jalaluddin Haqqani.

The squad of suicide bombers headed by Qari Hussain has a special status. Boys not older than seventeen were hailed by the Taliban as the ones restlessly waiting for their turn to strike against targets and embrace martyrdom. Baitullah Mehsud believes that the suicide bombers (fidayeen) are a force which can never be defeated. 'When these "fidayeen" are told that "hoors" (beautiful girls) are waiting, looking out of the windows in paradise to embrace them, these youngsters [became so impatient that] they all clamour to be the first to go on a mission. They want to see how many "hoors" out there are really waiting for them in paradise,' said one of the Taliban fighters.[1]

'They are my atom bombs. If the infidels have atom bombs, I have them too,' Baitullah Mehsud boasted in the presence of journalists who met him at a deserted government school in Spinkai, a desolate Pakistani village in South Waziristan. He also vowed his fight against the US and its allies would continue in Afghanistan.

Soon after May 2008 blitzkrieg-like operation Zalzala (literally, earthquake in Urdu), the Pakistan army took local and foreign journalists to a bombed house at Spinkai to show them 'evidence of suicide bomb factories'. Several days of fighting had left twenty-five militants and six soldiers dead, but the army claimed it had broken the back of TTP militants.

Brigadier Ali Abbas said his troops had recovered twelve detonation-ready suicide jackets, and many others being prepared (using ball bearings and steel nails) at a camp, which military officials said was a government-run school. The school was part of a large compound just outside the village that included a small mosque.[2] Major General Tariq Khan, the commander of the division that had captured the area, told the visiting journalists, 'It was like a factory [and it] had been recruiting nine to twelve-year-old boys and turning them into suicide bombers; [it also] manufactured IEDs [improvised explosive devices].'At another location military investigators found film footage on a DVD that they believed depicts children at the school being taught suicide training.[3]

The general said that, during operations in the area, soldiers had rounded up over fifty boys who were undergoing suicide attack training. Many of the boys had been kidnapped. Most of them were from the ethnic Pashtoon belt of the NWFP and some were locals from South Waziristan. 'The boys were handed to an NGO, Save the Children, to be looked after,' said General Khan.[4]

General Khan's claims notwithstanding, several suspects picked up by intelligence and security agencies in October and early November 2008 made startling revelations during interrogation. One young suicide bomber from Dera Ismail Khan, who collapsed as he approached a paramilitary camp on the outskirts of Swat in September, recounted the kind of fairy tales the trainers spun to entice children into becoming suicide bombers. 'My ustad [teacher] told me I would rocket into paradise once I press the button,' the boy explained, pointing to the trigger of the suicide jacket he had wrapped around his waist. A security official recalled that when the boy was taken to a military hospital for check-up he was visibly moved by the sight of the nurses dressed in white. He blurted out, 'My ustad had promised me "hoors" like these once I reached paradise.'

More information on these activities came from Imran alias Mansoor, a Taliban leader who was arrested during a shootout with security forces in the Mohmand agency in late October. The Mohmand Rifles, the local paramilitary force, arrested Imran only after serious injuries prevented him from escaping. Imran told his interrogators that a militant group in Karachi persuaded him to move to Dera Ismail Khan, the gateway to South Waziristan for training in manufacturing IEDs.[5] Following this training, Imran moved to Mohmand agency and stayed with TTP commander Omar Khalid's people there, where they concentrated on preparing cars and jackets for suicide strikes. A mechanic, Farooq Sattar, used to visit them in the camp to pack explosives into cars destined for strikes. 'We called him the Master Khudkush car [expert of suicide cars],' officials quoted Imran as saying.

Present in the camp were five Arabs, of whom two went down in a US-missile attack, while the other three—Dilbar, Abdul Samad and Israr—were still in Mohmand, living with Commander Abdul Hannan, the Al Qaeda pointman in the agency. The real mentor of these Arabs was Sheikh Usman, an expert in IEDs, who trained both Arabs and Pakistanis in the deadly art of suicide jackets and IEDs. All of them maintained good relations with Baitullah Mehsud who, according to local sources, occasionally helped the Mohmand Taliban with cash and goods.

This clearly pointed to Al Qaeda as a formidable enemy of the Pakistan army and the government through extremely motivated—and of course extensively brainwashed—youngsters recruited from all over the country.

South and North Waziristan and Bajaur in particular served as the staging posts for Afghan mujahideen who trained there before embarking on the mission of battling Soviet troops that had marched into Afghanistan in December 1979. The presence of training camps, which were supported by the American CIA and Pakistani ISI in these areas, enabled Arab, Afghan and other foreign fighters to establish links with the local tribes and build alliances. It was, therefore, natural for the foreign, or 'guest' fighters as they are sometimes called, to seek refuge in the two Waziristans and Bajaur once they were uprooted from Afghanistan after the fall of the Taliban regime in late 2001.

Scores of Al Qaeda Arabs and Chechens still reside in the Waziristan region, busy funding and motivating a new breed of fighters and potential suicide bombers.

Al Qaeda's Footprints

In a sensational interview with Pakistan's Geo TV, Mustafa Abu Yazid alias Sheikh Saeed, who heads Al Qaeda's operations in Afghanistan, said that suicide bombing was allowed in Islam. He declared the clerics who outlawed it were 'lackeys of the government'. The Egyptian militant gave an aggressive justification for suicide bombings as a 'legitimate weapon against the enemies of Islam'.[6]

Al Qaeda's involvement in the spiral of violence in Pakistan became evident in September 2007 when it vowed in a public statement to avenge the killing of a religious cleric and government's crackdown against the religious militants in Islamabad's Red Mosque in July 2007.

Since then, the Pakistani jihadis staged multiple suicide attacks against the army, air force, the ISI and other government personnel. In the six months following the assassination of former premier Benazir Bhutto on 27 December 2007, militants carried out about twenty suicide attacks at various locations.

An eminent Pakistani cleric, Maulana Rafi Usmani, together with fifty-two other scholars, had in 2005 declared suicide bombing was 'un-permissible in Islam' if it kills innocent people, but such religious decrees helped little in stemming the wave of Al Qaeda-led suicide bombings.

Before 11 September 2001, Al Qaeda did employ suicide missions as part of its global jihad, but in the aftermath of 9/11 the extremist interpretation of jihad has undergone a more radical change, degenerating into a cult of suicide bombing.

In their pre-martyrdom videos, bombers, while vowing commitment to God, also taunt their audiences with phrases such as 'while you Americans love life, we love death'. When these videos are shown on western television they evoke dislike, contempt and at times mockery, and also fuel anti-Islamic xenophobia in the west—which in turn attracts more recruits into the ranks of suicide bombers in countries like Iraq, Afghanistan and Pakistan.

The basic mindset of the new-look Al Qaeda and its extensions, as the eminent Pakistani journalist Khaled Ahmed explained in an article in the *Friday Times*, the message given to young jihadis is: 'You are not a good jihadi until you kill yourself in the act of killing many others.'

Developments since 2004 in particular highlight the footprints of Al Qaeda in the suicide bombings in Afghanistan and Pakistan; the mujahideen did not carry out a single suicide attack during the ten-year-long Afghan war against the Soviets. The assassination on 9 September 2001 of the Afghan Northern Alliance leader Ahmed Shah Massoud by suicide bombers was the first such Al Qaeda attack in Afghanistan.

Until early 2004, when the resurgent Taliban mounted six suicide attacks against US and Afghan forces, not a single such attack had been reported. But the subsequent years saw an explosion of suicide attacks in the country: twenty-one in 2005, 136 in 2006 and 137 in 2007. In 2006 there were 1100 casualties from suicide bombings and in 2007 the number rose to 1730. The Taliban aimed at exposed targets—900 Afghan policemen and forty Afghan aid workers were killed in 2008 in various acts of violence including suicide attacks.

New training techniques, including in the use and manufacture of IEDs and suicide jackets, spiritual guidance by Al Qaeda and support from narcotics trade tycoons continue to help the Taliban and Al Qaeda on both sides of the Durand Line enlist human resources and acquire hardware they need for attacks and propaganda. Money generated from drug trafficking and abductions for ransom also enable the militants to financially compensate families of young suicide bombers.

In Pakistan, local Taliban, effectively extensions of Al Qaeda, emulate their 'Afghan comrades'. Ensconced in the tribal areas of Pakistan, these Taliban are planning, preparing and conducting campaigns to destabilize the country; intelligence officials discovered that many of the initial suicide bombers used in the roughly eighty suicide attacks between January 2007 and July 2008 were Pakistanis and Afghans, many of them orphans or mentally unstable teenagers recruited from asylums, orphanages and Afghan refugee camps in Pakistan.

Whether it was the deadly attack on Pervez Musharraf in December 2004, or on then prime minister Shaukat Aziz in April 2005, or the massive detonation, probably by remote control, outside the Pakistan Ordnance Factories west of Islamabad, or the truck that a bomber drove into an assembly of tribal elders in Orakzai in October 2008, all these actions bore the hallmarks of Al Qaeda, which had successfully expanded the Taliban agenda against US-led foreign troops based in Afghanistan by bringing in issues such as Palestine and the Israeli repression. This seems to have added fuel to the simmering fire.

For Al Qaeda It Is Muslims Versus Infidels

'We were told to fight against Israel, America and non-Muslims,' said seventeen-year-old Muhammed Bakhtiar, when asked why he wanted to become a suicide bomber.[7]

Bakhtiar and his friend Miraj Ahmad left everything and everyone they knew in Buner, a district of the Malakand division of the NWFP, to join a madrassa near Lahore. A man had come to their boarding school and told there about the Markaz-e-Dawatul Irshad, run by the Jamatud Dawa, the charity linked to the Lashkar-e-Taiba, which shares the Al Qaeda ideology.

'We read about jihad in books and wanted to join,' said Ahmad. 'We wanted to go to the Muridke madrassa so we would have a better life in the hereafter.'

Once at the centre, the boys had the option of becoming freedom fighters or suicide bombers. The students were taught Islamic studies in the mornings and afternoons were reserved for sports after lunch. Jihad training was given in the evenings, two classes a night. 'The jihadi man who brought us to Muridke told us we would become great by fighting jihad,' said the clean-shaven Bakhtiar. 'We knew we could never become great if we stayed in Buner. I wanted to become great.'

When the parents of Bakhtiar and Ahmad learned the boys

had missed a week at their Buner boarding school, they panicked. They contacted relatives and friends, but everything led to a dead end. Even their principal, Abdur Rahman, expressed ignorance about their whereabouts. 'We don't support this; suicide attacks are murder; this is against Islam,' said Rahman. 'Those boys went to Muridke by themselves, they should have been here taking their exams, and I no longer want them back in my school,' he said.[8]

Eventually, the tribal elders intervened and brought Bakhtiar and Ahmad back home.

Bakhtiar and Ahmad were just a few of the lucky ones whom their parents could locate and retrieve from the Muridke seminar. But scores of youngsters, recruited from across the country, also from the tribal areas, simply lost their lives and souls to the jihadi parties; most could neither be rescued nor could they extricate themselves from the ideological web that is spun around them in exclusive sessions.

Overview of Suicide Bombings in Pakistan

The first suicide attack in Pakistan occurred in Islamabad in 1995 when a bomber rammed his explosives-laden truck into the embassy of Egypt, killing fourteen people. The bomber was Egyptian. The second suicide attack hit Karachi in 2002. There were twenty-two suicide attacks between 2002 and 2006. While PPP leader Benazir Bhutto's 27 December assassination was the most high-profile suicide strike of 2007, highly motivated youngsters staged at least fifty-six suicide attacks in 2007, compared to six in the previous year.

The 2007 strikes targeted mostly restaurants frequented by army men and policemen. A few strikes on mosques in Quetta, Rawalpindi and Multan appeared to be an attempt to cover them up in sectarian colour.

On 31 May 2005 a suicide bomb attack in Karachi during the evening prayers inside Ali Raza Imambargah killed nineteen and wounded thirty-eight. It also cracked the building's dome. This attack came just weeks after a suicide attack at another Shia mosque, which killed twenty-three and injured almost a hundred people during the Friday prayers. The Ali Raza Imambargah attack was probably in retaliation for the assassination of the Sunni Muslim head of Jamia Banuria in Karachi, Nizamuddin Shamzai, the previous day.

Being close to the border regions, cities like Peshawar and Kohat bore the brunt of Taliban-related violence, with three instances of two suicide attacks on a single day during 2007. The NWFP also witnessed the first suicide attack by a woman when, on 4 December 2007, a female suicide bomber blew herself up in a high-security zone in the provincial capital, Peshawar. Except for killing herself, the suicide bomber, who was said to be in her mid thirties, fortunately could not cause much damage, probably because of last-minute nerves.

A suicide attack near a Shia mosque in the heart of Peshawar in early December 2008 killed close to fifty people, more or less a repeat of an attack of the same intensity almost in the same area a year ago during the month of Shia mourning, Moharram al harram.

Those involved in suicide attacks can be categorized into two classes of Pakistani radical organizations. The first is based on sectarian influences—the most vociferous among them being the banned militant Sunni group, the Lashkar-e-Jhangvi and the Lashkar-e-Taiba. Their diehard zealots insist on carrying out their jihadi agenda inside Pakistan, while also extending support to their friends across the border; their leaders are mostly those who fought in Afghanistan, first against the Russian troops and then against the US-led allied forces along with the Taliban. For ideological guidance and inspiration they obviously look to Al Qaeda. Pakistani intelligence officials also traced several suicide bombings and attacks on Shia gatherings and mosques to Lashkar-e-Jhangvi activists, leaving no doubt on the close nexus that exists between the Pakistani militant groups and bin Laden's dreaded organization.

The second type of suicide attackers belong to the pro-Taliban groups who are also linked to the Al Qaeda mostly in the Waziristan region and are gathered under the leadership of Baitullah Mehsud. The agenda of this group, however, differs from the others; while the former seeks to give a purely religious spin to their war, the latter pursues a purely political agenda, one that aims at destabilizing Pakistan through acts of terror which do not distinguish between government, army, tribal or religious targets. The followers of this group are not concerned at the destruction of schools and hospitals, or about the lives of innocent citizens in pursuit of their relentless, violent campaign.

The Bomber Who Wavered

'We receive funds from Arab countries, therefore, we cannot carry out any attack there, and if we commit any wrong there, they will stop supply of funds to us.' This was the response of Abu Nasir al-Qahtani, a suicide bombing trainer, when one of his disciples, twenty-one-year-old Mansoor Khan Dawar, asked him through his local teacher whether suicide bombing was Islamic and was only Afghanistan and Pakistan the target of such attacks.

Born to Abdul Ghani Khan Dawar in Hurmaz, a small village near Miranshah in North Waziristan, Mansoor was picked up by Al Qaeda and Taliban recruiters from a village mosque in the spring of 2006.

'After several sessions at an isolated compound in Hurmaz, my teacher took me to Spinkai Raghzai for special training,' Mansoor told one of my close friends based in Miranshah. I had sent in Naeemullah (pseudonym) to interview youngsters who had undergone training for suicide bombing.

The camp was led by Qari Hussain, the TTP master-trainer of suicide bombers. If Mansoor Khan was to be believed, al-Qahtani, a Saudi national who, along with four other terrorists, had escaped from the Bagram prison north of Kabul during the summer of 2005, was staying with Hussain at that time.

After his escape from Bagram, the US-led air base and the detention centre, al-Qahtani fled to North Waziristan to continue attacks against NATO and Afghan forces fighting against the Taliban. There he joined forces with Abu Wafa, an expert in militant activities and became active in the Afghan provinces of Khost, Paktika and Paktia. 'A recently released CD shows al-Qahtani imparting military training, guiding the fighters with the help of computerized map to attack enemy bases and delivering a lengthy speech to wage jihad against "infidels" in Afghanistan and Iraq,' the *News* reported, before al-Qahtani[9] was recaptured in early November 2006 by Afghan and coalition forces in the eastern Afghan province of Khost.

'When I met al-Qahtani, he soon impressed me with his thoughts on Islam and America and I decided to become a suicide bomber,' Mansoor recalled, explaining why he opted to become a bomber. Mansoor was either unable to identify or perhaps did not want to name the place where he got his training. His description of the place, however, suggests the camp was located somewhere in the Shawal mountains that form a natural border between Afghanistan and Pakistan.

'I completed my training in the mountains in twenty days. Most of the time we were either training or praying and the speeches by al-Qahtani were also very emotional and motivating,' Mansoor told Naeemullah. 'Our instructors would show videos of atrocities on Muslims and also teach us verses of Holy Quran and Hadiths against the infidels,' recounted Mansoor, who said that he trained in a group of ten.

Once convinced the young boy was ready for the suicide mission, his mentors told him to visit his parents before embarking on the 'journey to eternity'.

Mansoor's parents were surprised, but also greatly relieved to see him again after an almost four-week absence. But the boy looked a different person; he had turned quiet and reclusive, thereby arousing their suspicion. 'After my father repeatedly asked me what I was up to, I told him about the training and the mission ahead of me, of my intention to carry out a suicide attack,' said Mansoor, who, according to the interviewer, also appeared nervous at the time of this conversation.

His father—Abdul Ghani Khan, a low-ranking government official—then engaged him in a long discussion, trying to explain the positive and negative aspects of the jihad Al Qaeda and Taliban were waging. He reminded his son of how the 'Americans and their Arab hosts were enjoying their lives in Saudi Arabia and other Muslim countries'. Why don't the militants target these Arabs and Americans? And is suicide bombing in accordance with the Islamic sharia?

'If they give you and me a satisfactory answer, I will not stop you from blowing yourself up,' Mansoor quoted his father as saying.

When the boy wavered a little, the father asked him to put these questions to his local teacher, who was a cleric at one of the mosques near Mirali, a North Waziristan town notorious for hosting foreigners. Mansoor travelled up to Mirali and put the same questions to him. A little embarrassed, the teacher rang up al-Qahtani (he was fluent in Arabic) and informed him of Mansoor's dilemma.

That is when al-Qahtani said, 'We receive funds from Arab countries, therefore, we cannot carry out any attack there, and if we commit any wrong there, they will stop supply of funds to us. But jihad in Pakistan and Afghanistan is lawful and even the Saudis believe so.'

Mansoor returned home after spending another few hours with the teacher, still undecided and confused. Once he sat down with his father, the fog of confusion disappeared but the fear of consequences of walking out of Al Qaeda made him shudder, he said.

The father eventually went to his son's teacher and managed to convince him that Mansoor was not firm any more and could back out at the last moment of a suicide mission.

The cleric somehow relented and allowed Abdul Ghani Khan to take his son back on the condition that they leave the village.

The family eventually moved to Bannu, a populous district of the NWFP that borders North Waziristan.[10]

The Making of Suicide Bombers

Several accounts have surfaced on the evolution of jihad into suicide bombing. In the Pakistan–Afghanistan border region, the ranks of suicide bombers swelled to unimaginable levels after the 6 September 2006 peace agreement in North Waziristan, which bound local tribal elders to disallow cross-border movement of militants to and from Afghanistan. The deal provided all shades of Taliban in North Waziristan with an opportunity to recuperate from the losses suffered at the hands of the military in the preceding months, and also to reorganize and enlist new recruits for their battle and suicide squads. With the deal, the militants got breathing space and their fears of being hunted by the military diminished, at least for the time being. Many disguised militants also received compensation for damages to their property during the military operation.

Residents of Miranshah, Makeen, Wana, Shawal and several other villages and hamlets in Waziristan often speak without condemnation, sometimes even with pride, of camps that motivate youngsters into blowing themselves up—all in the name of God and Islam. 'TTP and other outfits prey on youngsters and isolate them instantly if they find them fit for their mission,' said Ehsan Khan Daur from Mirali.

The would-be bombers are brainwashed to the extent that, they begin to dream of the 'glorious life afterwards'. They are prepared like grooms before the wedding ceremony, and emotionally 'motivated' in such a way that most of these boys rarely bother to think twice before putting on the lethal, locally improvised explosive-laden jackets that they explode when on the chosen site.

Enthusiastic and ingenuous teenagers are recruited, usually from mosques or seminaries, where jihadis hunt for potential bombers. They are moved from safe house to safe house and receive various forms of training. Bombers, for example, are taught to duck their heads when they pull the switch so their head is blown apart and is unrecognizable. Meanwhile separate teams choose the next targets in Afghanistan—a job done jointly by the Taliban and Al Qaeda; the former provide the manpower and the latter the explosives, packed either in a jacket meant for a suicide mission or a vehicle for a strike on a bigger and politically critical target.

'The martyr not dying physically and enjoying the pleasures of paradise is recorded in the Quran in relation to historical events which occasion the Revelation,' writes Khaled Ahmed. 'But the pivot of the suicide bomber phenomenon is religious extremism prevalent in the society from where the bomber is chosen. Extremism is not a specialization. It is flowing from the pulpit and TV screen in most Muslim states, including Pakistan. Research in Pakistan by an Islamabad doctor after interviewing the TNSM returnees from jihad against America in Afghanistan has found that the warriors were picked up from the mosque rather than the madrassa.'[11]

This determination, however, may be an overstatement for the simple reason that hunters may stumble upon their prey anywhere at any time; Taliban recruiters prowl both mosques and seminaries in search of potential bombers. But at times they pick up 'candidates' even from the roadside or from a friendly neighbourhood.

'"If we kill Americans through suicide bombing, America will not become Muslim. If we kill Pakistanis through suicide bombing, Pakistan will become a more strict adherent of Islam," [is the thought process that] seems to be the driving force behind Al Qaeda's suicide bombing campaign,' Ahmed says.

Rehman Wazir, a resident of Wana, recalled how some youngsters from his village spent a few weeks at one of the camps run by TTP zealot Qari Hussain. 'When they returned home, they were changed people, dreaming only of paradise,' Wazir said. They had been assigned numbers and were told to wait for their turn, he said.[12]

Government investigators claim almost all the suicide bombers in Pakistan are young men in their teens or twenties. Sources within the ranks of the Islamic militants corroborate this proudly saying that youngsters have responded most enthusiastically to the call to fight against the enemies of Islam.[13]

Intelligence officials in Peshawar told me about Adnash Gul, a twenty-three-year-old, who was intercepted in Dera Ismail Khan, one of the largest cities in the NWFP. Carrying a vest strapped with fifteen kilograms of explosives, Gul told interrogators he studied at a madrassa in Miranshah and was supposed to hand over the explosives-laden jacket to a man in Dera Ismail.

Devoid of basic facilities, poor education infrastructure and dismal employment opportunities make the tribal areas an ideal hunting ground of Islamic militants for young warriors. And they reap a rich harvest of teenagers, pumped with the zeal for jihad 'that will catapult them into heaven'.

'Despite allegations, there is no evidence that suicide bombers are paid to do the job,' said Rahimullah Yusufzai, analyst and expert on Afghan and tribal affairs. He had met with the families of three suicide bombers in the Shabqad area of Charsaddar district who told him that they did not receive any money after their young sons sacrificed their lives in Indian Kashmir and Afghanistan. Visits to the poverty-stricken homes of the bereaved families and interviews with neighbours supported this claim. The three young men killed themselves and many others while committing suicide bombings due to their belief that they were dying for a worthy and holy cause.[14]

However, according to the *Washington Times* the youngsters are recruited by the Taliban and paid Rs 1000 a day to become jihadis.[15]

Besides generating terror scares across the country, the Pakistani Taliban scored their greatest success with the assassination of Benazir Bhutto in Rawalpindi on 27 December 2007, ten days before the general elections. The mayhem and uncertainty following this tragedy forced a rescheduling of the polls to 18 February 2008, which Bhutto's Pakistan Peoples Party won.

Regardless of the army campaign against them, it seems the TTP and other outfits continue to run terror and suicide training camps, thereby churning out fresh squads of people who are ready to kill and die for the 'ultimate glory and the great life hereafter'.

Does Islam Permit Suicide Bombings?

In April 2007 I wrote a couple of special reports for the weekly *Friday Times* on whether suicide bombing is permissible in Islam. I spoke with several religious leaders and scholars, whose responses were wrapped in 'ifs and buts', rather than a straight appreciation or condemnation of suicide bombings. The following responses are insightful.

Qazi Hussein Ahmed, the mercurial chief of the Jamaat-e-Islami, was reluctant to speak on the issue 'because of its technicality'. Munawar Hassan, the party secretary general and a fiery orator and demagogue, however agreed to speak on behalf of the party.

'Pakistan supported infidels who carried out bombings on Bajaur and elsewhere . . . General Musharraf and infidels are allies and that is why they are facing similar reaction. Why are they supporting infidels? Why are they providing logistic support to them against the Taliban?' Hassan asked. However, he had little to say on whether the wrongdoings of leaders justified the murder of common people.

It merits mention that Mufti Nizamuddin Shamzai, the late spiritual mentor of the famous Binori Mosque and seminary in Karachi, had in 1998 decreed that killing Americans was justified. The Lashkar-e-Taiba too issued a similar proclamation soon after. This outfit had in fact launched the fidayeen attacks in the summer of 1998 as a ploy to pressurize the Indian government into retreat in Kashmir.

The ex-LeT chief Hafiz Saeed, put under house arrest on 10 December 2008 in the aftermath of the November terror attacks in Mumbai, used to take pride in patronizing suicide squads for Kashmir. But talking to a private television channel on 24 February 2007, Hafiz Saeed said 'killing innocent people was not permissible in Islam'. This appeared to be a departure from what he and his colleagues had devised and implemented through highly motivated fighters ready to die for their cause, the fidayeen attacks at the height of the LeT campaign in Kashmir.

Maulana Samiul Haq, former senator and chief of Darul Uloom Haqqania at Akora Khattak, about 100 kilometres north-west of Islamabad, said, 'They will kill me if I dare to issue a decree against suicide bombings.' But then he went on to rant in the typical conservative way. 'It is a reaction of what has been going on worldwide. An international coalition is conspiring to suppress those who are fighting for their identity and freedom.' He likened the suicide bombers as a legitimate party to the war.

Samiul Haq's seminary shot to international prominence for its role in the Afghan jihad as well as its connections with the Afghan Taliban leaders, many of whom had graduated from his school. As a self-proclaimed mentor, Maulana Haq would brag about his students' zeal and devotion to the cause of Afghan Taliban, at times employing gimmicks to impress visitors.

'Be quick and wind up filming lest the Taliban get angry,' the maulana had once told us during a shoot for a German television channel. This pretence exposed the duplicity of people like Maulana Haq because it is almost unthinkable that seminary students would take offence at something (like permission for filming) approved by their mentor.

Allama Sajid Ali Naqvi, the mysterious head of the defunct Shia religio-political party Tehreeke-Jafria Pakistan, which is suspected of promoting and protecting the Iranian brand of militant Islam, sounded candid, though ending with the same conclusion: 'Generally, killing others by blowing one's self up is prohibited in Islam but in particular circumstances you can't condemn such an act.'

Referring to a spate of suicide bombing that had erupted in Pakistan since mid January 2007, Naqvi said, 'Those attacks which are being carried out on a sectarian basis or against innocent people are completely un-Islamic, Islam doesn't permit them. But, if these are carried out to achieve major goals, for instance, to defeat evil powers or their puppets then one can't oppose it straight away.'

Hafiz Hussain Ahmed, a former member of parliament who once was the most vocal leader of the Sunni Deobandi Jamiat Ulmae Islam (JUI) of Maulana Fazlurrehman, was equally ambiguous, perhaps because Ahmed and Fazlurrehman possess a knack for 'pragmatic and business-like politics'. 'No doubt, such strikes are condemned in any religion but, instead of debating their legitimacy, we ought to look into the causes which force somebody, particularly youth, to end his life for such an act,' said Ahmed.

Like General Pervez Musharraf, Ahmed too regurgitates the causes that he believes underlie the anti-US emotion in the Islamic world.'The situation in Palestine, Kashmir, Afghanistan and Iraq does not let you issue a decree against such actions . . . We have been saying that Pakistan's coalition with US-led war on terror brought this menace in the country and that is why they must review their policy.'

Mufti Muneebur Rehman is considered a moderate and liberal religious scholar and frequently appears on national television channels. Asked for an opinion on the legitimacy of suicide bombings, Rehman said, 'Unlawful murder of any person is forbidden in Islam, whether it is a suicide attack or simple killing.' He was referring to his decree issued in 2006.

'There is no word for suicide bombing in shariat. It is just the unlawful killing that is forbidden . . . and would those who describe these attacks as a reaction to the turmoil in Waziristan tell us what was the sin of those clerics and people who were killed in a congregation in Nishtar Park [at Karachi in 2006] or elsewhere in similar attacks. Were these victims [of suicide attacks] responsible for ordering the military operation in tribal areas?' asked Mufti Rehman.

Hanif Jalandari, chief of the Multan-based Wifaqul-Madaris (the directorate for Sunni Deobandi schools), who lords over about 7500 seminaries across the country, offered a pragmatic explanation: 'Islam doesn't permit any Muslim to attack another Muslim or those non-Muslims living in a Muslim country. Recent suicide bombings in Pakistan are unlawful. It is not just the killing of a Muslim which is a sin, it is also a sin if one considers it legal, that is, sanctioned by Islam. It is an un-Islamic act and, according to Islamic scholars, such man is not a Muslim.'

Even though suicide bombers kept striking at public places and targeted army and government officials in big numbers throughout 2007 and 2008 (with more than 106 attacks altogether), none of the mainstream religious leaders openly condemned it.

Among the prominent religio-political leaders, only Maulana Hassan Jan had openly opposed suicide attacks. Jan, who had taught sharia law in Saudi Arabia and was an influential figure among Taliban leaders, had issued fatwas (religious decrees), calling suicide bombings 'un-Islamic'. Most probably to punish him for his opposition to what certain militant groups justify as 'legitimate tactics', unknown attackers shot Jan dead on 15 September 2007. Three people had asked him to accompany them to solemnize a wedding but they shot him in the evening on the outskirts of Peshawar city.

Against this backdrop, several religious scholars and clerics from twenty-eight religious groups gathered at a conference in Lahore to discuss the issue of suicide bombings on 14 October 2008. The low-key Muttahida Ulema Council of Pakistan organized the meeting at the Jamia Naeemia madrassa in Lahore. At the end of the talks, the council came up with a decree, which was part of a twenty-one-point declaration. Point 13 of the declaration said: 'It is the Ulemas' fatwa by consensus that suicide attacks inside Pakistan are haram [forbidden in Islam] and illegitimate.'

If taken at face value, the decree implies that such attacks are forbidden in Pakistan and permissible in other countries. Yet, when asked, none of the scholars offered any explanation as to why they specified that Pakistan was the only forbidden territory.

Regardless of their responses and the implications of the decree, the entire exercise meant little as far as addressing the masterminds of suicide bombings was concerned. The growing frequency of such strikes underscored that no religious decree or legal order would deter them from executing their mission.

Ironically, the head of Jamia Naeemia, Mufti Sarfraz Naeemi, was killed along with at least eight others when a suicide bomber struck at the mosque after the Friday prayers on 12 June 2009. Naeemi, sixty-one, was a reputed liberal scholar who had openly taken the lead in denouncing suicide bombings. A moderate cleric of the Barelvi branch of Islam and an outspoken critic of the Pakistani Taliban, Naeemi had told Reuters a few weeks before his death, 'The military must eliminate the Taliban once and for all otherwise they will capture the entire country which would be a catastrophe.' Naeemi had also participated in a conference of Islamic scholars convened by the government in May 2009, which criticized suicide attacks and the beheading of innocent Muslims as un-Islamic.

Concerned by the rise in suicide strike missions, several Indian Muslim clerics also took it upon themselves to devise a response.

Over 10,000 scholars and religious representatives of several sects and groups from all over India attended the Anti-terrorism Conference organized by the Islamic seminary Darul Uloom at Deoband, Uttar Pradesh (as reported by the Press Trust of India on 25 February 2008).

'Islam is a religion of mercy for all humanity. Islam prohibits killing of innocent people . . . Islam sternly condemns all kinds of oppression, violence and terrorism. It has regarded oppression, mischief, rioting and murder among severest sins and crimes,' said the declaration adopted at the end of the conference.

The gathering also denounced attempts to implicate Muslims and particularly religious institutions for terrorist acts.

'The disease [terrorism] has been diagnosed in a wrong way. Whenever there is any incident of terrorism, every possible attempt is made to link it to Muslims and particularly those who have studied in madrassas and some religious institutions. This is totally wrong,' said Adil Siddiqui, public relations officer of Darul Uloom, which is the prime source of guidance and inspiration for the Sunni Muslims (of Deobandi denomination).

8

The Evolution of Militant Organizations in Pakistan

Many of Pakistan's militant outfits took seed during the anti-Soviet jihad but subsequently evolved into lethal sectarian entities. The Harkatul Mujahideen, Lashkar-e-Taiba and Jaish-e-Mohammad also became heavily involved in the so-called 'jihad' in Kashmir and developed close ties with the Afghan Taliban as well. Most of these groups represent an obscurantist, pan-Islamist world view and are rabidly opposed to the western style of life as well as to India.

Events since 9/11 changed the rules of the game for militants and militant organizations, some of whom had traditionally enjoyed the support of the Pakistani establishment for the strategic objectives both in Afghanistan and the Indian part of Kashmir. Most of these groups had originated in central Pakistan, in the most populous province of Punjab, and sprouted from the Jamiat Ulami Pakistan of the Deobandi school of thought. They were know as 'guest organizations' in Kashmir, while in Afghanistan they revered, and owed allegiance to, the Taliban chief Mulla Omar and Osama bin Laden. Predominantly, these organizations drew people from the province and were thus known as the Punjabi factor in FATA.

Note: Besides Imtiaz Gul's book *The Unholy Nexus*, the information on Pakistani militant organizations is based on three other sources, the weekly *Friday Times*, Amir Mir's *The True Face of Jehadis* and Muhammad Amir Rana's *A to Z of Jihadi Organizations in Pakistan*.

Harkatul Mujahideen (Harkatul Ansar)

Harkatul Mujahideen emerged as Harkatul Ansar in the 1980s with a mission to fight the Soviet Union in Afghanistan. The organization was based on the belief that the Islamic system must be promulgated in Pakistan, and that those who are insincere to Islam and Pakistan must be killed. Its cadre received basic training inside Afghanistan and fought alongside the Afghan mujahideen against the Russian invaders. This religious militant group, though not involved in sectarian violence, strongly supported Sipahe Sahaba Pakistan's move against the Shia community. After the Soviet withdrawal from Afghanistan, the group reorganized its basic cadres and moved them into Kashmir under the patronage of Pakistani backers.

Its erstwhile chief, Maulana Fazlurrehman Khalil, appeared on the Kashmir scene in 1993–94. He is a big fan of Osama bin Laden and the Taliban. 'I saw him with an American Stinger missile in his hands,' said Maulana Fazlurrehman Khalil, when I asked him about his last encounter with Osama bin Laden during a meeting in Rawalpindi's lower-middle-class residential neighbourhood Khayaban-e-Sir Syed, in April 2000. 'Yes, Osama is a great Muslim mujahid. We fought together in Afghanistan against the Soviet-Russian troops but then I moved on to help Kashmir's Muslim liberation movement after the Russians left Afghanistan this month eleven years ago,' Khalil said. 'We have nothing in common any more,' he quickly added. The denial, however, had a hollow ring to it.

On 24 May 1998, one of his deputies, a trusted long-time aide and veteran of the Afghan war, code-named Allah Wasaya, arranged a trip for a few Pakistani journalists to Khost, in eastern Afghanistan, for a meeting with the Sheikh, a title they used for bin Laden. I was also invited, but backed out the day before the trip because I sensed the next couple of days were going to be crucial as Pakistan's preparations for nuclear tests were almost complete. Sources in one of the nuclear organizations had asked me to stay on for the 'big moment'. Pakistan exploded its nuclear devices on 28 and 30 May 1998.

Khalil, along with thousands of his zealots who idolize Osama bin Laden as their role model, vowed revenge on the United States after its Tomohawk missiles destroyed bin Laden's camp on the outskirts of the eastern Afghan city of Khost in August 1998, killing at least twenty-five people. The ostensible reason for this action was the terror strike on US diplomatic missions in Kenya and Tanzania a few days earlier, which the American establishment believed had been masterminded at bin Laden's camp in Khost. Nine of those killed were members of Khalil's Harkatul Mujahideen. Harkatul Ansar had changed to its present name after the US State Department banned it as a terrorist organization. In October 1999, the State Department listed the Harkatul Mujahideen as a terrorist organization along with twenty-eight others across the world.

The Harkatul Mujahideen was rated as the most lethal of the militant groups operating in the Indian-administered Kashmir. India insists the group acted in Kashmir with a mission from Pakistan's intelligence agency ISI. During 1999 alone, the group claimed to have killed forty-three officers and 1825 soldiers of the Indian army during attacks on convoys or military posts. They also killed ten alleged Indian spies and lost ninety-six of their own fighters during skirmishes with the Indian forces.

'They are all martyrs, we are proud of them because they gave their lives for a sacred cause,' Khalil said rejecting western allegations that his was a terrorist organization. 'I think this is the Indian propaganda that makes the world view us as terrorists. We condemn terrorism but we do believe in jihad for the liberation of Kashmir,' said the soft-spoken Khalil. He also took exception to the western definition of terrorism.

'Not a single person was declared a terrorist during the Afghan war against the Soviet-Russians. Instead, the Americans and other western nations welcomed and celebrated them as Islamic warriors. Osama bin Laden was one of these heroes of the west,' Khalil pointed out.

Harkatul Mujahideen continued training its fighters at the Rishkor camp on the outskirts of Kabul even after the 1998 missile attacks on its facilities in eastern Afghanistan. The proof came when one of the bombs dropped by the coalition jets hit a residential complex close to the Rishkor camp killing at least thirty-five Harkat people in late October 2001.

Jaish-e-Mohammad

When Maulana Masood Azhar was freed from an Indian jail and returned to Kandahar in southern Afghanistan on 31 December 1999 in exchange for the release of hostages aboard a hijacked Indian passenger jet, few in Pakistan or elsewhere had any inkling as to what the stocky fellow was up to. Soon afterwards, he emerged in Pakistan to a rousing reception. He announced his intention to raise an anti-India force—Jaish-e-Mohammad, or the Army of Mohammad—to liberate Kashmir. It was yet another Deobandi Sunni-militant organization created in the name of jihad against infidels. It enjoyed the blessings of Mufti Nizamuddin Shamzai, the spiritual head of a movement based in Karachi. Shamzai had in 1998 also declared that the killing of any American was 'legal and Islamic'.

Azhar's agenda also endeared him to the Afghan Taliban supreme leader Mulla Mohammad Omar, who eventually declared Azhar as his deputy for Pakistan.

Afghan Taliban officials used to extend full protocol to Azhar, who always carried a Kalashnikov, and moved with a dozen bodyguards. Until the rout of the Taliban regime, Azhar spent most of his time in Kandahar and Zabul, where he ran training camps for his Kashmir operations.

Interviews with intelligence officials, including Pakistani operatives based in Kandahar, yielded interesting revelations.

'I think we should also keep in mind our interests in Kashmir. These fighters have made the job much easier for us and they need our support,' a senior official of the ISI had observed when confronted with hard questions on the support for militancy.

Jaish-e-Mohammad was one of the sixteen organizations united under the umbrella of the United Jihad Council (UJC) to battle Indian troops in Kashmir.

Possibly two factors influenced Azhar's decision to go his own way; first, as it later turned out, the cleric from Bahawalpur had become more radical and rigid during his captivity in Tihar jail in India. Second, one of his associates told me at Rawalpindi shortly after the creation of Jaish-e-Mohammad, Azhar thought he could provide a fresh impetus to the insurgency in Kashmir with the help of the Afghan Taliban. Azhar's oratory and his close relations with the inner circle of the Afghan Taliban quickly won him scores of new members, and within a year or so the Jaish-e-Mohammad gradually outnumbered the Harkatul Mujahideen.

But the creation of the Jaish-e-Mohammad led to another complication: apparently while the Pakistani establishment supported the move, it also suspected Azhar of playing a double game. It thought Azhar might be acting on behalf of his former Indian captors because, while his jihadi outfit appeared more radical and motivated, it also further divided the Kashmiri militant movement. Also, his zealots openly admitted, and frequently at that, to acts of terrorism in Kashmir and India, including the attack on the Kashmiri legislative assembly.

The drifting apart of the mujahideen group had in fact begun two years earlier. The emergence of the Jaish-e-Mohammad marked virtually the fourth division within the Harkatul Mujahideen. In the initial years of jihad, the Harkatul Mujahideen and Harkatul Jihad-e-Islami (HJI) had merged into Harkatul Ansar after the US declared it as a terrorist organization. But the bond did not last and both resumed their original identities. This development encouraged Ilyas Kashmiri, who was leading the 313 brigade of the Harkatul Mujahideen in Kotli, to go independent in 1999. The launch of the Jaish-e-Mohammad in early 2000 was the most severe blow.

Azhar had been jailed in India for overstaying. It was believed that the Indian Airlines passenger plane had been hijacked primarily to secure the release of Azhar and two other militants. Indian Airlines Flight 814 (IC-814) took off from Kathmandu's

Tribhuvan International Airport for New Delhi's Indira Gandhi International Airport on 24 December 1999. The Airbus 320 with about 156 passengers was hijacked shortly after it entered the Indian airspace at about 5.30 p.m., when five Pakistani nationals seized control of the aircraft. Following refusal by Pakistani and UAE authorities, the aircraft ultimately landed at Kandahar airport, in south-western Afghanistan, where the hijackers released their hostages in exchange for the release of three extremists including Azhar on 31 December, after several rounds of talks with Indian negotiators.

Just a few days after his release, Azhar emerged in his hometown of Bahawalpur, southern Punjab, and received a hero's welcome from religious workers, mostly Harkatul Mujahideen followers. Soon after announcing his intention to raise tens of thousands of dollars for Jaish-e-Mohammad, Azhar undertook a whirlwind tour of the country, including Islamabad, where he received special attention from the intelligence agency's personnel, who could be easily identified at public meetings by their appearance and their stiff bearing. Jaish-e-Mohammad drew away hundreds of Harkatul Mujahideen activists. Once the party structure was in place, scores of new mosques and madrassas sprouted in the NWFP within months, where they attracted hundreds of jihad-oriented students from similar establishments of the rival groups. That Azhar had been in an Indian jail worked as a special pull; his top tier leaders used this fact to portray him as a great mujahid, whom 'we snatched from the jaws of India'.

Observers believed that the Pakistani backers of the Kashmiri militancy, and supporters of the Afghan Taliban, had found in Masood Azhar a new tool to reinforce the jihad in Kashmir after the setback in the Kargil war in the summer of 1999, where Pakistani special troops had to vacate Indian positions they had occupied in winter after crossing the border—the Line of Control that separates the Indian and Pakistani Kashmir.

Censured by the international community for violating the Line of Control, the then prime minister Nawaz Sharif was compelled to sign a pullout agreement in Washington on 4 July 1999 in the presence of the then US president Bill Clinton. Pakistan was still recovering from the Kargil humiliation when the hijacking took place. With the release of Azhar, the establishment hoped it could inject a new vigour in the demoralized mujahideen as well as the regular forces.

Azhar, therefore, moved to Afghanistan, received the blessings of the Taliban supreme commander Mulla Omar and began establishing camps there to train fighters. This was the first instance of Afghan Taliban acquiescing to a Pakistani militant outfit for objectives pursued elsewhere.

By the end of 2000, Azhar had managed to entrench himself in the NWFP and in southern Punjab. He turned Hangu, considered the most sensitive part of the region close to the Pakistan–Afghanistan border, with a history of Sunni–Shia hostilities, into his virtual headquarters. At several places, Sipahe Sahaba Pakistan, headed by the firebrand Maulana Azam Tariq, assisted Jaish-e-Mohammad in establishing new mosques and recruitment centres for those desirous of fighting in Kashmir. The SSP helped Azhar out in this region for two reasons. Both idolized the Afghan Taliban for their 'commitment to Islam' and the SSP was focused on Pakistan's internal politics and essentially thrived on its radical anti-Shia outlook whereas Azhar dreamed of 'liberating Kashmir'; hence there was no conflict of interest.

Hangu has a volatile mix of Shia and Sunni populations. The town is also a gateway to the Kurram and Orakzai agencies of the tribal belt bordering Afghanistan. Jamia Taleem-ul-Quran, a seminary set up by Maulana Masood Azhar's followers in Hangu, became the nucleus for his followers. It stands out as a landmark for those approaching the town. Sprawling over more than two hectares, the complex attracts money and people and substantial support and sympathy from officialdom.

From Kohat up to Bagato village in Hangu, one could observe highly provocative anti-Shia slogans and invitations for joining jihad by Jaish-e-Mohammad, Al-Badr, Harkatul Mujahideen and Hizbul Mujahideen, all of which are ideologically radically anti-Shia, and given to jihad in Kashmir. These organizations also offered military training to youngsters anxious to participate in jihad. The invitations were painted on hilltops, roadsides and walls of private homes in many other parts of the hilly NWFP.

Regardless of their rancour against the west, the expanding influence of the militants' outfits generally aroused concern among the people of Pakistan. 'It is not going to be without consequences for our society either,' said Dr Rasool Bakhsh Raees, an Islamabad-based expert on Afghan and international affairs. 'Religious indoctrination and the zeal of jihad inculcated a sense of self-righteousness, of being on the right path,' Dr Raees argued and, like many others, was unequivocal in maintaining that the mushrooming of dozens of training camps and madrassas across Pakistan and Afghanistan in the 1980s was directly related to America's proxy war against the Soviet Union in Afghanistan. 'American funding actually turned both Pakistan as well as Afghanistan into hotbeds of religious militancy that have now gone against the United States itself,' said Dr Raees.

It was like putting the Afghans and their Muslim brothers across the world on the drug of jihad and then asking them to self-detoxify after the objective—the Soviet pullout—was accomplished. Once the CIA shifted its interest from Afghanistan after the Soviet withdrawal in 1989, the committed veterans emerged to haunt the US and its allies as battle-hardened jihadi forces ready to take Islamic causes elsewhere. Be it Bosnia-Herzegovina, Chechnya, Uzbekistan, Tajikistan or Kashmir, they have been fighting alongside their oppressed brothers, ready to kill and die in the name of Islam.

Until it was banned in January 2002, the Jaish-e-Mohammad network was spread over seventy-eight districts in Pakistan. The biggest centre, Karachi, oversaw about a hundred subordinate offices. Bahawalpur and Multan centres followed, in size with fifty-five offices functioning in Bahawalpur and forty in Multan. Jaish-e-Mohammad also maintained large centres in the NWFP's Waziristan agency, Malakand, Kohat, Bannu and Dera Ismail, while Muzaffarabad used to be the largest Jaish-e-Mohammad establishment for Pakistan-administered Kashmir.

Tehreekul Irfan

In October 2001, Maulana Abdullah Shah Mazhar, the ameer of Sindh province, announced his separation from Jaish-e-Mohammad and the creation of his own movement, Tehreekul Irfan. Maulana Mazhar was the Karachi ameer of Harkatul Jehad-e-Islami before joining Jaish-e-Mohammad along with his entire group. He shot into prominence in Jaish-e-Mohammad and made himself known for his firebrand oratory and his name was included in the American list that declared four members of Jaish-e-Mohammad as dangerous criminals. He was considered close to Maulana Masood Azhar. The reason given for parting ways with JM was that the organization had failed in its goal of uniting all Deobandi parties, and that the disagreements had intensified instead.[7]

However, a member of Jaish-e-Mohammad, Lahore says that Maulana Mazhar was not happy with the sole imprint of Maulana Masood Azhar on the organization. He separated from the group along with his entire team, which is said to comprise a thousand individuals. His separation from Jaish-e-Mohammad was seen as the separation of Sindh Jaish from the Punjabi-dominated centre. Maulana Mazhar was arrested a week after creating the new organization.

Lashkar-e-Taiba

Lashkar-e-Taiba (LeT), widely believed by Indian intelligence agencies to be behind the Mumbai attacks of 26 November 2008, is the armed wing of the Pakistan-based religious organization Markaz-al-Daawatul Ershad, a Sunni anti-US missionary organization formed in 1989. The LeT is one of the four largest and best-trained groups fighting in Kashmir, besides Jaish-e-Mohammad, Harkatul Mujahideen and Hezbul Mujahideen, and is not connected to a political party. The organization has conducted a number of operations against Indian troops and civilian targets in Kashmir since 1993, and was also suspected of eight separate attacks in August 2001 that killed nearly a hundred, mostly Hindu Indians. LeT militants were suspected of kidnapping six persons in Akhala, India, in November 2000 and killing five of them. The organization collects donations from the Pakistani community in the Persian Gulf and United Kingdom, Islamic NGOs and Pakistani and Kashmiri businessmen. The amount of LeT funding is unknown. The Lashkar-e-Taiba maintains ties to religious/military groups around the world, ranging from the Philippines to the Middle East and Chechnya through the Markaz-al-Daawatul Ershad.

The man who made most of the headlines on the Kashmir front was the unassuming, slightly stocky Hafiz Mohammad Saeed, fifty-eight, who headed the LeT until 24 December 2002, when the ban on his organization and international pressure forced him to take a back seat within the organization. He had also been a staunch ally of the Afghan Taliban and like them considered photography un-Islamic.

Vociferous and unmoved by what his opponents say, Hafiz Saeed wears an entirely different look while at home or in meetings with guests. Saeed, father of a son and a daughter, appears down to earth, with his eyes mostly fixed on the floor, and interjects his answers with 'my brother, son, my dear'.

His soft demeanour hardly betrays the hyper-active, militant character of the organization he heads; even former prime minister Benazir Bhutto once took exception to LeT's activities when she accused it of 'muddying waters' in the Indian subcontinent. Western intelligence sources see the LeT as an arm of Pakistani intelligence agencies, but Hafiz Saeed brushes aside the allegation as 'mere Indian propaganda', saying the Indian establishment sees Pakistan's involvement 'even in accidental deaths in India'.

The organization's headquarters is in the Muridke sub-district near Lahore. It is a sprawling complex spread over 200 acres, and has a mujahideen colony with fifty houses, six fish farms and a rabbit farm that caters to the residents. Since religious education forms an important element of LeT's work, the complex boasts two model schools—one each for girls and boys—and the university Al-Dawat-al-Irshad. The students attending the university also learn horse-riding. Hundreds of them pass out every year, and hundreds more are swelling its ranks, essentially those driven by the LeT's ideology of living for God.

On 3 November 2000, Saeed thundered in the presence of tens of thousands of zealots that 'jihad is not about Kashmir only. About 15 years ago people might have found it ridiculous if someone had told them about the disintegration of the USSR (Union of Soviet Socialist Republic). Today, I announce the break-up of India, inshallah. We will not rest until the whole (of) India is dissolved into Pakistan.' Saeed promises a new war which will 'encompass all of India including Junagarh and Hyderabad', and his organization cites the bomb attack on Indian army soldiers at New Delhi's Mughal Red Fort in early 2001 as proof of that vow.

Sipahe Sahaba Pakistan

Sipahe Sahaba Pakistan (SSP) came into being in September 1984 in the deeply conservative district of Jhang in Pakistan's Punjab province. Its founder, Maulana Haq Nawaz Jhangvi, had been an active member of Jamiat Ulemae Islam (Fazalur Rehman group) before he went his own radical way. He had made an unsuccessful bid to become member of the National Assembly, losing it to a woman rival, Syeda Abida Hussain. However, his successor Maulana Azam Tariq has been able to make it several times to the Assembly, or Lower House of Pakistan's Parliament.

This organization has espoused the goal of restoration of Khilafat, or the system of a pan-Islamic rule of governance uniting all Muslim states under a single ruler, a system that followed the demise of Prophet Mohammad, a precedence that the Afghan Taliban had claimed to be practising. Being rabidly anti-Shia, the

SSP offers membership to any Muslim who regards Shia Muslims as 'infidels'.

Its anti-Shia campaign has had a terrible impact on Jhang and Faisalabad, a prosperous, industrial district in Punjab and adjacent areas. Many sub-districts became a battleground for militants of SSP and its Shia counterpart Sipahe Mohammad. During the mid 1990s these areas witnessed numerous 'sniper and terrorist attacks' on Shia and Sunni mosques and other religious centres, leaving more than 1000 people dead in three years, including two Iranian diplomats. Their rivalry had turned Punjab, Pakistan's most populous and politically influential province, into a hotbed of sectarian violence, until President Pervez Musharraf banned the two organizations in line with his policy to eliminate Islamic extremism in Pakistan.

Authorities would often declare curfew in Jhang to stop the movement of SSP and SM militants. Provocative graffiti against Shiites and other propaganda tactics were part of the SSP's activities. All members of the SSP were barred from joining any other movement or party and were required to always be ready for the holy war. Maulana Azam Tariq used to claim on the floor of the National Assembly that SSP fighters had directly participated in the Afghan jihad and had also trained on Afghan soil. 'Those acting against us must know that we have fought a jihad against the Soviet Russians, and know how to deal with our enemies,' Azam Tariq warned while discussing a motion on sectarian terrorism in the National Assembly in 1991. He himself fell to a barrage of bullets fired by unknown attackers in 2003 near Islamabad.

The SSP, characterized as a terrorist organization by the country's intelligence agencies, received huge financial assistance from Saudi Arabia and Iraq for their proxy war against Iran. Ziaurrehman Farooqi, the predecessor of Azam Tariq, stated in an interview that they receive funds from abroad but not from governments. 'It is just our sympathizers who donate to our cause,' Farooqi had said, shortly before he was assassinated in a bomb attack in Lahore in 1994, along with more than a dozen followers.

Pakistani intelligence sources used to consider the Saudi embassy in Islamabad a major conduit for the Saudi and American funding to the Afghan mujahideen between 1981 and 1998, but when insulted by the Taliban chief Mulla Omar over the Osama bin Laden issue, it terminated the funding. They recount secret visits to the embassy by SSP leaders, as well as indirect contact between them.

The overriding objective of the Saudi cooperation with SSP and other Sunni groups in Pakistan is seen as an effort to undermine growing Iranian influence and attempts by Tehran to reinforce its supporters both in Pakistan and in Afghanistan. For instance, in 1992 there was an unprecedented increase in the circulation of anti-Shia pamphlets, justifying their killing. Six of these pamphlets obtained by the *Friday Times* from the SSP's central distribution office at Lahore outlined the reasons for waging jihad against Shias. One pamphlet warns that 'if you are not a member of the SSP then you should be a very worried person'. The pamphlet also urges all 'Ahle Sunnah' or Sunni Muslims to unite against their common enemy, which by implication is a reference to the Shias. A pamphlet titled 'Why Shias are not Muslims' calls for a social boycott of the Shias as a religious duty for Sunnis because 'they (Shias) are kafirs (infidels)'. Another pamphlet ends in a particularly vicious fatwa from Darul Uloom Deoband, which says that anyone who marries a Shia, eats an animal slaughtered by them, participates in their nimaz-e-janaza (funeral prayers), or their annual Eid sacrifices, makes them witnesses to one's marriage, eats with them, offers prayers in their mosques or has any kind of social contact with them is an infidel. A postscript asserted that even voting for a Shia turns a Sunni into an infidel. A fourth pamphlet warned that Shias were an 'alarm bell for the entire Muslim Ummah', or Muslim brotherhood, saying Shias have been the greatest threat to Islam throughout Islamic history. It portrayed the Iranian revolution under Ayatollah Khomeini as the first major attempt by the Shias to spread their brand of Islam throughout Europe, Turkey and Russia and Central Asian Muslim states, all the way down to Sri Lanka through Pakistan. It appealed to the government to declare

Pakistan a Sunni state and Shias as non-Muslims, a favourite theme with the SSP. However, the SSP has presently mellowed down because of increased surveillance by security institutions and checks on their sources of financing.

Lashkar-e-Jhangvi

Lashkar-e-Jhangvi was created in 1996 with Riaz Basra as the head of its broadcast and publication wing. Basra believed in using force to further Maulana Haq Nawaz Jhangvi's mission. His complaint against SSP leadership was that they had abandoned the path of Maulana Jhangvi. Some say that Lashkar-e-Jhangvi was created by the SSP leadership to wash off the label of terrorism.

The SSP claims that it has nothing to do with Lashkar-e-Jhangvi but there has been contact between the two organizations. The two also share similar goals and views, whereas differences between them have been about organizational details. These differences are viewed with scepticism and it is said that the Lashkar-e-Jhangvi was created as a cover for activities of the SSP. As evidence, it is pointed out that Lashkar-e-Jhangvi activists used to stay in the mosques and madrassas that are considered hubs of SSP activities. Visits by SSP leaders to Lashkar-e-Jhangvi activists in jail are no secret either. When the LeT terrorist Sheikh Haq Nawaz was about to be hanged for the murder of the Iranian counsel Sadiq Ganji in March 2001, Maulana Azam Tariq offered to pay qisas (blood money) to Iran and threatened dire consequences if the hanging took place.

Lashkar-e-Jhangvi began its activities in 1996 and started targeting important Shia leaders and government officials. Its organizational network was strong and extremely complex. Its leader was given the title of Salar-e-A'ala, chief commander, with twelve salars or junior commanders under him and a shura (council) was formed to run the organization. Every activist of Lashkar-e-Jhangvi adopted aliases and had fake identity cards made under these names. An important leader of the Sipahe Sahaba Pakistan based in Jhang claims that Riaz Basra alone possessed twelve national identity cards under different names. A strong network was set up for the supply of arms from Afghanistan to Punjab and from there to Karachi. An official of the civilian Intelligence Bureau outfit told me in Lahore that the number of hardcore Lashkar-e-Jhangvi activists would not be more than a thousand. Yet, from the mid 1980s through to the late 1990s, they kept most of the security agencies on their heels.

Lashkar-e-Jhangvi activists are limited in number as it was mandatory to take a vow until death to complete the organization's mission and to break contact with all family and friends. Areas had been divided into different units for the purpose of terrorist activities. Under this scheme Gujranwala, Rawalpindi and Sargodha were under Riaz Basra's command; Faisalabad, Multan, Bahawalpur division and Bhakkar district under Malik Ishaq; and Karachi under Qari Abdul Hai's control.

By 2001 Lashkar-e-Jhangvi had been involved in 350 incidents of terrorism. The organization suffered the most difficult time during the second government of Mian Nawaz Sharif, when dozens of activists were killed during confrontations with the police between 1998 and 1999. There were reports at that time that Lashkar-e-Jhangvi had received 135 million rupees to assassinate prime minister Nawaz Sharif, the chief minister of Punjab Shahbaz Sharif and the federal minister of information, Syed Mushahid Hussein. The attempt on Nawaz Sharif's life by exploding a bomb on Raiwind Road in Lahore on 2 January 1999 is thought to be part of this plan.

Riaz Basra remained a challenge for law enforcement authorities for twelve years. He was wanted in 300 cases and carried a bounty of about USD 60,000 on his head. That is why Basra's presence in Afghanistan was also a source of friction between the Afghan Taliban and Pakistan. He kept in touch with newspapers on the phone and even gave media interviews while in hiding and on the run from law enforcement agencies. He was a dreaded figure and at times, because of threats, journalists saw to it that his messages were put across in newspapers. Basra was known to use ten aliases that included Shah Ji, Abdul' Rehman, Ashraf Butt, Sajjad, Pir Sahib, Bawa Ji, Chaudhry Sahib, Asif and Haji Sahib.

Former interior minister Moinuddin Haider told me he and his officials raised Basra's issue several times with Mulla Omar and his ministers. 'We had solid intelligence that suggested Basra's presence in Afghanistan and his close links with the Taliban. But every time we would raise the issue, Taliban ministers would either ignore it or brush it aside,' Haider told me. Finally, on 14 May 2002, Basra was killed in a police encounter in Mailsi in southern Punjab. He was accused of killing Sadiq Ganji; Sikander Shah, chairman of the Shia Political Party; and Syed Tajamul Hussein, commissioner, Sargodha. He was held responsible for the murder of twenty-five Shias at Mominpura, as well as the bomb explosion near Raiwind, both located near Lahore.

9

Profiles of Militants

W hile reliable material on militant leaders is hard to come by, over the years, through personal contacts with intelligence officials, journalists and from occasional reports in the press, I have put together this who's who of militants in FATA. The profiles explore how young tribesmen, driven by the Islamist jihadi rhetoric echoing from across the Durand Line and exploited by external and internal forces, became instrumental in an insurgency that has shaken the Pakistani society and is threatening the very foundations of a state that once used militants as tools of its foreign policy.

Baitullah Mehsud: The Most Dangerous Icon of Islamic Militancy

In its early May 2008 issue *Time* magazine listed Baitullah Mehsud among its hundred most influential individuals. The other luminary from Pakistan was the Chief of Army Staff (COAS) General Ashfaq Pervez Kayani. Both Kayani and Mehsud made it to the list of 'Leaders and Revolutionaries'. Commenting on this, General Talat Masood wrote, 'It also shows to what extent our political, cultural, academic and intellectual leadership has been marginalized and the power of the people diminished'.[1]

General Masood asked whether these individuals are 'truly the most influential in Pakistan's national scene today. Is this selection a fair assessment or merely a reflection of the US global agenda of pursuing their "war on terror"? The two "Leaders and Revolutionaries"—Kayani and Baitullah—represent the disproportionate ascendancy of militaristic and militant power in Pakistan. Clearly, it is also an indication of the high value placed on military power in the context of national and international security, although the most pressing security challenges in Pakistan and the region are in building constructive capacities as opposed to destructive ones.'

Regardless of the questions General Masood raised in his article, most intelligence officials working in FATA now regard Mehsud as the 'most dangerous person'. In his early thirties, Baitullah has three brothers, two of whom assist him in South Waziristan, while the third one lives in the Bajaur agency.[2] Mehsud is married but told reporters he has no children. He recently married for the third time, effectively quashing rumours of his death from diabetes. Waziristani journalists and supporters also call him the governor of South Waziristan because of his influence over the Mehsud areas of the agency. He hails from the Makeen village in South Waziristan, and had allegedly been behind most of the suicide bombings in 2006 and 2007.

The Tehreek-e-Taliban Pakistan also runs suicide training camps, located mostly in and around the Shawal area between North and South Waziristan. Spinkai Raghzai and Kotkai are some of the other locations where, officials said, training camps had existed.

Baitullah Mehsud defends suicide attacks as a 'viable form of self-defence equivalent to atomic bombs', yet he denied the existence of suicide training camps in the area. The Pakistan government also blames him for the assassination of Benazir Bhutto in Rawalpindi on 27 December 2007, but during his 24 May meeting with about thirty journalists somewhere in South Waziristan, Baitullah Mehsud denied his involvement in the case. 'We didn't kill Benazir Bhutto. We are not involved. She had not taken any action against us, so there was no need to harm such a person,' he told the group visiting him, in an apparent attempt to project his innocence.[3] Yet in effect, the two prime accused were believed to be associated with Baitullah Mehsud according to investigations and other sources.

'America is our enemy and we'll fight against it wherever it is possible . . . the Taliban could not negotiate with Americans, as Christians and Jews cannot be friends with Muslims, they are the enemies of Muslims,' he said.

Speaking to Al Jazeera TV in December 2007, Mehsud had declared that attacks on New York City and London were his ultimate aim. Earlier in January, a cell of Pakistanis was arrested in Barcelona for allegedly planning suicide operations in Spain and elsewhere in Europe on the behest of Mehsud.[4]

In his May 2008 encounter with journalists Baitullah claimed that Afghan Taliban made up 95 per cent of those leading the fight against US-led forces in Afghanistan. Pakistanis and other foreigners made up only 5 per cent of the insurgents.

Denying TTP's involvement in the kidnapping of Pakistan's ambassador to Afghanistan, Tariq Azizuddin, he said his organization had helped secure Azizuddin's release but had no knowledge of his location.[5]

'The real war is the media war . . . it is our desire to learn also how one should fight the media war,' Mehsud told journalists. He aimed to do this by acquiring the ability to upload videos on websites such as YouTube.[6]

One of Mehsud's colleagues, a non-Pashtoon and non-combatant member of the Taliban's media cell, told some journalists, 'we will soon be available on YouTube', demonstrating how mindful the militants have been of the necessity of 'outreach'.

The Taliban media cell has released video CDs showing horrific images, apparently with different aims. One such video, screened during an army media briefing on 18 May, shows a boy as young as ten firing shots at the head of a blindfolded man and beheading another.

In an attempt to win over reporters he said the murder of the private Express TV's correspondent Mohammad Ibrahim, which had happened just the day before, was 'unforgivable'. He assured journalists that his organization would 'hang the killers' of Ibrahim if they were identified.

A BBC reporter, Haroon Rashid, and another tribal journalist, Shams Mohmand, later told me that 'the media show put on by the Taliban simply reinforced the impression that the area is under "complete control of the militants".' They said that the show of strength was also an attempt to demonstrate how the army had been forced out of the area.

The Pakistani government struck a peace accord with Baitullah Mehsud at Sara Rogha weeks after his militants had swept the Sara Rogha and Laddha Forts in South Waziristan, which until then had been jointly manned by the FC and Pakistan army. The attack in January 2007 invited a military operation against him that lasted for a couple of weeks. The military operation failed to weaken his base, even though it had taken over important Mehsud towns like Sara Rogha, Laddha and Makeen.

The terrain in most of FATA, especially South Waziristan, is treacherous and inhospitable. Physically controlling the entire territory, that is, establishing real authority over these regions, is a formidable task. In most cases, the army and khasadars only control the main roads and some strategic hilltops, while most of the terrain remains ungoverned. Militants on the other hand are used to the conditions and can easily access their targets.

The journalists' trip that the TTP organized in May 2008 was, according to some members of the group, also meant to show them the destruction the military operation caused to residential and commercial centres in the Waziristan area. They took Baitullah Mehsud's claim of non-involvement in the assassination of Bhutto and in the abduction of the Pakistani ambassador as 'mere showmanship' because TTP activists did admit to several attacks and operations against the military.

Baitullah Mehsud is wanted on several counts, not only by the Pakistan army police, but also by the police in Dera Ismail Khan. A court in Rawalpindi, where Benazir Bhutto was assassinated, has declared him as an absconder in connection with Bhutto's murder.

Qari Hussain: Master of TTP Suicide Squads

Qari Hussain Mehsud is in charge of Baitullah Mehsud's suicide squad. The suicide squad camps, including those being run by the Haqqani family, are mostly in and around Shawal area in North Waziristan.

Hussain heads the anti-Shia operation in the Kurram agency, which is plagued by Sunni–Shia conflict. He was also a member of the now defunct rabidly anti-Shia outfit Sipahe Sahaba Pakistan based in the central Pakistani town of Jhang, which too was a hotbed of Shia–Sunni rivalry. He announced the formation of the TTP, and is often the contact person for media organizations.

Hussain, in his early thirties, is practically the deputy to Baitullah Mehsud and belongs to the Eshangi sub-clan of Mehsud tribe living in Kotkai village near Spinkai Raghza in South Waziristan. He was allegedly involved in the killing of a local bigwig, Amiruddin Khan, and his family on 31 May 2007. Amiruddin Khan was the political agent of Khyber agency and his family became the militant's target, reportedly for political reasons. Khan's brother, local sources said, also openly opposed Mehsud and his associates. Later on, Hussain was also involved in the kidnapping of twenty FC personnel and beheading one of them in August 2007.

Qari Hussain studied in the madrassa Jamia Farooqia Karachi for four years. He returned to his hometown in South Waziristan in 2003 when a military operation was launched there against non-Pakistani militants. During his stay at Jamia Farooqia in Jhang he joined the Sipahe Sahaba Pakistan. He commands the loyalty of four to five hundred personnel, slightly more than the force of two to three hundred that mid-level commanders usually maintain.

During their May 2008 visit to Baitullah Mehsud, journalists also met with Qari Hussain, who told them that he had 'by the grace of God' survived the Pakistan army clean-up Operation Zalzala in January. 'I am born to live and serve the Taliban,' Hussain, the grey-haired zealot said. During a briefing at Spinkai Raghzai on 18 May, the general officer in command, Brigadier Ali Abbas, had claimed that the Pakistan army had intercepted militants' wireless communication which suggested that Qari Hussain had been killed during the operation launched on 24 January. Hussain's mud-house in Kotkai had become a casualty of the army tanks and heavy artillery fire.

'Since my house was targeted and destroyed during the operation, some of my mujahideen may have said on wireless that I am dead and the military believed it.' Asked if he was still training suicide bombers, Qari Hussain did not respond directly and instead looked at the Taliban standing beside him. Hussain also hedged when asked if he was still a member of the banned militant organization Sipahe Sahaba Pakistan. 'I am with every Muslim group,' he said in the brief interview.[7]

TTP Leaders/Mehsud's Lieutenants

Noor Said: Leader of the local Taliban in Barwand area of South Waziristan and a close confidante and a deputy of Baitullah Mehsud, Noor Said led the eight-member Taliban group for negotiations with the Amiruddin Khan family, after TTP activists murdered several members of the Khan clan. Several rounds of negotiations between the Khans and the Taliban for a peace deal remained inconclusive and it seems that rather than asking for compensation, or going for retribution, the Khans have accepted the killing of Amiruddin Khan's family members as fait accompli. Noor Said participated in the jirga that secured the release of the fifteen Frontier Corps men and the Naib political tehsildar of Laddha on 28 August 2007.

Mufti Niamatullah: A militant commander affiliated with Baitullah Mehsud, Mufti Niamatullah was also part of the twenty-one-member jirga that negotiated the release of the fifteen Frontier Corps soldiers in August 2007. Baitullah Mehsud and Qari Hussain were also present during the negotiations with the jirga. At one point, Niamatullah lost his temper with the jirga members after repeated disagreements over the release of the soldiers. (Usually the jirga negotiators try to defend both parties and when they try to defend the opposite camp the young and hot-headed sometimes lose their cool.) Mufti Niamatullah asked the jirga members to leave immediately, but other militant commanders calmed him down.

Maulvi Shamim: The local Taliban commander in Laddha, South Waziristan; he runs a madrassa. In his mid-twenties, he is a Shaman Khel tribesman. He comes from a family of carpenters, and is reportedly quite unpredictable in his behaviour. In fact his men had briefly held hostage a Frontier Corps delegation led by a colonel when their talks stalled. The delegation had gone to negotiate the control of a paramilitary check post in the region.[8] The colonel and the soldiers were later released on the intervention of local tribal elders.

Hakeemullah Mehsud: A close confidante of Baitullah Mehsud, Hakeemullah Mehsud was caught by the coalition forces in Afghanistan during a raid inside Pakistani territory in Lowara Mandi, Shawal area of North Waziristan on 8 March 2007. He heads the anti-Shia campaign in the Orakzai agency and is also responsible for TTP operations in Khyber and Mohmand agency.

Journalists who met him somewhere in the Orakzai agency in the last week of November 2008 view Hakeemullah as the emerging deputy to Baitullah Mehsud. The TTP militant had invited journalists from Peshawar for the meeting. He said his targets included President Asif Ali Zardari and his allies for their 'pro-American' policies. He accused members of the ruling alliance at the centre and in the NWFP of 'working to break up Pakistan in collaboration with the US'.

Hakeemullah threatened to 'cut off' supplies to American forces in Afghanistan if US drone attacks continued. During the meeting his people displayed one of the two American Humvee military vehicles they had hijacked in Khyber agency on 10 November.

Asmatullah Shaheen: Another aide of Baitullah Mehsud. He was shot and injured during one of the campaigns in Afghanistan but is still very active. He was injured in a clash between local tribesmen of Jandola and his men when the latter tried to blow up a British-era bridge in the area on 5 October 2007.

Shah Faisal Barki: The Taliban commander in Saam village in Kanigoram, South Waziristan, Shah Faisal Barki kidnapped three Frontier Corps personnel including a colonel on 25 August 2007. He released them on 28 August after a jirga brokered a deal between the militants and the government of Pakistan.

Mulla Asmatullah: A self-proclaimed Taliban leader who has enforced his writ in several areas on the outskirts of Tank, Mulla Asmatullah has been in prison for the past few months. His deputy Jahanzeb, a Bhittani tribesman, runs the militant group's offices in Jandola, the headquarters of Tank.

Khan Gul Bhittani: A resident of Bubbakhel village, Bhittani is notorious as a criminal, known to be involved in kidnapping for ransom. But he too is a self-proclaimed Taliban after declaring allegiance to militant commanders in South Waziristan.

Non-TTP Taliban Leaders in South Waziristan

Mulla Nazir: At thirty-three, Mulla Nazir is the head of the Taliban in the Ahmadzai Wazir areas of South Waziristan. He had replaced Haji Omar in 2006. He belongs to the Kakakhel Wazir clan of the Zilikhel sub-tribe of the Ahmadzai Wazirs. He had earlier fought against the Afghan Northern Alliance alongside the Taliban on the Kunduz and Takhar (northern Afghanistan). He led a fierce campaign against Uzbek militants in the surrounding areas of Wana in March–April 2007.

Mulla Nazir turned his guns against the Uzbeks taking shelter in the area after they started kidnapping locals, attacking Pakistan military and forcing the locals to live according to the Uzbek dictates.

The TTP's hold in the Ahmadzai Wazir areas is practically non-existent, and the pro-Uzbek militant leaders had to flee from the area.

Some observers contest that Mulla Nazir actually led the fight against the Uzbeks from the front which was started by the Tojikhel tribesmen, but he hijacked the leadership halfway through the fight.

Following his anti-Uzbek operations, Nazir also became suspect for his alleged contacts with the Pakistani government, and rivals twice sent suicide bombers his way. Fortunately, Nazir's guards overpowered the first attacker before he could blow himself up near Nazir. The would-be assailant was arrested with explosives.[9]

Nazir also heads the five-member Taliban shura of South Waziristan that was reconstituted after the ouster of Uzbeks from the area.

Khanan Wazir: Khanan Wazir was the ameer of the Taliban in South Waziristan's Shakai valley. He too opposed the presence of Uzbeks in South Waziristan, and was killed in an ambush by Uzbek militants in early June 2008 (see Chapter 6).[10] In September 2006, Khanan had survived an ambush by his Uzbek detractors. So it was only natural that he extended support to Mulla Nazir's anti-Uzbek operation in March–April 2007. Khanan's supporters were attacked by Uzbek militants again in January 2008, after which tensions grew between Ahmadzai Wazir and Mehsud tribesmen because the latter are believed to be sheltering Uzbek militants. Khanan was part of the five-member Taliban shura of South

Waziristan that was reconstituted after the ouster of Uzbeks from the area.

Khanan's murder was a severe blow to Mulla Nazir because the former had established his control over the difficult Shakai valley, where the government had signed its first peace accord with Nek Mohammad in May 2004.

An aide to Qari Hussain had admitted to his group's involvement in the killing of Khanan for his 'association with the government'.

'All those acting for or on behalf of the US or its allies—whether the Afghan or Pakistan army—are our targets. They are damaging the cause of the Muslims in Afghanistan and other parts of the world. We will spare none,' said Qari Mudassir, an aide to Qari Hussain in a phone conversation recorded on 6 June 2008. A friend, whom Hussain himself had called, had recorded this phone conversation and he played me the audiotape during one of our meetings in Peshawar.

Haji Omar: Haji Omar, forty-seven, is a cousin and successor of the slain militant leader Nek Mohammad. He too belongs to the Ahmadzai (Yargulkhel) Wazir tribe and is a resident of the village Kaloosha near Azam Warsak in South Waziristan. A battle-hardened jihadi who has fought alongside the Taliban in Afghanistan, Haji Omar sided with the Uzbek militants during Mulla Nazir's fierce operation against the Central Asian militants in March–April 2007. Subsequently, Omar moved to North Waziristan and then took refuge in the Mehsud areas of South Waziristan which are under the leadership of Baitullah Mehsud. He is still active in cross-border insurgency in Afghanistan.

Haji Sharif: Haji Sharif is the brother of Haji Omar, and belongs to the village Kaloosha. Haji Sharif, in his mid-fifties, sided with Mulla Nazir after initially opposing him (though Omar and other brothers stood by the Uzbek militants). The exact circumstances surrounding the differences among the brothers over the Uzbek fighters were not clear, yet ideological affinity seemed to have played a key role in keeping the majority of these brothers on the side of the Central Asians.

Noorul Islam: Noorul Islam is another brother of Haji Omar and Haji Sharif. He has fought alongside the Taliban in Afghanistan in the past. He has spent a lot of time in the UAE as well. He is believed to be very close to Uzbek militants and is sheltering not only the militants but also their families. Noorul Islam fiercely supported the Uzbek militants during their clashes with Ahmadzai Wazir tribesmen led by Mulla Nazir in March–April 2007.

Zawal Khan: A Zillikhel Wazir by tribe, Zawal Khan belongs to Khanghi village near Angoor Adda. He is believed to be a supporter of Uzbek militants.

Maulvi Abdul Aziz: A Yargulkhel Wazir by tribe, Maulvi Abdul Aziz is a resident of village Ghwakha in South Waziristan. Besides being the administrator of a madrassa at Azam Warsak, he is also a school teacher at the Government Middle School, Ghwakha. He got his religious education from the madrassa of Maulana Noor Mohammad, a former member of the National Assembly from South Waziristan. A strong supporter of the Taliban in the area, Maulvi Aziz took out a procession on 31 March 1999 in favour of the Afghan Taliban and their Pakistani supporters in Waziristan. He is a cousin of Haji Sharif and was also affiliated once with the Tehreek-e-Nifaze Shariate Mohammadi.

Maulvi Abbas: A veteran Taliban commander who was controlling the Ahmadzai Wazir areas of South Waziristan alongside Nek Mohammad, Maulvi Abbas belongs to the Malik Khel Wazir tribe and resides in the Kaloosha area. He is believed to be in his mid-forties. He got his religious education from Darul Uloom Haqqania in Akora Khattak, one of the largest seminaries in the NWFP, established in 1947 by Maulvi Abdul Haq.

Interestingly, the current head of the Darul Uloom Haqqania, Senator Maulana Sami-ul-Haq, is believed to have immensely benefited from money the CIA and ISI funelled into the anti-Soviet-Russian resistance; during the 1980s this seminary kept churning out fighters for the CIA-sponsored jihad. Several mujahideen commanders, including Jalaluddin Haqqani, had studied in the seminary. Many Afghan Taliban leaders also received their degrees from this institution.

Maulvi Abbas is a supporter of Haji Sharif. He fell out with Al Qaeda after differences over the Uzbek militants' raid on the Pakistan military at Zari Noor on 8–9 January 2004.

Maulvi Javed Karmazkhel: Maulvi Javed is an Ahmadzai Wazir Taliban commander and he supported Uzbeks during March–April 2007 fighting between Uzbeks and local militants. In February 2007 a group of alleged Lashkar-e-Jhangvi associated suicide bombers had reportedly confessed to being trained in a training camp run by Maulvi Javed and Maulvi Abbas.

Shireen Jan: A militant commander who sided with Mulla Nazir in the standoff between locals and Uzbeks in March–April 2007.

Mittha Khan: A member of the reconstituted Ahmadzai Wazir shura after the ouster of the Uzbeks, Mittha Khan was seriously injured in a bomb blast on 2 September 2007. He was reportedly treated in an FC hospital for his injuries, and later on in the Combined Military Hospital, Peshawar. He fought alongside Mulla Nazir to oust Uzbeks from the Ahmadzai Wazir areas of South Waziristan.

Malang: Malang Wazir is a low-profile member of the Ahmadzai Wazir shura led by Mulla Nazir. Following the murder of Khanan Wazir by Uzbek militants, Malang Wazir became a member of the shura. Not much is known about this aide to Mulla Nazir.

Haleemullah: Haleemullah belongs to the Tojikhel sub-tribe of the Ahmadzai Wazir tribe. He was formerly associated with Haji Nazir but now has an independent command in the Tojikhel area of Kirkot, but is still a member of the Mulla Nazir-led Taliban shura of South Waziristan.

Ghulam Khan: An Ahmadzai Wazir tribesman believed to be very close to Uzbek militants in the area, Ghulam Khan sided with the Uzbeks during their clashes with locals in Azam Warsak, Shin Warsak and Kaloosha areas in March–April 2007.

Younas: A part-time journalist turned Taliban, Younes used to call Online news agency in the past for news coverage from the area. He is now close to Uzbek militants, and largely out of the news for security reasons.

Abdullah Mehsud: Hailing from Nano village in the Makin area, Abdullah Mehsud was a Guantanamo Bay detainee and rose to prominence after he abducted two Chinese engineers and killed one of them. He was killed in a raid by the security forces in the town of Zhob (Balochistan) on 24 July 2007.

Wali-ur-Rehman: One of the key deputies of Baitullah Mehsud, Wali-ur-Rehman took active part in the negotiations with the jirga for the release of over 250 soldiers who had been taken hostage by Baitullah Mehsud's militants in August 2007. Wali-ur-Rehman heads a chapter of TTP in Bajaur agency.

Militants in North Waziristan

Maulana Sadiq Noor: Maulana Sadiq Noor is in his mid-forties and hails from Khati-Kelay, a small village in the suburbs of Miranshah along the Tochi river in North Waziristan. He belongs to the Daur tribe of North Waziristan. He is an experienced warrior who fought on the Bagram front in Afghanistan against the Northern Alliance. He is also believed to support anti-US entities in Khost, Afghanistan. For the past fifteen years, Sadiq Noor has operated a seminary in Khati-Kelay. Sadiq Noor hit the headlines in 2006 when Pakistani troops conducted an operation against his compound to flush out foreign terrorists (Uzbeks and Arabs) he was suspected of hosting. He refused to give in and started organizing his men to resist the army. However, after the military operation in North Waziristan in July–October 2007, Sadiq Noor reportedly ceased to support foreign militants and is cooperating with the security forces for restoring peace in and around Miranshah, where Noor's supporters patrol the streets to keep militants away. Probably because of his close links with the security forces, Noor is reportedly not member of the local Taliban shura of North Waziristan any more.

Maulvi Abdul Khaliq Haqqani: A Daur by tribe, Maulvi Abdul Khaliq Haqqani is a mulla of a mosque in Miranshah Bazaar and thrives on delivering speeches against Pervez Musharraf and George W. Bush. He came into the limelight in March 2006 when his men captured the telephone exchange and other government buildings at his orders. In the crossfire that ensued, his mosque and seminary were pounded with heavy artillery, substantially damaging it. By May 2008 the complex had been repaired and restored to the pre-operation condition.

Haji Gul Bahadur: A Madakhel Wazir by tribe belonging to the southern part of North Waziristan, Hafiz Gul Bahadur is a very powerful local Taliban commander and is the main leader of pro-Taliban militants and the local shura of Taliban in North Waziristan. Hafiz Gul Bahadur entered into a peace deal with the Pakistan army after the military operation against the militants in North Waziristan in July–October 2007. His commitment not to attack Pakistani security forces was tested when Baitullah

Mehsud asked him in January 2008 for help against the Pakistan army, which in those days was scouring and bombing the area to cleanse it of Baitullah-led militants.

Gul Bahadur refused to cooperate with Baitullah Mehsud, ostensibly to keep his commitment to the Pakistan army as well as to keep North Waziristan out of the army–Baitullah conflict. During the army operation in South Waziristan, Baitullah kept requesting Gul Bahadur through emissaries for help. He also urged Gul Bahadur to start attacking military targets which might ease pressure on him but Gul Bahadur refused. Instead, he advised Baitullah against taking on the military in the Shawal area of North Waziristan, which Bahadur considered his territory.

In early July 2008, Bahadur forged an alliance with Mulla Nazir of South Waziristan. They named the alliance Taliban Ittehad and vowed to keep up their anti-US campaign, also triggering speculation they might have acted to facilitate the government's desire to isolate Baitullah Mehsud in his Mehsud region. In late July Bahadur was re-elected as the chief of the Taliban in North Waziristan. Over 800 Taliban attended the meeting held at Razmak, seventy-five kilometres south of Miranshah.

By August 2008, Bahadur had forged an alliance with Maulvi Abdul Khaliq, which also maintained good relations with Mulla Nazir. This meant Baitullah Mehsud stood isolated.

The following leaders are independent power brokers in North Waziristan, many of them fence-sitters, sometimes siding with one or the other group and at other times opposing them. This way they maintain their 'nuisance value'.

Sangeen Khan Zadran: An Afghan belonging to the Jadran tribe in Khost, supervising the Taliban in Shawal, Sangeen Khan Zadran claimed in late November 2006 that his group had provided forty suicide bombers for attacks that occurred in Afghanistan.

Maulana Siddique Darpakhel: Hails from the Darpakhel area of North Waziristan and a prominent militant leader.

Waheedullah: The Taliban shura member assigned the responsibility of administering the Miranshah town on behalf of the Taliban. A college educated Taliban, Waheedullah was killed in a CIA-operated drone attack in South Waziristan (where he had gone on a visit) in October 2008.

Haleem Khan: A militant known to have links with foreigners, especially Uzbeks, and believed to be involved in targeted killings in the area.

Dr Isa Khan: Dr Isa Khan, in an informal interview with the *News* on behalf of Baitullah Mehsud, claimed that Baitullah Mehsud had nothing to do with the 18 October 2007 suicide bombing of the procession in Karachi that former premier Benazir Bhutto was leading after returning from exile.

Abu Okash: An Iraqi Arab militant, who has gained considerable influence in parts of North Waziristan, like Mirali and Miranshah. His name, according to some sources, is Abu Kashif but he has gained fame locally with the name Abu Okash. There were reports that he had been injured in an extensive aerial bombardment on villages around Mirali in October 2007. In early 2008 though, Abu Okash released his first videotape calling for jihad against the infidel.

Bajaur Agency

Maulvi Sufi Mohammad: Sufi Mohammad was the founder of the defunct Tehreek-e-Nifaze Shariate Mohammadi (TNSM). On 21 April 2008, Mohammad was released from Dera Ismail Khan prison after over six years in jail to facilitate a deal between the Taliban and the administration. He had been jailed in late 2001 for sending several thousand armed fighters for jihad to Afghanistan soon after the US launched its anti-Al Qaeda campaign on 7 October 2001.

In 1994 TNSM had launched a campaign in Bajaur and Malakand to establish sharia in the region. There are conflicting reports about his native village, with some claiming it is the Kumbar village in Bajaur agency and others that he belongs to the Maidan area of Dir.

Though Sufi Mohammad's influence had waned over the years, it is now expected that he will play a role in calming the situation down in the Swat/Malakand division, where the followers of Mohammad's estranged son-in-law, Maulana Fazlullah, had run amok in the latter part of 2007, triggering a vicious army reaction.

Maulvi Faqir Mohammad: Maulvi Faqir Mohammad used to be the deputy of Maulvi Sufi Mohammad but eventually grew out of his shadow and is now the deputy to Baitullah Mehsud for Bajaur agency, with several thousand militants at his disposal. After the release of Sufi Mohammad in April, Faqir Mohammad had openly played it down saying 'talking to Sufi will not bring peace to FATA'.[10]

Last year, Faqir Mohammad, in his early forties, had also condemned the Red Mosque operation and held President Pervez Musharraf responsible for it. 'If Musharraf doesn't stop promoting the US agenda, peace may return to Kashmir and Afghanistan but the situation in Pakistan will worsen. The government is trying to divide the Taliban and backtracking on its commitments with them,' the militant commander told reporters.[11]

Faqir Mohammad was born in Changai Bala village in the Damadola area of Bajaur agency, about nine kilometres north of Khaar. He is a graduate of the strictly Wahabist 'Punj Pir' seminary near Swabi. He fought against the Soviets alongside the mujahideen in Afghanistan in the 1980s. He is one of the most wanted men in Bajaur on suspicion of supporting Taliban and Al Qaeda—especially after they escaped from Tora Bora in 2001–02—but he can still be seen in public addressing rallies, etc. He had expressed his resolve to wage jihad against the coalition forces in Afghanistan and the Musharraf administration in Pakistan, and to establish sharia in Bajaur agency and adjacent districts a number of times. He was also among the first few of the FATA militants to pledge support to the Red Mosque administration when the issue emerged in March 2007. As the leader of TNSM and the successor of Sufi Mohammad, Maulvi Faqir Mohammad is believed to be behind most terrorist incidents in Bajaur and the adjacent districts, including attacks on security forces.

Khyber Agency

Mufti Munir Shakir: The founder of the strictly Wahabist organization Lashkar-e-Islam, Mufti Munir Shakir originally belongs to Kurram agency. He left his home after a family feud which left his mother dead. Some say he killed his mother while others are of the view that she was killed while trying to save him from his father with whom he had a stormy relationship. He then moved to another city (most probably Karachi) and eventually came to Bara. Some accounts also suggest that he is actually from Karak but his family was settled in Lower Kurram.

In late 2005, Shakir's Lashkar-e-Islam developed serious differences with Ansarul Islam, a Barelvi organization led by Pir Saifurrehman. Both the groups incited hatred against each other through their illegal FM radio stations. The differences between the two groups were often violent, and remain so even to this date. Mufti Munir Shakir left Khyber agency in the last week of February 2006, after the political administration conveyed a stern warning to him through a tribal jirga after gruelling negotiations. He was arrested soon after he left Khyber by Pakistani intelligence agents and was sentenced to an indefinite jail term.

Mangal Bagh Afridi: Mangal Bagh Afridi became the successor to Mufti Munir Shakir to lead Lashkar-e-Islam. He comes from a humble background, and officials often deride him as a 'trucker's helper'. Afridi is also an ultra-conservative cleric considered close to the administration. He enjoys considerable support of the people because of his daring, religious decrees against criminals; when the government fails, Afridi steps in to maintain law and order or deliver justice. In the process he has gained formidable clout among local tribes. That is why he at times comes across as an independent and high-handed cleric. This also causes ripples in his covert relations with the political administration every now and then. For instance, in June 2006, Lashkar-e-Islam ran into trouble after the political administration disagreed with the peace committees that Afridi had set up for maintaining law and order in the area. The disagreement led to tensions and resulted in the closure of local markets for a few weeks.

Afridi has been dispensing vigilante justice from time to time, and has administered public punishments to people he declared as criminals for dealing in liquor and drugs, running murderous gangs, committing adultery, etc. Besides, his illegal FM radio station keeps delivering sermons and urging people to take to the right path, that is, join the Lashkar-e-Islam for serving God and Islam.

In the absence of effective government control, Afridi has grown enormously in strength. Some locals suggest that, depending on the situation, the government sometimes ignores Afridi's militant activities and indirectly supports him whenever the state machinery is unable to fix a problem.

Under the leadership of Mangal Bagh Afridi, the Lashkar-e-Islam has occasionally picked battles with some of the local sub-tribes. In April 2008, his men had a skirmish with the powerful Kukikhel tribesmen of Jamrud because the Kukikhels wanted to indulge in some businesses which Afridi considered un-Islamic.

In brazen disregard to the law, on 3 March 2008, Lashkar-e-Islam militants attacked a controversial shrine in the Bara Sheikhan village on the outskirts of Peshawar and killed about eighteen locals. The organization said that the controversial shrine was being used by drug peddlers and addicts. After repeated warnings, the Lashkar-e-Islam leadership finally attacked the shrine, which led to a shoot-out between the alleged drugs dealers and the militants, resulting in several deaths.

Afridi's group has some connection with the Taliban movement in Afghanistan but contacts with Al Qaeda cannot be established. Publicly, Lashkar-e-Islam expresses solidarity with the Afghan Taliban and Osama bin Laden, but it is difficult to ascertain whether this relationship extends beyond verbal expressions of support. Afridi did maintain good contacts with Haji Naamdar, who was an avowed opponent of the TTP and Al Qaeda in the area.

In November 2007, Afghan Taliban leaders mediated a dispute between Lashkar-e-Islam and their rivals Ansarul Islam. Moreover, even if Mangal Bagh is not sending his men to fight in Afghanistan, his state within the state does provide another safe haven for those like-minded Taliban.

Pir Saifurrehman: Pir Saifurrehman, an Afghan who lived in Khyber agency from 1977 to 2006, is the founder of the religious-cum-militant group Ansarul Islam. Since late 2005, his group has been involved in hate-mongering through illegal FM radio stations and violent clashes with the rival Lashkar-e-Islam.

He was forced to leave the tribal area after the political authorities of Khyber agency detained about forty of his supporters in the first week of February 2006 as his verbal attacks on Mufti Munir Shakir had led to violence in the agency. Pir Saifurrehman reportedly moved to central Punjab for shelter, where he might be staying at one of the safe houses of the Lashkar-e-Taiba or Jamatud Dawa.

Haji Naamdar: Haji Naamdar founded the Amar bil Maroof wa Nahi Analmunkir (Promotion of Virtue and Prevention of Vice). Inspired by the Afghan Taliban supreme leader Mulla Omar, Naamdar espoused the enforcement of Islamic sharia in Pakistan (just as Mulla Omar wants it for Afghanistan). He was shot dead by an assassin on 13 August 2008. He was in his mid-thirties.

Although Naamdar launched his organization to cleanse the society of infidels and criminals, he often talked of the 'foreign occupation of Afghanistan'.

'Naamdar does nothing inside Pakistan and is interested only in Afghanistan. He runs his own prisons, and his utterances are treated as final, like that of Mulla Omar,' a senior government official said after a meeting with Naamdar in late April 2008.[12]

Naamdar opposed suicide attacks inside Pakistan, but justified them as the 'best weapon' against the enemy. 'We have to finish our enemy in Afghanistan by any means and suicide bombing is the best weapon.'

Naamdar acknowledged the presence of Taliban militants and their 'active participation' in cross-border anti-US jihad, underscoring the fact that even Khyber agency has begun providing militants for such activities.

A day after surviving a suicide attack Naamdar told the media that he was helping to 'detoxify' militants staying with him through 'Islamic classes', which teach them that attacking Pakistani forces, people or state installations 'is no jihad at all' and that rather, by 'doing so, we are strengthening anti-Islamic forces'.[13]

'I am reforming these mujahideen as Islam does not allow jihad against Muslims,' said Naamdar.

What, however, turned Naamdar into a half collaborator of the Pakistani authorities was his criticism of attacks on Pakistani people—both civilians and government officials.

'These [mujahideen] leaders brainwash teenagers, telling them that each and every Pakistani is their enemy and his or her killing is justified. Are they not killing innocent Pakistanis?' asked Naamdar of militants targeting Pakistani forces.[14]

'We will never wage jihad inside Pakistan. Afghanistan needs mujahideen to liberate that country from United States-led foreign occupation. We do attack the US forces across the border and that is what real jihad is all about,' he admitted. 'The way [US]

President [George W.] Bush is waging a crusade against Islam, we will hit the US wherever and whenever it is possible. Our jihad against the US in Afghanistan goes on . . . Why should mujahideen target Pakistan when this country provides everything for jihad in Afghanistan,' Naamdar was quoted as saying.[15]

Naamdar's influence was restricted to the Bara Kambarkhel tribe, but he played host to various tribal and foreign militants, and that had made him a potentially influential commander in a region through which food and fuel supply flows to the US and NATO forces based in Afghanistan.

Mehbubul Haq: Successor to Pir Saifurrehman. He lives a low-profile life in the remote Tirah valley. He graduated from a madrassa and is inspired by the philosophy of Mulla Omar.

Maulana Mustamin: One of the main leaders of Ansarul Islam. In January 2007 he was reported to have blocked the supply route for his rival group at Naree Baba, which left ordinary people of the area facing shortage of food supplies and other essentials. He was killed by the rival Lashkar-e-Islam militants on 20 May 2008.

Maulana Hazrat Nabi: Maulana Hazrat Nabi (also known as Tamanche Mulla) is the prayer leader of the Quba mosque, one of the main mosques in Landi Kotal. In September 2007, he organized local Taliban and took out their processions condemning obscenity and un-Islamic activities. He and his supporters have vowed to eradicate such ills of the society if the political administration do not take due action. In November, there were reports about his followers distributing leaflets in Landikotal bazaar warning people against selling CDs and ordering women not to go unaccompanied in public places.

Farmanullah: The purported spokesman of the local Taliban of Landikotal. He is the brother of Maulana Hazrat Nabi.

Mohmand Agency

Abdul Wali Raghib: Abdul Wali Raghib, in his early forties, is the top Taliban commander in Mohmand agency, and the deputy ameer of TTP for the Mohmand area. Known as Umar Khalid, Raghib is a resident of Kared (Lukro tehsil). His father is known as Haji Sahib. He had been affiliated with the Harkatul Mujahideen in 1990–91 and was involved in jihadi activities in Kashmir and Afghanistan. He used to sit in Mianmundi as a local commander of Mohmand agency. He was famous for the recitation of revolutionary poetry among his colleagues.

Close associates describe Umar Khalid as a 'born jihadi' who has glorified the fight against 'infidels' through his poetry which is all about jihad.[16]

Formerly a journalist, Khalid worked for pro-jihad publications *Zarb-e-Momin* and the daily *Islam* in the 1990s before he joined the 'freedom struggle' of the Kashmiri people against Indian rule of Kashmir. Local journalists said his membership of the Ghalanai Press Club was revoked after he became involved in militant activities.

'Umar Khalid was the Harkatul Mujahideen chief in the Mohmand Agency before becoming a Taliban commander. According to his associates, his journey towards extremism began with a journey to Azad Jammu and Kashmir. He was in Muzaffarabad on personal business when Azad Jammu and Kashmir jihadis contacted him. Since then, Khalid's sole concern has been jihad,' reported the *Daily Times*.[17]

Ghalanai administration officials maintain that Khalid and his people usually engage American forces in the eastern Afghan province of Kunar and closely coordinate their actions with Maulvi Faqir Mohammad of Bajaur agency, though unlike the latter Khalid 'does not host foreign militants' in Mohmand.

Khalid reportedly commands at least 25,000 trained militants, though figures are difficult to verify, said Mukkaram Khan.

Sangeen Khan Kandahari: The Taliban associated with Sangeen Khan Kandahari had abducted ten Frontier Corps men including a major (carrying Rs 260,000 cash, the salaries of the FC men deployed in the Mohammad Gat area) on 2 September 2007. He made certain demands for the release of the FC personnel but released them apparently unconditionally on 4 September 2007.

Abu Nuhman Sungri: Also known as Dr Assad, Sungri is one of TTP's strongmen in Mohmand. He also liases with the media, but few people know him by face.

Orakzai Agency

Apart from Hakeemullah Mehsud, the following militants operate in Orakzai agency.

Maulana Mohammad Nabi Orakzai: Unconfirmed reports put him as the local TTP representative. There is not much available information about him. He is also responsible for TTP affairs in the neighbouring Kurram agency.

Islam Gul and *Hassamuddin*: Both are considered as the local TTP operatives, drawing guidance from Hakeemullah Mehsud.

Kurram Agency

Maulana Fazal Saeed is reportedly the local TTP operative in the lower and central Kurram area. Both Hakeemullah Mehsud and Qari Hussain have their footprints here as well. These TTP leaders have reportedly been at the forefront of the anti-Shia campaign that left hundreds of tribesmen dead in dozens of direct clashes and gory incidents of slaughter during most of 2008.

Swat

Maulana Fazlullah: Born on 1 March 1975 in the small village of Imam Derai near Kanjoo, Fazlullah, the son-in-law of Maulvi Sufi Mohammad, is the new face of Al Qaeda in the Swat region. He was not appointed by Baitullah Mehsud. Militants from other regions, particularly from areas like Waziristan and some foreign countries, simply rallied around Maulana Fazlullah because of his charisma. Because of his strength in the area, locals and outsiders alike must establish contact with him or his people for a clear passage through the areas outside Mingora. He also enjoys support within the security establishment of Pakistan because of his role in the Afghan Taliban movement. In the Bajaur and Malakand regions, he is considered as dangerous as Baitullah Mehsud.

He was also arrested with Sufi Mohammad and scores of others late in 2001 for their daring attempt to help the Taliban against the US-led coalition in October 2001. Fazlullah spent seventeen months in D.I. Khan jail before being released. He essentially resurrected the once forgotten TNSM when he started criticizing the government's pro-western policies but is now considered a full-fledged part of TTP.

He has nothing to do with the TNSM any more. Instead he used the TNSM cadres to raise his own army, provoking the TNSM to disown him right from the beginning, particularly after he began spewing hatred against the government and the army through his FM radio station. He is now TTP and has made it evident on many an occasion by linking peace in Swat to peace in Waziristan. He primarily acts as Baitullah Mehsud's deputy for the Bajaur and Malakand regions.

Fazlullah made international headlines in October 2007, when the government of Pakistan took military action against Fazlullah's supporters to restore the writ of the state in Swat district. The confrontation continued for a couple of months, and claimed the lives of many of Fazlullah's supporters—including his brother Fazle Ahad—as well as security forces' personnel.

Fazlullah is still on the run along with his hardline supporters, while many of his supporters are also surrendering to military forces or are getting captured. He was reported to be very popular among women as well because of his emotional speeches aired over his illegal FM radio station. In January 2007 he collected approximately USD 19,000 for the construction of a seminary in Imam Derai in Nikpikhel area of lower Swat from the residents of Mingora. A large number of people volunteered for the construction work of his madrassa, which is a sprawling fifty-acre compound with a hundred square feet hall for a mosque, separate compounds for madrassas and an idgah, where followers offer their Friday and post-Ramadan prayers.

One of his younger brothers, Fazle Wahid, was killed along with eighty-three others in the Pakistan military's strike on a seminary at Chenagai village in Bajaur agency on 30 October 2006. After the Red Mosque operation in July 2007, Maulana Fazlullah started anti-government propaganda through his illegal FM radio station and incited violence against security forces in the area, which eventually prompted a military operation in October 2007, restoring the government partially. Following elections on 18 February 2008, the provincial government signed a peace deal with Fazlullah's militants to buy some time, though these Taliban continued to impose sharia justice in Piochar, Janikhel and Imam Derai areas, considered to be still out of bound for government officials.[18]

Maulana Fazlullah says he set up the FM radio for the reformation of society and he has been campaigning against TV, VCR, CDs, etc. and termed these things 'sources of evil that promote obscenity and vulgarity'. On a number of occasions during 2007, following his appeal hundreds of people burnt their TV sets and VCRs publicly all over Swat. He then began giving Islamic names to villages and also turned against female education, urging people not to send their daughters and sisters to schools, an action that he termed 'un-Islamic'. His appeal prompted parents in Swat to remove about 1,700 girl students from schools within two to three months.

As many as sixty-seven girls' schools were destroyed or damaged by unknown attackers between November 2007 and July 2008. The first public burnings of TVs and VCRs, orchestrated by Fazlullah's zealots began in early 2006 and continue till date.

Maulana Fazlullah went as far as declaring polio drops as 'un-Islamic practice' and asked people in his area not to get their children vaccinated, saying that it is a conspiracy by the west to make them infertile. Interestingly, the maulana also argued that there was no concept of a cure for the disease in Islam. Yet, socio-political pressures forced Fazlullah to allow a three-day anti-polio vaccination drive in Swat in July 2008, though he kept threatening suicide attacks if the army did not pull out of the area. In late July, when the army mounted attacks on the TTP militants and their hideouts, Fazlullah again disappeared to guide the militancy from underground.

Maulana Shah Dauran: Dauran hails from Qambar village in Swat. He is the deputy head of the Swat Taliban led by Maulana Fazlullah. Since the summer of 2008, Dauran has been one of the most dreaded names because of the evening show that he does on Fazlullah's FM radio station. He ridicules Pakistani leaders as well as the army and also issues harsh pronouncements even on common citizens and welfare workers associated with NGOs.

Sirajuddin: A cousin of Fazlullah's and a resident of Mamdheray, Sirajuddin was once member of a leftist student group—the democratic students' organization. Now in his early thirties, he champions Fazlullah's hardline Islam, ready to kill and die for the Taliban cause. He is in charge of areas which were once prime tourist attractions like the skiing resort of Malam Jabba.

Muslim Khan: Khan is the spokesman for the Swat Taliban, an extension of the TTP. In his early forties, Khan was once a member of the progressive Pakistan Peoples Party of the slain premier Benazir Bhutto. He also spent some time in the United States before returning to Swat, where he joined Fazlullah. Besides his mother tongue Pashto, Khan is also conversant in Urdu and English.

Defending the TTP as an alliance of mujahideen struggling against the 'cruel policies of America and Pakistan', Khan vows to continue the 'jihad'.

In February 2009, Muslim Khan released a list—also mentioned during Shah Dauran's radio programme, of forty-five people and their family members, eighty-six in all—who he said were wanted for their opposition to the Taliban. He offered these people an opportunity to clear their names by appearing in one of the forty sharia courts which he calls a 'forum for dispute settlement'.

Said Rahman alias Fateh: Fateh became the Taliban's field operations' commander after Hussain Ali alias Tor Mullah was killed during a raid by the security forces. Fateh, in his mid-thirties, is also a graduate of a seminary.

Ibn-e-Amin: An emerging Taliban commander in his late twenties, Amin has injected terror in the residents of the Matta sub-district of Swat by decreeing harsh punishments to rivals and government functionaries.

Mohammad Alam Khan: He is known as Mulla Binori because he headed a mosque in the Binori village near the Khwaza Khel sub-district. Like Shah Dauran, Alam Khan also uses the FM radio to spread his message of fear and terror.

Maulana Saifullah: Maulana Saifullah is the ameer of TNSM in Malakand. Addressing TNSM workers in Matta on 25 March 2007, Saifullah had set a seventy-two-hour deadline for the government to release Sufi Mohammad and warned that a hundred suicide bombers were ready to strike targets inside Pakistan if he was not released.

Two Taliban militants belonging to North Waziristan and caught in Afghanistan had testified that they were sent across the border by Maulvi Saifullah after the signing of the peace deal in September 2006.

The ISI Factor

The Inter-Services Intelligence, Pakistan's powerful spy service, has remained in the international spotlight, particularly since the US-and Saudi-funded anti-Soviet jihad, where it executed operations with the help of its proxies in Afghanistan. No state intelligence is as controversial and it is widely believed that the ISI conducts the covert war in Indian Kashmir and maintains ties with the Afghan Taliban. Many Pakistanis believe that the ISI watches them and at times punishes them for stepping out of line, while the Indian and Afghan establishments hold the ISI responsible for the terrorist violence that takes place in their countries. The ISI trained and funded Afghan mujahideen for years before many of these switched to the jihad in the Indian Kashmir. The involvement in the anti-Soviet operation turned the ISI into an overzealous organization which not only indulged in domestic politics but also turned its attention to the 'liberation of Indian-administered Kashmir'. It also threw its weight behind the Taliban, hoping they would act as Pakistan's satellite pliant state, and thus provide Pakistan the so-called strategic depth to its west in order to counter threats from the east. Pakistan's quest for political domination of Afghanistan gained strength after Indian military intervention severed its eastern wing as independent Bangladesh in a civil war in 1971. The ISI was in fact credited with creating and supporting the Taliban movement to realize the goal of securing strategic depth through a friendly government in Afghanistan.

Relentless American pressure in 2003–04, however, forced the then president Pervez Musharraf to demobilize most Kashmiri militant outfits, order the closure of many camps and restrict them from carrying out operations on the other side of the Line of Control, the de facto border between the Indian and Pakistan-controlled Kashmirs. The spotlight fell on the ISI again after the deadly attack on the Indian embassy in Kabul in July 2008 and the 26 November terror attacks in Mumbai which the Indian authorities claimed were carried out with the consent of the ISI.

The Pakistan army and its affiliated security institutions, particularly the ISI, continue to suffer from, and be haunted by, their role in prosecuting the CIA-funded jihad fought in the 1980s to free Afghanistan of Soviet occupation. The triumph of that jihad encouraged them to try to repeat the experience of manipulating religious zeal to humilate an overbearing power in the arena of Indian Kashmir through a sixteen-member Muttahida Jihad Council (MJC). But the muddle that followed the Red Army's departure from Afghanistan in February 1989, and Washington's 'hands-off' Afghanistan policy, also muddied the image of Pakistan, its army and the ISI.

What came across as possibly the worst embarrassment to Pakistan was a *New York Times* report of 30 July 2008, during Prime Minister Yousuf Raza Gilani's Washington visit, which linked the agency with the Taliban and Al Qaeda operating in the Pakistan–Afghanistan border regions. Only two days earlier, the then president George W. Bush and Gilani had exchanged vows to cooperate in the war on terror, but the *New York Times* report dropped a bombshell on the entire entourage, greatly dampening the spirit of the visit.

The report said some CIA officials had travelled secretly to Islamabad on 12 July and presented evidence to Pakistan's most senior officials showing that members of the ISI had deepened their ties with some militant groups operating in FATA which were responsible for a surge of violence in Afghanistan, possibly including the suicide bombing in early July 2008 of the Indian embassy in Kabul.[1] 'The decision to confront Pakistan with what the officials described as a new C.I.A. assessment of the spy service's activities seemed to be the bluntest American warning to Pakistan since shortly after the Sept. 11 attacks about the ties between the spy service and Islamic militants. The C.I.A. assessment specifically points to links between members of the spy service, the Directorate for Inter-Services Intelligence, or ISI, and the militant network led by Maulavi Jalaluddin Haqqani, which American officials believe maintains close ties to senior figures of Al Qaeda in Pakistan's tribal areas,' the report said.

Two days later, Siraj Haqqani, the most active son of Jalaluddin Haqqani, snubbed the *New York Times* report. 'I have nothing to do with the ISI,' Haqqani junior said in a statement he issued from somewhere in North Waziristan.[2]

Prime Minister Gilani too rejected links between the ISI and militants. In the aftermath of the 9/11 attack and especially since 19 September 2001, when Pervez Musharraf declared 'unconditional support to the international coalition against terrorism' (whose members grew to forty-one by July 2008), the CIA and the Federal Bureau of Investigation (FBI) have been heavily dependent on the human assets of the ISI for operations and surveillance with regard to the war on terror.

The visit was in the wake of the deadly suicide attack on the Indian embassy in Kabul, which killed forty-one people on 7 July. Afghan President Hamid Kargai lost no time in publicy pointing fingers at the ISI for the attack.

Two days before Gilani's meeting with Bush in Washington, Lieutenant General Martin E. Dempsey, the acting commander of American CENTCOM forces in south-west Asia, visited Rawalpindi, headquarters of the Pakistan army, to discuss the situation in tribal areas. General Dempsey also met with Pakistani commanders in Miranshah, where units of Pakistan's 11th Army Corps and the paramilitary Frontier Corps are headquartered, for discussions on the deteriorating security situation in the region, the *New York Times* reported. Even today, North Waziristan remains the focus of the US and NATO forces because they consider it the hub of Al Qaeda and other foreign fighters, who are sheltered and protected by the Haqqani network. Pakistani troops and US drones continue to target mosques and seminaries directly or indirectly associated with the Al Qaeda network.

According to a statement issued by the Inter Services Public Relations (ISPR), Dempsey met with General Tariq Majeed, chairman, Joint Chiefs of Staff Committee, a largely ceremonious position, to convey his concerns. Majeed bluntly referred to the six missiles that the US forces had lobbed into Azam Warsak, in South Waziristan, the same morning. The attack was the fourth in July.

As far as Pakistan's army was concerned, the 'uninformed strikes' were not welcome at all. 'Expressing concern over repeated cross-border missile attacks/artillery and mortar firing by coalition and Afghan forces, General Tariq Majeed said that "our sovereignty and territorial integrity must be respected,"' the ISPR statement quoted Tariq as telling Dempsey. 'Any violation in this regard could be detrimental to bilateral relations.'[3]

'It was a very pointed message saying, "Look, we know there's a connection, not just with Haqqani but also with other bad guys and ISI, and we think you could do more and we want you to do more about it,"' one senior American official said of the message to Pakistan.[4] The Al Qaeda, nevertheless, was not specifically mentioned because evidence on direct involvement of Al Qaeda is scanty and because most attacks on US and NATO targets inside Afghanistan have been carried out by Haqqani's and Hekmetyar's militants.

The *Los Angeles Times* quoted an American counter-terrorism official as saying there were 'genuine and longstanding concerns about Pakistan's ties to the Haqqani network, which of course has links to Al Qaeda.'[5]

Six months earlier Mike McConnell, the director of national intelligence, and Michael V. Hayden, the CIA director, had made a similar trip to Islamabad for meetings with the then president Pervez Musharraf and other army officials to seek for the CIA and US forces based across the border 'greater latitude' to operate, particularly in the Waziristan region which US military believes serves as the base for Taliban and Al Qaeda terrorists.[6]

In an even more damning report the *New York Times* said American intelligence agencies had conclusive proof that ISI had helped plan the bombing of India's embassy in Kabul. 'The conclusion was based on intercepted communications between Pakistani intelligence officers and militants who carried out the attack, the officials said, providing the clearest evidence to date that Pakistani intelligence officers are actively undermining American efforts to combat militants in the region.'[7]

The American officials also said there was new information showing that members of the Pakistani intelligence service were increasingly providing militants with details about the American campaign against them, in some cases allowing militants to avoid American missile strikes in Pakistan's tribal areas. Such reports, particularly when the Pakistani prime minister had just concluded his maiden Washington visit, not only embarrassed the leadership but also amounted to a public indictment of the ISI, which President Bush and others held responsible for the chaos in Afghanistan.

Pakistani government and military officials, notwithstanding all the confusion around the question as to who controls the ISI, hit back and brushed aside US administration's allegations. 'All elements sympathetic to Taliban and the likes of them have been shunted out and we stand committed to the war on terror,' Major General Athar Abbas, head of ISPR, said.[8] In fact senior intelligence officials also put up a strong defence of their policy towards some of the Pakistani and Afghan militants, some also wanted by the Americans. The *News* said, 'Pakistani military leaders rubbished the American information and evidence on the Kabul bombing but provided some rationale for keeping a window open with Haqqani, just as the British government had decided to open talks with some Taliban leaders in southern Afghanistan last year.'

Admiral Mullen and Kappes were also informed on the activities of the Indian consulates in Kandahar and Jalalabad and asked how the CIA does not know that both Indian consulates are manned by Indian Intelligence who plot against Pakistan round the clock.[9] 'A US official who just returned from a fact-finding trip to South Asia said Pakistan is particularly perturbed about India's growing ties to the Afghan government and its establishment of as many as five consular offices in the country, which it believes are being used as intelligence hubs. The Indians set up one of these missions in Kandahar, just across our border, and that one is really driving the Pakistanis crazy,' the official said.

The American visitors were also told that the government of Pakistan sought help from Taliban commanders such as Sirajuddin Haqqani for the release of its kidnapped ambassador Tariq Azizuddin, after the US-backed Karzai administration failed to secure Azizuddin's release from his captors in Afghanistan. Azizuddin himself refused to divulge how his ninety-seven-day-long ordeal at Taliban hideouts in Waziristan mountains came to an end, yet he admitted several channels worked overtime to secure his release from Baitullah Mehsud.[10] It was pointed out that before opening new channels of communication with the Taliban in Helmand province in March, the British and NATO forces had also been talking to leading Taliban leaders through Michael Semple, the acting head of the European Union mission to Afghanistan, and Mervyn Patterson, a senior UN official.[11] The Afghan government unceremoniously expelled both Semple and Patterson in January 2008 on charges of maintaining contacts with Taliban and thereby undermining 'the war on terror'.

The ISI's image took an unusual beating both at home and abroad after 9/11, despite Pakistan's frontline support in the US-declared war on terror and reconciliation replacing acrimony between India and Pakistan over Kashmir. Interviews with locals in the past and a survey by the Centre for Research and Security

Studies (CRSS) in April–May 2008[12] revealed that Muslim separatists from across the border were openly trained in Pakistan-administered Kashmir and in FATA at least until 15 March 2004 when the Pakistan army lost dozens of soldiers and officers in a bloody encounter with the fighters of the Islamic Movement of Uzbekistan (IMU) at Sheen Warsak near Wana.

Residents also identified Islamist militant groups such as Jaish-e-Mohammad, Harkatul Mujahideen, Lashkar-e-Taiba and Lashkar-e-Jhangvi as beneficiaries of the military and ISI-led establishment's largesse. They believe that these outfits ran either their own complexes in FATA or used the hospitality of the local Taliban and mujahideen outfits such as Tehreek-e-Nifaze Shariate Mohammadi and Lashkar-e-Islam for their operations.

Maulana Jalaluddin Haqqani, the Afghan war veteran, and his son Siraj Haqqani, have also been hosting like-minded pan-Islamist fighters for almost a decade in North Waziristan. Since the senior and junior Haqqanis pop in and out of Miranshah without hinderance, it suggests that their presence and regular visits to friends and families on the Pakistani side of the border enjoy tacit approval of Pakistani authorities.

Residents of the Waziristan region and other FATA areas insist that without the tacit support of the ISI and other intelligence outfits, none of the Pakistani, Afghan, Arab or Uzbek militant outfits can survive in the tribal areas. 'If the ISI is not supporting them, how come they move so freely in our areas?' many residents of the area interviewed by the CRSS asked.

The most prevalent perception is that intelligence agencies look the other way, if not actively assist, when local and Afghan Taliban and Al Qaeda operatives and leaders meet, move or murder pro-government Pakistani and Afghan officials and tribesmen.

In June 2008 the US think tank RAND Corp. concluded in a report that Pakistani intelligence agents and paramilitary forces have helped train Taliban insurgents and have given them information about American troop movements in Afghanistan.[13] The study, 'Counterinsurgency in Afghanistan', found some active and former officials in ISI and the Frontier Corps provided direct assistance to Taliban militants and helped secure medical care for wounded fighters. It said NATO officials have uncovered several instances of Pakistani intelligence agents providing information to Taliban fighters, even 'tipping off Taliban forces about the location and movement of Afghan and coalition forces, which undermined several US and NATO anti-Taliban military operations'. No timeframes were given, though. The study was funded by the US Defense Department, and was apparently used as a reference during PM Gilani's US visit.

A statement by Ahmed Mukhtar, Pakistani defence minister, can be taken as confirmation of this. 'The Americans told us that vital intelligence is leaked ahead of operations, and that people within the ISI do it on purpose,' Mukhtar told the media after meetings with US officials, including US Defense Secretary Robert Gates.

Hamid Karzai, the Afghan President, holds similar views. Without naming the Pakistani military or the ISI, Karzai believes these organizations are still backing militants. 'I don't hold the civilian government responsible but I just address the prime minister of Pakistan when I want to convey a message and I get the response to it when the prime minister speaks,' Karzai said in an interview at his palace in Kabul.[14]

'Whenever these kinds of places are identified, action is taken . . . there are umpteen examples in the past where action has been taken against these insurgents, or, for that matter, foreigners,' Pakistan military spokesman Major General Athar Abbas said in response to the RAND Corp. report.

'Therefore, we reject this claim of sanctuary being aided by Pakistan's army or intelligence agencies,' General Abbas said, in a press release by ISPR.

The current Pakistani ambassador to the US, Husain Haqqani, maintained in several of his articles and his book *Between Mulla and Military*, on the relationship between the Islamists and the Pakistani security forces written during his stay with American think tanks, that Pakistani military and intelligence services have for decades used religious parties as a convenient instrument to keep domestic political opponents at bay and for foreign policy adventures, such as the US-backed jihad in Afghanistan and anti-India insurgency in Kashmir. 'The religious parties provide them with recruits, personnel, cover and deniability . . . They trained the people who are at the heart of it all, and they have done nothing to roll back their protégés,' states Haqqani, who served rival political governments in Pakistan in the 1990s.

The ISI has been linked by its detractors to violent struggles in Bangladesh, Sri Lanka and Nepal as well.

America's STRATFOR intelligence analysis service, sometimes called the CIA's 'cousin', reported in April 2007 that 'Pakistan is fuelling the growing Islamization in South Asia and had a strong nexus with Bangladesh intelligence agencies in laying a militant trap for India which is fighting a growing Maoist movement'.

The STRATFOR forecast titled 'India: The Islamization of the Northeast', observed that there is a growing Islamization in the region, spurred by ISI and instability in neighbouring Bangladesh which is giving foreign powers (China, Pakistan) a whole range of exploitative secessionist movements to use to prevent India from emerging as a major global player.

The STRATFOR report claims that there exists a strong nexus between the ISI and Bangladesh's intelligence agencies. ISI, in cooperation with Bangladesh's Directorate General of Forces Intelligence (DGFI), appears to be investing a considerable amount of resources in solidifying India's militant corridor. There are growing indications, says the report, that these two agencies are working clandestinely in Bangladesh to bring all the insurgent outfits based in India's north-east and jihadist elements under one umbrella. 'The ISI has facilitated cooperation between United Liberation Front of Asom (ULFA) and other northeastern militant outfits with the Liberation Tigers of Tamil Eelam (LTTE) in Sri Lanka, Islamist militant groups in Kashmir, Islamist groups in Bangladesh and a growing number of Al Qaeda-linked jihadist groups operating in the region.'[15]

The Indian government too has continuously blamed most acts of terrorism in Kashmir and elsewhere in India on the ISI. In early 2003 it promised in Parliament to present a white paper on the ISI's activities inside India, but reversed the decision four years later saying the move would jeopardize national security. Former Indian prime minister Atal Bihari Vajpayee had also openly spoken of the 'nexus that exists between the ISI and Bangladesh', which though denied by the Bangladesh government kept reverberating in the media, vitiating the bilateral relationship.

On 26 November 2008 the multiple bloody terror strikes including those on the Taj and Oberoi Trident Hotels in Mumbai—eleven in all—once again shook the entire region. These acts of terror provided Indian officials and media with another opportunity to point a finger at the ISI.

Earlier, on 10 October 2006, the American Council on Foreign Relations had come out with a stinging analysis of the ISI role in the region. It quoted experts as saying the ISI has supported a number of militant groups in the disputed Kashmir region between Pakistan and India, some of which are on the State Department's foreign terrorist organizations list. Though the level of assistance to these groups has varied, Kathy Gannon, who covered the region for decades for the Associated Press, says previous support consisted of money, weapons and training. 'Though Pakistani officials deny any current support for the Taliban—which the State Department does not deem a terrorist group—the ISI certainly has supported Afghan insurgents in the past.'[16] And in late September, the BBC received a leaked copy of a report from the British Defence Academy, a think tank run by Britain's Ministry of Defence, which stated 'Indirectly Pakistan (through the ISI) has been supporting terrorism and extremism—whether in London on 7/7, or in Afghanistan, or Iraq.' Just days later, Mumbai's police chief claimed to have proof that the ISI planned the 11 July bombing of the Indian city's commuter rail system, which was carried out by the Kashmir-based militant group Lashkar-e-Taiba.

In a sort of rebuttal to the leak, President Pervez Musharraf underscored the importance of his nation's role: 'Remember my words: if the ISI is not with you and Pakistan is not with you, you [America] will lose in Afghanistan.'[17] And on 1 October in an appearance on NBC's *Meet the Press*, Musharraf acknowledged some retired ISI operatives could be abetting the Taliban insurgency in Afghanistan.

President Musharraf's anger was understandable. He was being distrusted by the very western powers he was helping. And his help to the west had made him unpopular with his countrymen as well as a target of assassination attempts by Islamic militants. All of which had served to destabilize Pakistan.

As far back as September 2003, Russian deputy foreign minister Vyacheslav Trubnikov had named the ISI as the force responsible for the resurgence of remnants of the Taliban in Afghanistan.[18]

'These attacks are occurring frequently which is proof that Taliban is not yet liquidated . . . during our contact with Pakistanis and meetings within the Russia-US joint working groups, we have insisted that Pakistani leadership consistently follow the line of pressurizing the Taliban elements, and the ISI, which is overtly assisting the process of reorganization of the Taliban,' the *Indian Express* quoted Trubnikov as saying.

Until 9/11, western powers had almost abandoned ISI to its own devices following the Soviets' humiliating departure from Afghanistan. But the west needed the ISI's services again to fight the global war on terror when the US resolved to finish the demon the Afghan jihad had created.

The Pakistan army's and ISI's stock rose as they cooperated in the war on terror and turned over close to 800 Taliban and Al Qaeda operators, known or suspected. But this cooperation started souring, particularly after the start of the US invasion of Iraq in 2003, as the US and its coalition partners increasingly accused ISI of playing a double game by protecting the agents it had cultivated during Afghan jihad days.

Under the new terms of cooperation with the US, the FBI and the CIA in late 2001, General Pervez Musharraf had to purge the ISI of its Islamic leanings to make the organization do as the US said in the war on terror. Still, the allegations thrown at Musharraf and ISI from all sides, at home and abroad, stuck.

According to a 2003 Global Intelligence report, the CIA was close to the ISI during the Cold War and this relationship was rekindled after 9/11. Agents of the purged ISI were quick to seize the suspected killers of the *Wall Street Journal* journalist Daniel Pearl. And in early April 2002 more than sixty Al Qaeda operatives were arrested in Faisalabad, along with Abu Zubayda, Al Qaeda's third highest ranking member.[19]

But the accusations only grew as did punitive actions by the coalition forces in Afghanistan and in Pakistan's tribal areas.

Although forced into cooperation, most CIA veterans agree that the relationship between CIA and ISI is like a bad marriage, in which both sides have long stopped trusting each other but would never think of breaking up because they have become so mutually dependent, said the *New York Times*.[20]

While the CIA makes noises about dealing with Pakistan's ISI, there is a certain 'grudging reverence' for the spy services' scheming qualities. Some former spies even talk about the ISI with a mix of awe and professional jealousy. But a web of competing interests complicates the relationship. 'The top American goal in the region is to shore up Afghanistan's government and security services to better fight the ISI's traditional proxies (the Taliban and former mujahideen) there. Inside Pakistan, America's primary interest is to dismantle a Taliban and Al Qaeda safe haven in the mountainous tribal lands,' the *New York Times* said.

The *New York Times* report noted that even the ISI 'has difficulties collecting information in the tribal lands, the home of fiercely independent Pashtun tribes. For this reason, the I.S.I. has long been forced to rely on Pashtun tribal leaders—and in some cases Pashtun militants—as key informants. Given the natural disadvantages, C.I.A. officers try to get any edge they can through technology, the one advantage they have over local spies. The Pakistan government has long restricted the areas where the C.I.A. can fly Predator surveillance drones inside Pakistan, limiting paths to approved "boxes" on a grid map.'

The Background

The US administration's suspicion and mistrust of ISI is rooted in thirty-two documents that the US Defence Intelligence Agency (DIA) of the Pentagon had compiled in September 1999, and placed for public scrutiny in 2002 on the anniversary of the 11 September 2001 attacks.

The information contained in these documents clearly shows that the US State Department and the DIA knew of the role of the ISI in sponsoring not only the Taliban but also Al Qaeda.[21]

After General Musharraf seized power on 12 October 1999, the documents say, the presence of the Pakistani intelligence in the Taliban-controlled territory increased and Afghanistan became a veritable Pakistani colony, which was facilitated by the past ties of many mullas of the Taliban with Pakistan's military–intelligence establishment. Yet, the Bush administration chose to close its eyes to the complicity of Pakistan and projected General Pervez Musharraf to the international community as a frontline ally in the war against terrorism.

Since becoming an essential element of the international anti-terror war, the ISI has undergone quite a transformation; its Afghan cell does not exist any more. Most of the Afghan-related officers now interact with the FBI. Even retired ISI officers are working for the US agencies. Yet suspicion abounds that within ISI several elements are still maintaining contacts with people like the Haqqanis, Mulla Omar, Hekmetyar and several Pakistani militant outfits.

While the ISI stopped funding the operations of the outfits battling Indian forces in Kashmir, it also curtailed its tentacles in Afghanistan. Out of strategic considerations, the organization maintains contacts with the Kashmiri outfits, but whether it disconnected itself from the Afghan and Pakistani Taliban remains a mystery.

Sources in Peshawar, who are familiar with the jihadi leadership, claim that most of Hekmetyar's leaders and activists are quietly living in Peshawar. His family members have been even attending weddings of relatives. 'I would say that the intelligence agencies do know about these people but are probably keeping quiet as a policy of tolerance,' a Pakistani journalist with close links to Hekmetyar's Hezb-e-Islami said, requesting anonymity.[22]

Discussions with the Afghan President Karzai and his deputy interior minister Abdul Hadi Khalid in June 2008 also yielded similar impressions; their arguments are deeply embedded in the belief that the ISI is manipulating militants like Baitullah Mehsud and Fazlullah to destabilize Afghanistan.

Some cynics even went to the extent of suggesting that the abduction of Ambassador Tariq Azizuddin by Baitullah Mehsud's Taliban was also stage-managed by the ISI, perhaps to impress on the Americans that Pakistan was also a victim, or to send out a message that militants were not under the control of Pakistani intelligence any more.

In this context, the big challenge facing Pakistan is to convince the world that the ISI as a counter-insurgency agency is safeguarding only the legitimate interests of the country. It requires a lot of hard work to prove that the ISI is working against and not for radical fundamentalist groups, which now pose a direct threat to the Pakistani society as such.

'If the FBI and MI6 are here in the region to look after their interests how can the ISI remain oblivious to the situation in its neighbourhood?' asked General Talat Masood, a defence and political analyst. Indeed, the ISI needs to purge its ranks of pan-Islamists. 'It must get rid of the sympathizers and supporters of Al Qaeda and Taliban but it would fail in its duty if it left its job to foreigners,' Masood said.[23]

The stigma of 'abetting terrorist groups' is deep and would require much more effort to remove.

Probably to appease the US administration on these concerns, Prime Minister Gilani, a few hours before embarking on his Washington visit on 26 July, made an ill-conceived attempt to put the ISI under the ministry of interior. Theoretically, the ISI has been reporting to the prime minister, the chief executive, and it did so, particularly from October 1999 to December 2007, when President Pervez Musharraf also headed the military.

But being a force exclusively drawn from the military, the ISI never trusted civilian prime ministers like Benazir Bhutto and Nawaz Sharif; on the contrary, politicians accused it of plotting against the civilian governments and undermining their authority.

That is why even the Pakistan Peoples Party-led civilian government of Gilani has also been struggling to assert control over the ISI. It also grew wary of the accusations and suspicions coming out of Washington and London, and thus the attempt— a faux pas at best—to tame it through the interior ministry. The army hit back, and within hours, the notification was withdrawn.

'Two emergency calls from Rawalpindi to London forced Prime Minister Gilani to change the decision of placing the Inter-Services Intelligence (ISI) under the Interior Ministry within a few hours, causing serious embarrassment for him,' the *News* said.

Shaheen Sehbai, the group editor for the *News*, confirmed the motives of the coup against the ISI.

'The politically ill-advised developments in Islamabad to take over control of the otherwise notorious ISI are deeply linked to Prime Minister Gilani's US visit . . . and he was more than eager to take some decision on who would control the ISI before landing at the Andrews Air Force Base on the outskirts of Washington.'[24]

Bad timing and ill-advice notwithstanding, the reversal of the prime ministerial orders not only tarnished Gilani's image in and outside the country but also exposed the hidden differences between different state organs responsible for national security.

The generals, both at the ISI and at the General Headquarters in Rawalpindi, probably found it hard to swallow the prospect of being made accountable to civilian bureaucrats, and thus the manoeuvring behind the scenes that scuttled their 'subjugation' to the ministry of interior.

That is why foreign ministry diplomats, analysts and politicians alike hold the ISI responsible for Pakistan's foreign policy failures, which they believe stem from a tactical, suspicious mindset, deeply mired in the cold war tactics of securing a safe border in the west through a friendly government in Kabul, keeping India bogged down in Kashmir through the scores of militant organizations that operate there and keeping those politicians and intellectuals in check who are averse to such a big standing army.

The most serious problem stems from the attempt to muzzle freedom of thought as to whether the country needs such a big army at all, and to indirectly intimidate the intelligentsia. I wrote an article in 1996 for the *Friday Times* on how poorly the intelligence agencies operate in Pakistan-administered Kashmir. As a result, not only did the ISI put me on a 'security risk list' but also barred me from all army-related functions and ceremonies in 1997. The ban was finally lifted in 1998 after I approached the ISI through highly placed sources telling it that whatever I wrote was in good faith.

The case of Najam Sethi, the chief editor of the *Friday Times*, also exemplifies how those considered 'anti-Pakistan' are treated. He was picked up in April 1999 by Civilian Intelligence Bureau operatives but was eventually handed over to the ISI who kept him in illegal detention for several weeks.

One of the tools which allows the ISI to pick up people is the Pakistan Armed Forces' Act, which is applied to civilians to keep them quiet. Luckily, in Sethi's case, for the first time the Supreme Court rejected the government position that the army can arrest a person under the act and also detain him indefinitely. Sethi was released under tremendous international pressure, but had he been a lesser-known journalist, he would possibly have come out a shattered man. In the following years, though, Sethi enjoyed good rapport with the military ruler General Pervez Musharraf until the latter resigned in August 2008. (Musharraf had ousted Premier Nawaz Sharif in October 1999.)

As far as foreign policy is concerned, the ISI, though under the prime minister/chief executive, has apparently never allowed political governments to devise an independent Afghan or India policy. In fact military rule from the time of General Zia ul-Haq onward has never really allowed political governments to think on their own on these two fronts. The Afghan war, and the CIA's support of it, provided Zia and his associates an opportunity to expand the ISI into a monolithic organization with tentacles reaching into all provinces of Afghanistan, aligning all sorts of tribal leaders and fighters as commanders. But as the disengagement in Afghanistan got under way following the Soviet pull-out in February 1989, the forces which the CIA and ISI had gathered for the jihad began realizing their importance for jihad elsewhere.

In Jalalabad and outside Kabul, we met members of Hezb-e-Islami (Hekmetyar), a faction close to the ISI and which believes in militancy to spread Islam (like the Akhwanul-Muslimeen movement) who had been fighting in Azerbaijan, Bosnia-Herzegovina, Tajikistan and Kashmir.

It was a boon for the ISI because it had a ready corps of hardened, indoctrinated militants ready to fight anywhere for the Muslim cause. These people continue to fight and draw strength from the ISI, though none of the groups admits it.

Apart from guidance from ISI, these groups received a lot of funding from the Arab world, a fact borne out by the Arabic fluency of some of the top leaders of these groups—mujahideen, Taliban and the groups active in Indian Kashmir.

Gulbuddin Hekmetyar, Burhanuddin Rabbani and Professor Abdurrab Rasool Sayyaf are all conversant in Arabic, probably because of their close ties to the House of Sauds, the rulers of the

Saudi royal kingdom. Similalry, several leaders engaged in the Kashmir insurgency are also fluent speakers of Arabic, and regularly visit Saudi Arabia.

I know a few of these leaders personally, and they too told me that, after the ISI froze funding following US pressures in 2003, they managed to get financial resources from some Middle Eastern countries to keep their 'body and soul together'.

If some anti-army officials are to be taken seriously, the ISI had for quite some time viewed 'India . . . like an encroaching elephant and to stop its invasion and expansion, [we must] dig potholes in its way to obstruct its movement.' A former bureaucrat, who was among Zia ul-Haq's advisers, told me this philosophy was actually born during Haq's time, and was pursued until 2003, when the United States applied pressure and the Pakistan army promised to shut down training facilities for Kashmiri militants. President Musharraf gave these assurances to the then deputy secretary of state Richard Armitage and his deputy for Asia, Christina Rocca, after their lengthy meetings at Rawalpindi. Armitage in fact made these assurances public at an interaction with the media at the ministry of foreign affairs in Islamabad a few hours later.

With this, the ISI was told to restrict its interaction with Kashmiri militant organizations. 'We were told to hold back and wait for better times,' the head of a Kashmiri outfit told me at his Rawalpindi residence.

In fact the CIA and FBI had helped ISI grow into a monolithic organization because of the anti-Soviet jihad, little realizing what this could mean for the country's future. Nobody could at that time envision the prospect of a Pakistan infested with religious zealots, a country that would turn into a nightmare for their own former mentors.

What the CIA leaked out to the *New York Times* during Prime Minister Gilani's Washington visit, therefore, came as no surprise. This had been in the making, and the US establishment used the occasion to vent its frustration with the ISI in order to mount pressure on it for a clearer and more proactive role in hunting terrorists.

All the efforts that the army and ISI had put in to create a new image of the ISI—through large-scale transfers, retirements and interaction with the media—seemed to have done little to paint it in a better light.

ISI: The Taliban Connection

The ISI received flak from all over the world on two counts: its support for the post-mujahideen militia in Afghanistan—the Taliban—and for its close links with Muslim separatists in the Himalayan state of Kashmir.

Let us first see how Pakistan, led by the ISI, responded to the emergence of the Taliban in October 1994.

In 1993, when Benazir Bhutto returned to power for a second time, and made Naseerullah Babar the home minister, Babar visited Herat to meet with Ismail Khan, the independent Tajik warlord supporting Ahmed Shah Masood, and went to Kandahar to meet with the emerging Taliban and other warlords to discuss with them an end to war and the rehabilitation of the highways into Central Asia.[25]

Babar followed it up with a convoy of trucks loaded with medicines through the Pakistan border post of Chaman, aiming to continue onto the Afghan cities of Kandahar and Herat on the route to Turkmenistan. Babar kept insisting that since Benazir Bhutto was on her way to the Turkmenistan capital, Ashkabad, he wanted the way clear for the goods as well as the foreign diplomats' convoy to show the world that the road was open.

'We thought that if this route was open to the Central Asian republics, they would be able to get their economic independence after depending on Russia for more than seventy years,' Babar said of the rationale behind the caravan.

The convoy was dispatched against the advice of the foreign office and intelligence officials who had been warned by the Taliban

leader Mulla Mohammed Omar to expect trouble from the
warlords. 'I met Omar in the second half of October at Spin Boldak
where he advised me not to bring the convoy because the situation
was not fully under control,' said a former ISI colonel. Predictably,
the trucks were stopped right on the border by some rogue
commanders of Professor Rasool Sayyaf, one of the seven key
mujahideen leaders.

'We put pressure on Sayyaf, whose people had intercepted our
convoy. I put all his family at Jalozai and let him know that they
had to get the caravan released,' Babar said. Jalozai is a deserted
area near Peshawar that became infamous in 2001 for extremely
poor standards of living when Afghans fleeing drought and hunger
settled in the spot in late 2000.

The colonel returned to Omar for help but he advised him to
get safe passage guarantees from all Afghan leaders, whose
commanders had erected at least forty checkpoints between Spin
Boldak, the Afghan frontier town, and Kandahar. It took three
days, and then the convoy moved from Chaman.

That was when regular contacts between the Taliban and the
ISI were established. Until then, the ISI had bothered little about
southern Afghanistan. Nor was the Pakistani establishment any
more active after the virtual demise of the Islamabad, Peshawar
and Jalalabad peace accords among the mujahideen factions,
which had failed to end the bloody fighting in and around Kabul.

Since southern Afghanistan traditionally had been pro-monarchy,
and was not the hotbed of 'jihad' against the Soviets, Pakistan never
really devised a strategy for this region. That is why the Taliban
emergence came as a surprise to the Pakistani establishment.

The contacts with the Taliban grew as its fighters took one
province after the other, and swiftly moved northwards towards
the capital. Once the Taliban entrenched themselves in Kandahar
in late 1994 and looked set to storm past the opposition, the
Pakistani establishment decided to extend whatever support it
could to the new 'hope' for Afghanistan. Islamabad saw it as a
chance also for ensuring a friendly government in Afghanistan.

The first quarter of 1995 saw an influx of ISI and Pakistan army officials on a variety of missions. By 2000 the ISI presence in Kandahar had grown to about half a dozen officers, with a string of local informers including officials of Mulla Omar's secretariat and his ministry of foreign affairs.

In February 1995, while on an assignment to cover the then 'mysterious' movement and its leaders in their bastion of Kandahar, I could see several plain-clothed Pakistan army officers across the border starting from Spin Boldak all the way to Kandahar. One could easily tell these officers from the rugged Afghans; their gait, appearance and overall demeanour was visibly different.

Led by Naseerullah Babar, inspired by the 'access-to-Central-Asia' vision of Foreign Minister Sardar Assef Ahmed Ali and lured by the 'dream-come-true' analysis of the emerging situation, the Pakistani establishment rushed to extend whatever support it could to the Taliban. It was Benazir Bhutto's second government, and with the emergence of the ethnic Pashtoon Taliban, Pakistan's civilian and military establishment thought the time for reaching out to the resource-rich Central Asia had perhaps arrived. A friendly and peaceful Afghanistan offered the shortest access route to Turkmenistan's Daulatabad oil and gas fields. Hence Pakistan's eagerness to explore and exploit possibilities of establishing contacts with Central Asia via Afghanistan.

One of the major things Babar did was revive the Afghan Trade and Development Cell (ATDC) at the ministry of foreign affairs in Islamabad. The initial annual funding for the cell amounted to Rs 300 million, which by 2001 had shrunk to a paltry Rs 40 million.

Babar also ordered several practical steps to help the Taliban rehabilitate the tattered infrastructure. Engineers from Pakistan's Water and Power Development Authority (WAPDA) were sent to Herat, Kabul and Jalalabad to repair and make operable the power stations. Experts from the telecommunications department were sent across into Taliban-controlled areas and provided with a high frequency telephone system accessible through code numbers for the Pakistani cities of Peshawar, Quetta (the capital of Balochistan province) and Islamabad. They also helped restore the internal phone network.

Aviation experts from Pakistan were supposed to upgrade some of the Afghan airports for international flights, and its engineers did carry out some work at the Kandahar airport. The National Bank of Pakistan and the Utility Stores Corporation were to open branches in Afghanistan.

In all, by summer 2001, Pakistan had provided more than a hundred high frequency phone lines to Afghanistan; Kabul, Jalalabad, Mazar-e-Sharif, Kandahar and Herat were all accessible through the Pakistani phone network. More than 60 per cent of the connections were with the Taliban's ministry of foreign affairs, aviation and the core leadership, including Mulla Omar. Pakistani officials in Afghanistan said plans were afoot to increase connections to Afghanistan to 1500 to improve communication.

In Kabul at least five connections were with the Embassy of Pakistan, at least twenty-five with the Taliban government departments and ministries, the official Bakhtar News Agency and Ariana Airlines. In Kandahar at least four lines were serving Pakistani diplomats, and a minimum of fourteen were at the disposal of Taliban leaders and ministers. Out of the five connections in the western town of Herat reached from Islamabad as local numbers, the governor, the mayor and the corps commander shared one number each and two were with Pakistani diplomats.

The lines from Peshawar, for instance, connected Kabul and Jalalabad through a radio satellite high frequency system with Pakistan and the rest of the world through the old Afghan telecommunication network Mukhabirat. A high-power satellite booster with solar batteries atop the Lattaband Pass between Jalalabad and Kabul was also installed to ensure better communication.

Residents in Kabul, Jalalabad and Kandahar also had interesting stories to tell about the users of these phone lines; many Taliban leaders/ministers who had Pakistani phone connections used them as public call offices after office hours as an additional source of income. 'That is why their bills are running into tens of thousands of rupees which they pay very regularly,' a Pakistan Telecom official said during a chance meeting in Kabul in early 2001, pointing to the heavy bills the connections in Afghanistan were running.

'They are also charging ten Pakistan rupees a minute for incoming calls from Europe and the Gulf where thousands of Afghans have either found refuge or are working and call up their relatives in these big towns,' said a Pakistani diplomat posted in Afghanistan for many years.

On Islamabad's military assistance to the Taliban, the Human Rights Watch (HRW) report says: 'In April and May 2001 Human Rights Watch sources reported that as many as thirty trucks a day were crossing the Pakistan border; sources inside Afghanistan reported that some of these convoys were carrying artillery shells, tank rounds, and rocket-propelled grenades. Such deliveries are in direct violation of UN sanctions. Pakistani landmines have been found in Afghanistan; they include both antipersonnel and anti-vehicle mines. Pakistan's army and intelligence services, principally the Inter-Services Intelligence Directorate (ISI), contribute to making the Taliban a highly effective military force. While these Pakistani agencies do not direct the policies of the IEA [Islamic Emirate of Afghanistan], senior Pakistani military and intelligence officers help plan and execute major military operations. In addition, private-sector actors in Pakistan provide financial assistance to the Taliban.'[26]

Sources for this part of the report were a 1997 UN secretary-general's report, as well as an unnamed military expert with experience in Afghanistan. Part of it is based on what Anthony Davis has been reporting for Jane's Intelligence Review (JIR). Interestingly, Davis himself wrote in one of his JIR 2001 reports that there was no 'incriminating evidence available on the Pakistan military's involvement with the Taliban'.

At another place, while commenting on the 'presence of Pakistani military advisers performing command and control functions for the Taliban offensive prior to and following the fall of Mazar-i-Sharif in August 1998', the HRW relied for confirmation on a separate e-mail communication in September 1998 with a Pakistani source.

The HRW also relied on interviews with western diplomatic sources and military experts, and with journalists and other observers in the region in 1999 and 2000. HRW spoke with a Taliban official in Kabul in 2000 who confirmed that senior Pakistan army and intelligence officers were involved in planning Taliban offensives. Interestingly, all these sources requested anonymity.

Pakistan was also helping the Afghans in rehabilitating the agricultural sector. The prime example is the Ghaziabad farm outside the eastern town of Jalalabad where lack of care, water and fertilizer had left the vast olive, almond and orange orchards barren.

'We provided them with 700,000 olive plants, and are also training their farmers and agronomists at a couple of places in Peshawar,' Arif Ayub, the Pakistani ambassador, told me during an interview in summer 2001 at his embassy office in Kabul. He said agricultural training was also given to the Afghans to rehabilitate these orchards and the results of this training had been very encouraging. They were also doing road repairs. Interestingly, Ayub was the first Pakistani diplomat who refused to grow a beard before or after arrival in Kabul to assume charge; almost all other diplomats and support staff grew beards to avoid trouble from the Taliban.

'Agriculture is one innocent sector in which we believe we can and should help the Afghans,' said another Pakistani diplomat, adding that the Afghans had flooded the Pakistani mission with requests for training and guidance in the agricultural sector. But with Pakistan itself facing financial problems, the budget of the country's foreign ministry allocated for Afghanistan during the 2000–01 fiscal was a mere 40 million rupees—less than $700,000.

At the height of their interaction with the Taliban regime, ISI functionaries and the army representatives posted inside

Afghanistan had greater access to the Taliban nucleus of power compared to the civilian diplomats.

'We have had to wait for weeks to get an audience with Mulla Omar or his closest aides but the army people get the appointments instantly,' said one of the Pakistani diplomats posted in Kandahar. He was wary of the fact that the Pakistan army officers would sometime hold meetings with the Taliban leadership on their own, without taking the senior-most civilian diplomats like the consul general in Kandahar and the ambassador in Kabul into confidence.[27]

'ISI officials always excluded civilians from their meetings with Afghans. On several occasions we came to know about their meetings only afterwards,' said one of the senior-most diplomats posted in Kandahar during the Taliban rule.

Those were days when ISI functionaries, particularly those posted there, considered Afghanistan a crucial hotbed for militants fighting in Kashmir. Major militants groups—Lashkar-e-Taiba, Jaish-e-Mohammad and Harkatul Mujahideen—ran their training facilities in the Taliban-controlled areas. They all enjoyed unusual access into the Taliban power centres as well as with Pakistani ISI officials. I recall an interesting exchange of arguments with one of the military officials posted in Kandahar in early 2001; once he ran out of arguments in support of Pakistan's Taliban policy, the officer said, 'We also have to think of the struggle in Kashmir.' This, in a way, was an indirect admission that since the Taliban were taking care of the militants active in Kashmir we have to live with them.

As far as intelligence cooperation with the Taliban is concerned, senior officials used to stick their necks out by regularly visiting the Taliban stronghold of Kandahar. One of the officials, Faiz Jeelani, a major general, would fly to Chaman in a helicopter and then be picked up by the Taliban on the way to Kandahar, where the ISI had also taken over the consular section in the summer of 2001, a Taliban official told me at his Kandahar residence in March 2001.

Tayyab Agha, and one Mulla Ahmedi from Ghazni, both trusted aides of Mulla Omar, as well as the Kandahar governor Mulla Hassan Rehman, and the deputy defence minister Mulla Akhtar Usmani would attend most of the meetings. Not many civilian officials would even come to know about these consultations.

After a meeting that Moinuddin Haider, the then interior minister, had with Mulla Omar in March 2001, one of Omar's aides took a Pakistani intelligence official aside and asked, 'Does he really know what he is talking about? He is clueless about what is going on.' The aide did not elaborate but the incident at least underlined the close links that existed between the Pakistan army officials and the Taliban. It also explained that the military and intelligence community kept civilian diplomats out of their dealings with the Taliban leadership. But whether the latter ever listened to Pakistan is questionable because, as one diplomat put it, 'most Pakistanis were seen as untrustworthy partners who could betray the Taliban whenever the crunch came'.

Colonel Sultan Ameer Imam, a former ISI officer who had been involved with the Afghan mujahideen since Pakistan agreed to play host and teacher to the Muslim resistance on the instance of the CIA, had briefly trained Mulla Omar as a young mujahid in the mid 1980s near Quetta, the capital of Pakistan's south-western Balochistan province.

Following his retirement from the army, Imam, who one Pakistan foreign secretary had once described as an 'asset for his long involvement in Afghanistan and tremendous rapport with scores of Afghans', served as the consul general in Herat until the fall of the Taliban. Imam knows many Afghan leaders and commanders.

According to officials at one of the border posts in Balochistan, Imam visited Afghanistan even in the second week of October, just a couple of days after the American and British planes had launched Operation Enduring Freedom by bombing Afghanistan. It was a time when, officially, no Pakistani official was supposed to enter Afghanistan as all the diplomatic staff had already been recalled after General Musharraf broke alliance with the Taliban on 19 September 2001 and pledged unconditional support to the US-led war on terror.

The Kashmir Connection

Complaints about the ISI have not been restricted to the support for Taliban and insurgents in Afghanistan; Kashmiri militants have no qualms talking about the extent of ISI's influence over, and the support for, these fighters. Driven by the desire to free Kashmir from Indian rule, these jihadis took Pakistan army officers as they were: God-fearing, staunch and practising Muslims. 'I was really disappointed to know that the officer who used to sermonize us on the Quran and the teachings of Islam and criticized the west, had TV sets and music systems at home,' said a militant of an ISI officer who had good rapport with his organization.[28]

ISI officials stunned even Benazir Bhutto. During a visit to the ISI headquarters in the mid 1990s as prime minister, the Kashmir cell made a presentation to her on how the mujahideen were being trained and infiltrated into Indian Kashmir.[29] 'Are we really doing this?' asked a baffled Bhutto, who until then had parroted what the ministry of foreign affairs would tell her—that Pakistan is extending just political, moral and diplomatic support to Kashmiris.

This also explained, and later illustrated, the differences between Nawaz Sharif and General Pervez Musharraf over Kargil, on how the army and the ISI kept the civilian government out of the loop as far as its involvement in Kashmir and Afghanistan was concerned.

Bruce Riedel, aide to the then president Bill Clinton, also gave a detailed account of how distraught and wary Nawaz Sharif appeared when he went to Washington on 4 July 1999, to seek the president's help in diffusing an alarming situation that had arisen out of Pakistan army's occupation of certain peaks in the Kargil sector of Kashmir.[30]

ISI's Kashmir-related tactics suffered another blow when Christina Rocca, the then US assistant secretary of state for South

Asia, visited Islamabad in May 2002, followed by Richard Armitage, the deputy secretary of state, both on the mission of pressurizing Pakistan into changing gear on its support for Kashmir. Rocca's visit coincided with the killing of more than three dozen Kashmiris in Srinagar, and before she arrived in Islamabad the ISI called up all the components of the United Jihad Council (UJC) for a briefing. 'International pressure on us is becoming increasingly unbearable. You will have to halt the operations across the Line of Control,' one of the participants recalled in a personal interview at an obscure home on the outskirts of Islamabad.

The perceived Indian bellicosity that stemmed from international backing had raised temperatures on the LoC, and was the other reason a senior army officer gave the UJC members to slow down their movement. 'Alarmed by the warning, we asked whether there was any change in the Kashmir policy. No, it is just a change of tactic for the next three months. We will see afterwards,' one of the Kashmiri militants quoted an officer as reassuring the entire Kashmiri militant leadership.[31] As a result, the infiltration—or the launching of mujahideen, as the groups referred to the movement of fighters across the LoC—came down.

As General Musharraf responded positively to India's statement for 'actions and not words on the issue of infiltration', the cross-border movement by mid June in 2003 dropped by three fourths. Even the radio communication centre near the world's second highest peak, K-2, was cut off for fear of interception by American satellites and Indian surveillance along the LoC. 'We are really going to suffer this summer and fall as far as launching is concerned,' an anxious in-charge of operations of one outfit told me at his Islamabad seminary-cum-guesthouse.

Reporting on the escape of Ahmed al-Khadir, a close associate of Osama bin Laden who was wanted for the 1995 bombing of the Egyptian embassy in Islamabad, *Time* magazine minced no words while accusing the ISI of complicity with the Taliban. After weeks of highly risky surveillance work Egyptian investigators had tracked al-Khadir down to a safe house in Peshawar. The

Egyptians notified the ISI chief General Mahmood Ahmed, who promised swift action.

'It was swift, but not in the way the Egyptians had expected. That night last summer, the Pakistani security forces never turned up. Instead, a car with diplomatic plates full of Taliban roared up to the Peshawar house, grabbed al-Khadir and drove him over the Khyber Pass to safety in Afghanistan—beyond the Egyptians' grasp. Put bluntly, the Pakistani spy agency, known as the Inter-Services Intelligence, had betrayed the Egyptians.' The next day, the ISI called up and said, 'The man gave us the slip,' a diplomat recalls. 'It was a lie,' *Time* magazine reported.[32] Such incidents heavily stigmatized Pakistan with little acceptance of the explanations it has been offering on the role of the ISI in Afghanistan.

Senior diplomats at the ministry of foreign affairs in Islamabad would often oppose the ISI's strident and largely independent approach towards Kashmir and Afghanistan. Since Pakistan's claims of non-involvement in Kashmir failed to stand scrutiny, the international community continues to view Pakistan with suspicion. 'We lost face in Kashmir because of the overt support to the militants. Why should the world believe that we are not having a good time at the hands of Taliban any more?' a former senior diplomat posted in Kabul said.[33]

The September 1999 analysis by the Defence Intelligence Assessment contains quite a damning account of Pakistan's role as the real host of bin Laden and his Al Qaeda members in Afghanistan. It says, 'bin Laden's Al Qaeda network was able to expand under the safe sanctuary extended by the Taliban following Pakistan directives. If there is any doubt on that issue, consider the location of bin Laden's camp targeted by US cruise missiles, Zahawa (August 1998). Positioned on the border between Afghanistan and Pakistan (in Paktia province of Afghanistan) it was built by Pakistani contractors, funded by Pakistan's Inter-Services Intelligence (ISI) directorate and protected under the patronage of a local and influential tribal leader, Jalaluddin Haqqani. However, the real host in that facility was the Pakistani ISI.'[34]

In 2001, in a spate of scathing attacks on Pakistan's prime intelligence agencies for destabilizing political governments, Benazir Bhutto called for a truth and reconciliation commission to investigate their conduct. She bemoaned the fact that 'now we have seven intelligence agencies playing politics right down to the tehsil [village] level . . . this has led to the destabilization of political governments, the collapse of the economy and has undermined our standing in the international community', Zulfiqar Ali Khan, former air force chief, recalled during our meeting at his Islamabad residence in January 2001.

Bhutto was particularly incensed over the role the ISI and the Military Intelligence, both army outfits mandated with internal and external security operations and counter-intelligence, played against her governments. Listing names of former army chief General Aslam Beg, and ex-ISI chief Hameed Gul, and General Asad Durrani, Bhutto had claimed the ISI and MI had been doling out money and promising incentives to lure MPs away from the party as the army establishment was uncomfortable with her foreign policy and security agenda.

Benazir Bhutto had appointed Zulfiqar Ali Khan, who also served as Pakistan's ambassador to the United States during her first government in the late 1980s, to head an enquiry commission in 1989 to look into the working of various intelligence agencies including the ISI, the Intelligence Bureau (a civilian intelligence gathering outfit), the Federal Investigation Agency (FIA) as well as the Special Branch of the police and to also recommend measures to improve their performance and keep them away from the political arena.[35] Khan had suggested scrapping of the political wing of the ISI, a demand that reverberates within Pakistan even today.

Similar exercises were undertaken earlier as well: General Yahya Khan (who briefly ruled Pakistan 1969–December 1971) did it for Field Marshal Ayub Khan; Rafi Reza, a former federal secretary, conducted a study for Zulfiqar Ali Bhutto; and Sahabzada Yakub Khan, former foreign minister, did it for General Zia ul-Haq. But there was little movement on the implementation of recommendations of these commissions simply because the military-led security establishment towered over other institutions and political parties.

Even General Pervez Musharraf, a few months after seizing power in October 1999, had desired better coordination among various intelligence outfits. 'Musharraf had suggested that the interior ministry should act as the main coordinator for all the intelligence agencies for the effective utilization of resources and for de-politicizing them,' recalls Ansar Abassi, a senior Pakistani journalist.[36] Political expedience, however, came in the way of all these endeavours, said Abassi.

The events of 9/11, which once again sucked the ISI into the Afghan imbroglio, made it even more difficult for Musharraf and his civilian partners to even think of reforming the ISI and the entire intelligence apparatus. On the contrary, while the ISI stepped forward to help the US forces, FBI and CIA to dismantle the terror network that had taken roots in Afghanistan, the agency also turned inwards; the ISI indulged in unprecedented wheeling-dealings with political parties to the benefit of General Musharraf and reportedly also manipulated the formation of the government born out of the October 2002 elections. It is doubtful whether even a change of ISI command can radically alter the fundamental outlook of the ISI in the short term.

While he was prime minister, Nawaz Sharif had handpicked serving generals to head the ISI in 1991 and 1999 but neither could save him when he angered the military establishment by seeking civilian supremacy over the armed forces through constitutional amendments. On both occasions, the ISI chiefs, who are supposed to report to and support the prime minister, sided with the General Headquarters led by the chief of the army staff for the simple reason that the ISI predominantly draws on manpower from the armed forces.

'The reason is that the ISI is a military institution wedded to the military's institutional outlook and concerns about power and security. All its staff look up to the army chief and not the prime

minister or defence minister for their promotions and careers,'
concluded the *Friday Times*.[37] In Pakistan's political context, a
purely military organization is not likely to be comfortable with the
civilian leadership, which has been struggling (in vain) to establish
its credentials as responsible and sincere stakeholders in the
country's political system. The perpetual imbalance in the civil–
military equation continues to distort the political landscape, and
in the civil–military struggle for supremacy the most organized
institution—the army—almost always emerges successful vis-à-vis
a fragmented, short-sighted and polarized political elite.

Officials from the United States and India too openly spoke
of the need to reform the ISI. In September 2008, for instance,
Richard Boucher, the US assistant secretary of state, told the
Reuters news agency, 'It needs reform but there is no indication
of this happening yet.' The 26/11 Mumbai terror attacks provided
Boucher as well as the Indian authorities with another opportunity
to publicly criticize the ISI. Indian leaders insisted that the Lashkar-
e-Taiba terrorists involved in the attacks and their masterminds
acted under ISI instructions.

On numerous occasions, Indian officials and even Prime
Minister Manmohan Singh himself spoke of a 'thin line between
the state and non-state actors', when responding to the Pakistani
position that the terror acts were perpetrated by non-state actors.

On 18 January, the ISI was again on Boucher's agenda; the ISI
has links with the terrorist outfits based in the country and the
US is making an all out effort to ensure that these links are cut off
completely, the Indian news agency Asian News International said
in a report it lifted from the Pakistani newspaper the *Daily Times*.
Severing the link of the ISI from Pakistan-based terrorist groups
is a work in progress and the United States will make sure that it
is done effectively, Boucher said.

The Indian view that the perpetrators of the Mumbai attacks
had the support of Pakistan's state agencies is also supported by
the Afghan establishment and Pashtoon nationalists on both sides
of the Durand Line, and this breeds suspicions and fuels resentment

in both countries. The Indians and Afghans—followed by the US military and intelligence establishment as well—are paranoid about the role of the ISI in the region which they see as the root cause of all evils in the region, and thus needs to be controlled.

Pakistanis on the other hand proffer their own defence to these misgivings; most ISI officials I have been speaking to privately no longer deny their past involvement with militant groups such as the LeT, JeM or HM. They also acknowledge to previous contacts with Mulla Omar, Haqqani and Hekmetyar, and even to some of their Pakistani admirers currently known as the Taliban.

'Since the March 2004 Kaloosha operation the outlook on these militants has changed quite a bit,' a senior ISI official told me in early February 2009. 'Nobody wants the dark-age Taliban-style rule in Pakistan. Why would we support such forces which have now become a direct threat to our own existence', asked the official, while explaining the current thinking within the organization. He pointed out that sons and daughters of scores of senior ISI and army officers are studying either abroad or at prestigious Pakistani institutions. Why would they want radical and obscurantist militants to rule Afghanistan or Pakistan, asked the officer in a reference to thousands of Pakistani students, among them a big number from military families, studying in the American, Canadian and European universities.

During my meeting in January 2009 with General Kayani, we discussed the issue at length. One could not wish for Afghanistan what one did not want for Pakistan, Kayani said when I drew his attention to the much talked about 'doctrine of strategic depth in Afghanistan' that the ISI has allegedly been pursuing since the mid 1970s. The explanation that General Kayani offered was perhaps the first candid response by a serving army chief.

'We have been misunderstood as far as the notion of strategic depth is concerned. All we have been interested in is a stable and peaceful Afghanistan, a border that we don't have to worry about. I don't think anybody had ever even dreamed of occupying and treating Afghanistan as Pakistan's surrogate,' said the general.

'But we must be mindful to what is happening in our immediate neighbourhood,' Kayani emphasized.

The general went on to explain how the ISI, under his command as director general (between October 2004 and October 2007) and as the army chief since November 2007, has undergone a transformation in outlook and approach.

Regardless of the past relationships, implied the general, the ISI must move on in the national and regional interest. 'We cannot allow the likes of Baitullah Mehsud and Maulana Fazlullah to dictate to us on issues such as religion and governance. Neither do we want Afghanistan to descend into obscurantism,' explained the general.

Senior ISI officials at its walled headquarters in Islamabad, however, insist that as a counter-intelligence outfit they have to perform their primary tasks. 'Outsiders cannot deny us the right of doing what they themselves do,' said an official, pointing to the CIA, the MI6, Mosad and Indian intelligence outfits, which he said operate wherever they deem fit.

Only the months and years to come will demonstrate to what extent the ISI has really changed in outlook and approach and whether the US-led efforts to reform this institution will bear any fruit. Addressing the Indian concerns would be another challenge to an organization whom the United States extensively used twice— first for mounting the jihad against the Soviet Union in the 1980s and then for undoing the consequences of that jihad: waging the war against Al Qaeda and its hosts, the Afghan Taliban.

Who Funds Militancy in FATA?

There is little proof available on the foreign funding for Pakistani militants, but based on circumstantial evidence it is possible to point out the possible bankers of the insurgency that is taking place in an area that has become a battlefield for the competing interests of different nations—USA, Pakistan, India, Russia and Iran. In addition, indirectly, substantial amounts of USAID and donor money that is being routed through the Pakistani authorities at times end up with militants—either through ransom money given to criminal gangs for the release of hostages or to fund agreements aimed at peaceful coexistence.

In August 2008, Pakistan's mighty establishment came out with its 'own assessment' of the situation in the region, particularly in the context of the 7 July 2008 suicide bombing outside the Indian embassy in Kabul. A story in the mass circulation daily *News* (5 August 2008) quoted 'impeccable official sources' as saying that the military leadership provided 'strong circumstantial evidence of American acquiescence to terrorism inside Pakistan' to US Chairman Joint Chiefs of Staff Admiral Michael Mullen and CIA Deputy Director Stephen R. Kappes during their unscheduled visit to Rawalpindi on 12 July.

The establishment cited the case of Brahamdagh Bugti. Brahamdagh Bugti is one of Nawab Akbar Khan Bugti's grandsons and a prominent leader of the Jamhoori Watan Party, largely based in the south-western province of Balochistan. Nawab Akbar Khan Bugti was a veteran Baloch leader and a former governor of the province. Following differences with the federal government over provincial financial rights, Bugti had retreated into a cave in the Marri area, where he was later killed by military commandos in August 2006 under controversial circumstances.

Besides providing strong evidence on Bugti's presence in Afghan intelligence safe houses in Kabul, Pakistan army officials also placed his photographed visits to New Delhi and his written orders for terrorism in Balochistan before the American visitors to prove their point. Admiral Mullen and Kappes were also asked 'why the CIA-run predators and the US military did not swing into action when they were provided the exact location of Baitullah Mehsud' for example in May 2008, when Mehsud drove to a remote South Waziristan mountain post in his Toyota Land Cruiser to address the press and returned to his safe abode. About thirty journalists from Islamabad and Peshawar travelled to south Waziristan on Mehsud's invitation and this trip had become the subject of discussion at national and international levels because of the freedom with which Mehsud and his people moved.

Highly encrypted communications are available with Baitullah Mehsud, which enables him to collect real-time information on Pakistani troop movement from an unidentified foreign source without being intercepted by Pakistani intelligence, the papers wrote, raising suspicion for the first time to the possible involvement of the Americans with the militants. Several journalists, who were part of the delegation, also appeared surprised over the organizational abilities as well as the presence of the state-of-the-art means of communication. 'They appear ever ready and in an operational condition, something that is not possible without good financial resources,' recalled Shams Mohmand, who too was part of the journalists delegation in May. 'Baitullah's men told us they change vehicles after using them for a year or so because they have to be in top condition in this rugged and hilly terrain.'[1]

Where would they get all these things from, one of the journalists wondered after the visit; he gathered from the fighters accompanying Mehsud that their salaries start from USD 100 a month for foot-soldiers and USD 200 a month for senior ranks. Other organizations reportedly pay similar allowances, but they do not match the financial resources that the TTP possesses. However, they rely more on their ideological wherewithal and less on monetary incentives. Baitullah reportedly used to provide a travel allowance for fighters' missions into Afghanistan. Survivors would get a hefty payment after successful missions that lasted between four to six weeks.[2]

Suspicion on the possible backers of the militancy drives and dominates discussions within political and security circles, more so in Peshawar, where most of the security apparatus comprises locals, and who view things differently. 'We believe the Americans also have their fingers in the pie,' a very senior intelligence official had told me in Peshawar shortly after the journalists' interaction with Mehsud. He too recalled that the American drones rarely spare Al Qaeda operatives hiding in the tribal areas, evidenced from the five dozen missile strikes (during 2008) on targets in the Waziristan region that took out people like Abu Lait el Libi, Hamza Rabia and Abu Khabab al-Masri. Libi, who served as the Al Qaeda spokesman, was killed on 29 January 2008. Rabia was Al Qaeda's third in command while al-Masri was considered the top bomb-maker and explosives expert and carried a USD 5 million bounty on his head.

During an informal discussion at his official residence in Rawalpindi the army chief General Kayani opened his heart to a few journalists and vented his frustration. He admitted that the Americans 'embarrass us with precise locations of militants and their movements they obtain via their satellites . . . They confront us with satellite videos which track militants' movement from our areas into Afghanistan and vice versa, quite precise surveillance,'[3] explaining that American troops regularly coordinate with Pakistani forces this side of the border and usually have a 'very close track of things happening here'.

'US satellite and drone help is just a call away,' General Ahmed Shuja Pasha, director general military operations, said while explaining the precision with which the American technology hits its targets. This offer is part of the cooperation in the war against terrorism, he said. [4]

But many within the Pakistani establishment question why the US and NATO troops cannot use such 'actionable intelligence' against Taliban, and whether the Americans use these images only to embarrass Pakistani military top brass in order to extract more cooperation on Al Qaeda. Pakistani security officials have in fact intercepted a number of Afghan and Pakistani informers who were carrying gadgets that look ordinary but are extremely hi-tech, able to pinpoint locations and lead drones to suspects and their hideouts. Why are these tools not employed against Pakistani militants, is a million dollar question. Is it lack of American will, capability, shortage of resources, a matter of priorities or all by design? Do the Americans want to bleed the Pakistan army by ignoring the Taliban, who have given an extremely rough time to the army in Bajaur, Swat and Mohmand since November 2007?

A lot of speculation also goes into who is actually funding the militancy. Is it the Americans, the Indians, Iranians, the drug lords, the Afghans or the ISI itself? Or are the Taliban generating financial resources on their own through peace deals, abductions of important locals and foreigners and compromises that hinge on huge payments as 'compensation' to the victims and those affected by military operations?

During the Bajaur operation that continued through February 2009, army and intelligence officials also found traces of the shoulder-fired Stella missile, which is produced in Russia. In one of the incidents there, militants destroyed two Pakistan army tanks with the help of a Milan rocket, a shoulder-fired missile used by the Italian, French and the Indian armies. 'That the militants have access to these weapons also underscores the fact that they are certainly getting guidance, if not direct support, from elsewhere,' Ikram Sehgal, who specializes in security affairs and also owns Pakistan's largest private security agency, SMS, told me in Islamabad.

Based on what has appeared in the press so far, the question yields an interesting study.

Funding from Poppy Cultivation

Owais Ahmed Ghani, the governor of NWFP, believes that Baitullah Mehsud spends between Pakistani Rs 2.5–3 billion (USD 31–37 million) yearly on procurement of weapons, equipment and vehicles, and to maintain the families of injured or killed militants.

Talking to a national English daily in May 2008, Ghani opined that 'narco-dollars' were also feeding the militancy in both Pakistan and Afghanistan.[5]

A report on Afghanistan published by the US Bureau of International Narcotics and Law Enforcement Affairs in March 2008 had also concluded that 'Narcotics traffickers provide revenue and arms to the Taliban, while the Taliban provide protection to growers and traffickers and keep the government from interfering with their activities.'[6]

In 2007, the report pointed out, Afghanistan provided 93 per cent of the world's opium poppies, the raw material for producing heroin. Despite repeated calls for action against some very prominent figures, part of or indirectly linked with the Karzai government, nothing happened on the front. 'Drug lords benefit from chaos and insurgency whether in Afghanistan or tribal areas. Why wouldn't they spend part of their income on keeping the conditions volatile?' asked a security official in Peshawar.

Ghani said that continuous strife had turned Afghanistan practically into a narco state, with even influential people allied with the United States actively supporting and benefiting from it. He elaborated, 'Some sixty per cent of its economy is narcotics based, it's supplying ninety-five per cent of the world's demand for heroin and is valued by the United Nations at over 50 billion dollars per annum. Now that is a huge vested interest there. We think this one factor has totally negated all the gains that have been made. That is why much of the violence in Afghanistan is based on narcotics—their warlords, their drug lords.'[7]

He said the US and United Kingdom had ignored his 'early warning of serious repercussions if poppy cultivation was not curtailed after the outer of the Taliban regime'. The easy availability of narco dollars would not help end the militancy, he had warned.

In his 4 November 2008 meeting with US assistant secretary of state Richard Boucher at Islamabad, Pakistan President Asif Ali Zardari pointed out that Afghan drug traffickers were funding terrorists in Pakistan's tribal areas. Ever since Pakistan had stopped Afghan drug dealers from using its territory for smuggling, the smugglers had leaned on terrorists so that they could continue their trade. 'He urged the US to take action and to stop the infiltration of terrorists from Afghanistan into Pakistan,' an official at the President's House told the author. Boucher assured the President of 'all possible help'.

Frontier Corps: Also a Culprit?

Suspicions of abetment in violence and criminal activities under the cover of Taliban also fall on the paramilitary Frontier Corps (FC). 'We cannot rely on Pakistan to stop the traffic of terrorists crossing that border despite the strong statements of its leaders,' Senator Carl Levin, the Michigan Democrat who chairs the US Senate's committee on armed forces, told journalists after visits to Afghanistan and Pakistan.[8] Levin and other US defence officials suspected that Taliban fighters may also be getting assistance from Pakistan's army. They hinted that if suspicions were true, it might also jeopardize a multi-million-dollar US assistance package for the FC. 'If that's our intelligence assessment, then there's a real question as to whether or not we should be putting money into strengthening the Frontier Corps on the Pakistan side because if anything there's some evidence that the Pakistan army is providing support to the Taliban,' Levin was quoted as saying.

The United States set up a programme in 2007 to train and equip the paramilitary Frontier Corps, which comprises fifty-seven wings and recruits its manpower largely from within the tribal areas for border security and counter-terrorism. Under the programme, Washington planned to supply equipment like helmets and flak vests to the Frontier Corps, but would not provide weapons or ammunition.[9] The US army trainers were to instruct the paramilitary force for which Washington allocated USD 52.6 million in 2007, and a defence spending authorization bill for the 2009 fiscal year, which starts on 1 October, included USD 75 million for Frontier Corps training at the headquarters of the Swat Scouts in Warsak. The Americans also funded the construction of new quarters for the two dozen US military trainers who would routinely visit the facility as master trainers.

Timber Mafia?

Hameedullah Jan Afridi, the minister for environment from Khyber agency, offers his own interesting analysis. The 'timber mafia' is responsible for funding militancy in the NWFP and the provincial government is devising a strategy to crack down on the covert industry, the minister told Dawn News TV. The timber mafia is one of the many collaborators of the militants who help the merchants transport their goods safely. Yet people familiar with the tribal insurgency say that kidnappings for ransom, collection of transit fees and road taxes in areas under their control, or money collected in the name of compensation to the areas affected by military operations are all effective sources of income for the militants. 'We could discern from our conversations with Baitullah aides that he received 2.5 million dollars in return for the release of ambassador Tariq Azizuddin,' said one journalist who visited Kotkai for a meeting with the militant leader and spent two days with Baitullah and his fighters. 'Some of the Coalition Support Funds that Pakistan receives in return for the services it provides to the partners of the coalition against terrorism are also

used to pay ransom for the release of kidnapped civilian and
government officials,' said a local journalist, with good access to
the FATA secretariat.[10]

Foreign Sponsors: The USA?

Pakistani intelligence officials often speak of American designs
for the region. The theory of conspiracy essentially runs along
these lines: US forces are in Afghanistan for the long haul. They
also plan to expand their presence in Pakistan and to justify that
the US intelligence and security apparatus keeps churning out stories
on 'FATA as the sanctuary of the Taliban and Al Qaeda'. This, say
officials, would provide them with a justification to physically
intrude into Pakistani territory, even if apparently only for surgical
operations. Pakistanis fear the US establishment might also engineer
the balkanization and denuclearization of their country.

'A redrawn map of South Asia initially circulated as a theoretical
exercise in some American neoconservative circles precipitated
these apprehensions because it shows [Pakistan] truncated, reduced
to an elongated sliver of land with the big bulk of India to the east,
and an enlarged Afghanistan to the west,' said a report in the
New York Times on 23 November 2008. It added, 'It has fuelled a
belief among Pakistanis, including members of the armed forces,
that what the United States really wants is the break-up of Pakistan,
the only Muslim country with nuclear arms.'

The report alluded to the fears of the Pakistani military
planners that India and Afganistan are together out to destroy
Pakistan—with support from the United States.

'Some commentators suggest that the United States is actually
financing some of the Taliban factions. The point is to tie down
the Pakistani Army, they say, leaving the way open for the Americans
to grab Pakistan's nuclear weapons,' the paper said.

To keep the situation on the boil, say officials within the security
establishment as well as many Pakistani analysts, the US intelligence
agencies would like to use outfits like the TTP of Baitullah Mehsud.

He is being used as an instrument of America's Pakistan policy, which, these officials believe, also includes providing financial resources to Mehsud. 'Being responsible for the area, I often know where Baitullah is. Why is it impossible for the Americans to track and take him down?' asked a civilian intelligence official.[11]

These officials also raise questions over the unusually large number of American FBI and CIA spies present in Pakistan; by mid 2008, the number of US expatriates at the embassy in Islamabad had swollen to over 150, with dozens of them popping in and out of Peshawar at frequent intervals. The US consulate at Peshawar, local journalists point out, has also been buzzing with activity, and officials based there have been unusually enthusiastic about the government that is led by the ethnic Pashtoon nationalist and secularist Awami National Party (ANP). The ANP once looked up to Moscow for political ideological guidance and inspiration. But exclusion from power for over three decades, and US overtures, probably affected its socialist outlook. A long visit to the United States by the party chief Asfandyar Wali Khan and his close associates laid the foundation for a broader and more comprehensive understanding between the ANP and the US.

Soon after the 18 February 2008 elections, the ANP formed the government in the North West Frontier Province and US diplomats based both in Peshawar and in Islamabad demonstrated an unusual concern for the ANP government. Based on my personal experience, I can quote here with authority that the US diplomats not only promised long-term financial assistance to the provincial government, but also lobbied with intelligentsia and media professionals to assist the ANP in media management. 'We would like somebody to help the provincial government set up a permanent professional media management capacity,' a senior US diplomat based in Peshawar told me.

Pakistan security officials often speak about the position of Wackenhut, a US private security company, in Pakistan. In late 2007 Wackenhut's parent company, G4S, a mega US security agency, acquired over 50 per cent of the stake in SMS, a Karachi-based Pakistani private security company, and got an equal shareholding in Wackenhut, of which 86 per cent is owned by G4S.

Ikram Sehgal, who now also looks after the Wackenhut operations, told me that the US law requires its diplomatic missions to be guarded by an American company, hence the SMS and G4S deal. As a result of this deal, most SMS top management, particularly in Peshawar, underwent almost a complete change and a new set of officers took charge. Police sources confirmed that the new look SMS–G4S guards meanwhile man a number of buildings in the Hayatabad and Town residential townships, mostly housing US diplomats, USAID workers and businessmen. 'It all shows that the Americans have something up their sleeves and thus are converging in Peshawar,' opined Saleem Durrani, a retired ISI colonel, who told me that another US firm, Blackwater, which won notoriety in Iraq, was already in Pakistan, busy training Pakistani paramilitary Scouts at a facility, some twenty-two kilometres north-west of Peshawar.

'The current American agenda revolves around two points, that is, preventing a second 9/11 inside the United States and destroying those who possess the will and wherewithal to do so,' says Dr Farrukh Saleem, analyst and executive director of the Centre for Research and Security Studies, Islamabad.[12] To achieve these objectives, says Brigadier Mehmood Shah, a former security secretary for FATA, the Americans can co-opt some of the militants into their operational strategy and try to fix the anti-US Al Qaeda from within. If that happens, US funding would become a necessity for some of the militant outfits.

An Indian Hand?

Another theory singles out India as a source of funding for the militancy. Pakistan first allegedly supported the Sikh insurgency in eastern Punjab in the early 1980s and then created the Kashmir insurgency for India in the late 1980s. This is the line of argument according to which the Indian establishment would like to settle scores with its neighbour. The mounting Indian engagements in Afghanistan—monetary support worth over 500 million dollars between 2002 and 2007, personnel training and reconstruction projects—are all held out as the manifestation of an Indian desire to undermine Pakistani influence in Afghanistan.

The Indian establishment has always viewed Pakistan and its intelligence–security apparatus with great scepticism as far as its role in Kashmir is concerned. It believed that the ISI was deeply involved in the hijacking of the Indian passenger aircraft to Kandahar in December 1999.

The Pakistani establishment's suspicion of India has also been rooted in history, fuelled by the break-up of Pakistan in 1971, when its eastern wing became Bangladesh following months of insurgency, and a war with India. Pakistanis at that time had accused India of direct support to Bengali secessionists led by the nationalist Bengali leader Shaikh Mujeebur Rahman. 'India essentially mid-wifed the birth of Bangladesh by helping Mujeebur Rahman,' says Mushahid Hussein, former editor of the *Muslim* and a syndicated columnist turned politician.

I happened to be at Kandahar to cover the hijacking incident as it drew to a close on 31 December.

Shortly after successfully negotiating the release of some 150 countrymen onboard the hijacked Indian Airbus, one of India's senior negotiators wondered where the four militants swapped with the hostages and the hijackers themselves would end up and how this would affect the image of Pakistan. As expected, at least three of the released prisoners ended up in Pakistan, including Omar Saeed Sheikh (who was convicted for involvement in the execution of the American journalist Daniel Pearl), Maulana Masood Azhar and Mushtaq Zargar. So did the hijackers, presumably because the deal had provided them about ten hours to leave Afghanistan. And none of them ever reported at the Iranian border.

The hijacking episode severely bruised the Indian ego; despite agreeing to release militants from Indian jails, the then foreign minister Jaswant Singh sounded furious when responding to pointed questions by journalists present inside the Kandahar airport. 'We will never surrender to terrorists,' Singh said. 'But sir you have just surrendered to them by setting four terrorists free,' an American journalist replied. Keeping his cool, Singh chose not to respond to this observation and turned to another questioner.

These were testing times for the entire Indian team of negotiators. They managed the release of the aircraft and its passengers, but at a price. The hijacking, however, also opened the way for an Indo-US strategic dialogue, which contained counter-terrorism cooperation as one of the key components. 'We will absorb what you have done to us,' a senior member of the Indian team at Kandahar told me pointing to the aircraft, which was being readied for the flight back. 'But you will not be able to absorb what we might do to you.' His words clearly implied his belief that Pakistani agencies were behind the aircraft hijacking.

Subsequent to the hijacking, India focused on building extremely useful ties with the Karzai administration. The Indian official I had spoken with at Kandahar was also part of the Indian diplomatic offensive to win the hearts and minds of common Afghans; three Airbus aircraft, 400 passenger buses, almost a hundred vehicles—trucks, waste disposal trolleys, etc.—were donated to the Kabul municipality, and tens of thousands of tonnes of edibles were given along with the promise for cooperation in numerous fields. During 2002 and 2006 India was also credited for diverting Afghan government telecommunication to Indian satellites. Not only do the governmental communication routes go through the Indian satellites but even the official Radio and Television Afghanistan (RTA) uses the same satellite link for its TV and dozens of FM radio stations across Afghanistan. India also provides crucial training to certain wings of the Afghan forces, probably to the intelligence wing of the Afghan police. It is also currently constructing the new Parliament building in Kabul.

A civilian Pakistani intelligence official in Kabul[13] says that Indian diplomats played a crucial role in cultivating Afghan and

Pakistani human assets, which they believe have been in cahoots with people like Baitullah Mehsud to destabilize Pakistan. Interestingly, some of Baitullah's aides themselves brought up the issue of Indian involvement when the thirty-odd journalists travelled to South Waziristan in May 2008 for a meeting with their chief. 'The ameer [Baitullah] told us he declined an offer of support from India when his talks for a peace deal in South Waziristan with the Pakistan authorities hit snags,' one of the journalists, requesting anonymity, quoted a masked Mehsud fighter as saying.[14]

The offer, said the militant, came in March, when their people were in talks for the release of Tariq Azizuddin, the Pakistani ambassador to Kabul, through close associates of Jalaluddin Haqqani, the Afghan jihad and Taliban veteran. 'Baitullah mentioned this to the captive ambassador as well,' the TTP fighter told the journalist in question. The veracity of such statements obviously remains suspect until directly confirmed by the people or parties involved. Even Ambassador Azizuddin, during our meeting in Kabul in June, refused to comment on the issue, saying he would not like to add fuel to an already explosive situation. He restricted himself to what has been public knowledge for a couple of years, reiterating the Pakistan government's position that they suspect the Indian diplomatic missions in Afghanistan to be working against Pakistan's interest through militant groups. Most Pakistanis—civilian and military alike—believe that India, through its diplomats and agencies, has helped mount insurgencies on Pakistan—one in FATA and the other one in Balochistan. They believe the mysterious Balochistan Liberation Army receives financial and technical support from India, and that the Indian consulates in Jalalabad and Kandahar in particular are using anti-Pakistan elements to 'settle scores with Pakistan for its involvement with the Kashmir militancy'. The Pakistani establishment also draws on Indian media reports and expert opinions expressed therein to reinforce its allegations of Indian involvement in FATA and Balochistan.

A cover story of the *India Today* magazine (19 January 2009) appears quite instructive as far as Pakistan is concerned. 'There are lessons that India should learn from the 1971 conflict that was a result of careful strategy and planning. What the current situation calls for is a similar massive effort with a clear end goal in sight. If the 1971 objectives was to dismember Pakistan then the 2009 game plan should be to neutralise Pakistan so that it can no longer pose a threat to India,' wrote the magazine.

One of the four points of the action plan the magazine suggests is to 'exploit the divisions within Pakistan and expose its weaknesses in Balochistan, the FATA and POK. Drive a wedge between the army and the jihadis. Also win over the moderate democratic forces.'

The magazine also quotes G. Parthasarthy, former envoy to Pakistan, on how to deal with Pakistan: 'We need to build covert capabilities in Pakistan and mount psychological war. We should not shy away from political destabilization and inflicting economic damage to Pakistan. The time has come for us to say that Pakistan's border with Afghanistan is disputed.'

Such thoughts in one of India's most prestigious news magazines obviously works as canon fodder for those Pakistani institutions and individual groups which insist that politically strong and influential lobbies inside India are out to undermine Pakistan. They use these statements and articles to reinforce their argument that India is funding militants in FATA and Balochistan to bleed Pakistan.

Is the ISI in Cahoots with Militants?

Among the liberal political elite is the view that the Inter-Services Intelligence and the army sponsor militants to counter the US and retain their contacts with them for the day when the US might physically intervene in FATA or the Frontier Province.

'Militants—whether Haji Naamdar or Baitullah Mehsud— still serve as the extensions of a conservative and hawkish Pakistani establishment which keeps knitting alliances with them as and when necessary to pursue its objectives,' Afrasiab Khattak, the firebrand central leader of the Awami Nationalist Party now ruling the NWFP says. 'The entire world is astounded by our fixation with the cold war mode. We have developed an incredible capacity to live in unreality. This is indeed dangerous for any state system but it can be catastrophic for a state dancing in a minefield,' Khattak wrote in an article distributed over the net by Professor Barnett Rubin, the US expert of Afghan affairs.[15]

The ANP also resonates with accusations made in Washington and Kabul: the Al Qaeda sanctuaries in FATA are a direct source of instability and threat to the entire world and Pakistan needs to do more to destroy these havens of terrorists.

But both the army chief General Ashfaq Kayani and the head of the ISI, General Ahmed Shuja Pasha, have repeatedly spurned these allegations. 'Baitullah Mehsud is certainly not a friend. We will take him out whenever possible,' Kayani said, when I specifically asked him whether Mehsud and his affiliates were friends or foes, during a meeting in January 2009 at his Rawalpindi residence.

'I have also heard these perceptions. My field commanders and civilians keep conveying to me anecdotal evidence about the ISI's contacts and cooperation with militants like Mehsud and Fazlullah in Swat. But let me tell you categorically, we have nothing to do with these people, and there is little I can do about perceptions,' said the general, who also recalled a meeting with the civilian home ministry and police officials during which he instructed the ISI and Military Intelligence officials not to meddle in the work of police.

'When I was heading the ISI, I requested a meeting with the civilian security apparatus in the home ministry and also took the military field officers along. In the presence of everyone, I told the secretary interior and the entire police high command that if someone from the ISI interferes in your work, call me directly on my cell,' Kayani explained.

General Pasha was equally vociferous in his rejection of his organization's links with militants. 'We would obviously like to fix these rogues. They are killing our own people and are certainly not the friends of this country,' Pasha told me during a meeting at the General Headquarters in Rawalpindi in early October 2008.

In late November 2008, I had an interesting encounter with a FATA journalist. To my repeated queries on possible motives for the ISI to support militants, my journalist friend came up with answers that were premised in the period between 2004 and 2007. He quoted ISI and military officials and also referred to the contents of several meetings with them to support his arguments on the involvement of ISI with militants such as Baitullah Mehsud and Afghan war veterans like Jalaluddin Haqqani.

Time and again during the conversation, I drew his attention to the massive casualties that the Pakistan army has taken, particularly since early 2007, including the abduction of over 250 soldiers by TTP in South Waziristan in August that year. I repeatedly confronted him with more or less the same question: will the ISI and the military still support a force which is striking the very foundation of the country, destroying schools and hospitals, butchering and executing soldiers, killing civilians and slaughtering even tribal elders? I also recalled that more than half the suicide attacks during 2008 had clearly targeted armed forces personnel and government servants. Is the ISI itself becoming the nemesis of Pakistan by indulging with a force as destructive as the TTP?

When left with no argument, the journalist asked, 'What about the possibility of the ISI being on the payroll of the American CIA? Perhaps the CIA is paying our intelligence to create unrest and turmoil in Pakistan?' Realizing I could not possibly influence deep-seated perceptions grounded in recent history, I thanked my friend for his thoughts and left his office.

Compensation or Appeasement?

The print and electronic media in late May 2008 highlighted the news of large amounts of money being handed to Baitullah's aides, following their withdrawal from areas like Makeen, Kotkai and Spinkai Raghzai; under an understanding, the Pakistan army and the political administration provided tens of millions of rupees in compensation, albeit through Baitullah's people. The latter had insisted that the government distribute the compensation through him. He distributed Rs 10 million among the affected tribes in Kotkai town, which suffered badly during the military operation with almost half the buildings in the town destroyed.

A Pashtoon journalist who spent a few days in Wana, South Waziristan, quoted a Pakistani official who wanted to remain anonymous as saying that the government paid some Rs 200 million (USD 2.5 million) to the Taliban to compensate for the dead and wounded in the Zalzala operation. Only half the amount, he said, was ultimately used for compensation.

Sources in Wana claim that Mulla Nazir, who drove out Uzbek militants wary of Pakistan army in a fierce battle in March 2007, also received several million rupees in recognition of his services.

Personal friends and sources in the region also say Baitullah Mehsud too has received several acknowledgements from authorities, including a big piece of land in Dera Ismail Khan, and several development schemes through his cover men, who also act as interlocutors in talks with the government, which prompts one to ask whether these are bribes to militants, their appeasement, or an indirect funding of their activities.

A lot of foreign development funds for FATA are being routed either through the FATA secretariat or through various security outfits including the FC. 'And this is the money that is usually used as payouts to the militants as part of deals or unwritten understanding,' insisted a friend privy to how the Taliban have been extracting money from government officials. He believes that donor agencies do know where some of their funding ends up. But the 'burden of circumstances' makes them accept this.

All negotiations or undeclared deals for 'peaceful existence' between the government and militants usually encompass hefty payments to the Taliban and their leaders. While some of the 'schemes approved by the government' might be under execution, most existed only on paper, says a source from Wana and Makeen, South Waziristan. Here are some examples:

- In November 2007, Baitullah Mehsud received Rs 50 million (USD 600,000) for the release of about 280 soldiers whom he had ambushed in late August 2007, in exchange for the release of twenty-five of his associates charged with various crimes.
- In early 2008, Malik Amir Mohammad, a close aide to Baitullah Mehsud, received funds in the name of several development schemes including for animal husbandry and the construction of schools and roads in his area.
- Noor Wali, in charge of Baitullah Mehsud's vice and virtue department in the Gurgury village (South Waziristan), received Rs 9 million (USD 12,500) in the name of a water development scheme.
- Azmatullah, Baitullah Mehsud's commander at Spinkai village, received Rs 10 million (USD 125,000) in the name of a water supply scheme.
- Maulana Ikramuddin, considered a trusted aide to Baitullah Mehsud, was given several million rupees for the installation of a tube well, the construction of a road and a school in the area. He was also promised a job to any of his nominees in the local militia force called Khasadars.
- Malik Masood Mehsud Khan, another close aide to Baitullah Mehsud, was rewarded with funds for animal husbandry and a hospital.
- Malik Roman Malikshahi, also a Baitullah Mehsud associate, was given funds for a medical dispensary and a water channel at his village, Danga.
- Mailk Saifurrehman, another trusted aide to Baitullah Mehsud, got funds for a middle school and tube well.
- Sangeen Zadran, an Afghan aide to Baitullah Mehsud, also got a road construction contract worth Rs 800 million.

As for other militants, Mulla Nazir, head of his own Tehreek-e-Taliban (Wana valley), receives a 50,000-rupee monthly stipend from the administration. For his drive against Uzbeks in March 2007, Nazir received Rs 5 million as personal reward from the authorities.

One of Nazir's allies, Mulla Sharif, gets Rs 25,000 monthly while the authorities gave him Rs 20 million for constructing a hospital in his hamlet, Sheen Warsak near Wana.

'A good part of these payments usually end up with Baitullah Mehsud and constitute an important source of funding for him,' said a journalist from the area, now settled in Peshawar, requesting anonymity. It is certainly appeasement, if not a direct source of financing for the TTP, he said.[16]

The Pakistan military spokesman Major General Athar Abbas denied any connection with the payments to the militants. 'As far as I know, the FATA Secretariat and political administration are involved in the process of compensating people affected by the conflict,' Abbas told a daily.[17] Officials at the FATA secretariat, which functions under the direct supervision of the provincial governor in Peshawar, also rebutted media reports that TTP and other Taliban militants were paid huge sums as 'appeasement'. Even if this has happened, it would hardly go into the books because these payments are done from discretionary funds of the political agent or from the secret funds available to intelligence agencies.[18]

Journalists and intelligence officials based in Peshawar and other NWFP districts such as Kohat, Dera Ismail Khan and Bannu insist that narcotics and abductions for ransom are also a big source of funding for the militants.

'Smaller kidnapping gangs sell their hostages to bigger ones if they fear they have kidnapped someone too high profile for them to hold. This is what happened to Tariq Azizuddin [the Pakistani ambassador to Kabul],' wrote the monthly magazine *Herald*, published from Karachi, in its October 2008 issue.

The reporter, Zahir Shah, also quoted a Taliban commander on how they use drugs money for their jihad. 'A Taliban leader based in Mohmand agency tells the *Herald* that the use and sale of drugs for serving the cause of "jihad" is not *haram* [forbidden]. He claims that this cash crop is god's gift to fight the infidels. Protection has also been provided to timber and trucking mafia involved in transporting smuggled goods,' wrote the magazine, corroborating what the federal minister Hameedullah Jan Afridi believes.

As a whole, the presence of American and international troops across the Durand Line, the activities and shelters of the Al Qaeda and Taliban militants in FATA, the massive deployment of Pakistani troops on the 2560-kilometre border with Afghanistan, the increasing desire on India's part to assert itself as a major regional player, the Iranian proximity to an American-dominated Afghanistan and the omnipresent narcotics trade have turned the entire tribal region into a battlefield of competing interests, with many players fighting for their piece of pie. This war of interests also obscures the view, making it difficult to pinpoint who is working for whom and at whose cost. What is nevertheless easier to assess is Al Qaeda's presence in FATA which it has turned into a hunting and training ground for recruits it deploys against the United States and other NATO members; these western allies ostracize Al Qaeda for its 'global anti-western campaign' and project it as the single largest threat to world peace. Al Qaeda, on the other hand, curses the entire west as 'evil and threat to the Muslim world'. In between, several players are fighting it out against one another.

This confusion was best exemplified by one of my friends in the security establishment. During several sittings on the nature and components of the insurgency in FATA, I confronted him with provoking questions but at the end of our last session on the subject my friend admitted in frustration, 'I am probably as confused as you are . . . it is murky and obscure . . . sorry.'

Epilogue
FATA Terror Spreads All Over

'In the nearly eight years since 9/11, al Qaeda and its extremist allies have moved across the border to the remote areas of the Pakistani frontier. This almost certainly includes al Qaeda's leadership: Osama bin Laden and Ayman al-Zawahiri. They have used this mountainous terrain as a safe haven to hide, train terrorists, communicate with followers, plot attacks, and send fighters to support the insurgency in Afghanistan. For the American people, this border region has become the most dangerous place in the world.'

This conclusion drawn by the US President Barack Obama in his 27 March 2009 speech summed up FATA's journey in the past few decades—from a launching pad for the US-led anti-Soviet Russian jihad in the early 1980s to a 'safe haven and sanctuary for international terrorists aligned under the al Qaeda flagship' in 2009.

While announcing his new strategy for Afghanistan and Pakistan—also called the Af-Pak—Obama said the forces holed up in the tribal areas were not 'simply an American problem— far from it'. 'It is, instead, an international security challenge of the highest order. Terrorist attacks in London and Bali were tied to al Qaeda and its allies in Pakistan, as were attacks in North Africa and the Middle East, in Islamabad and Kabul. If there is a major attack on an Asian, European, or African city, it—too—is likely to have ties to al Qaeda's leadership in Pakistan. The safety of people around the world is at stake,' Obama declared.

This pronouncement underscored a bitter reality for Pakistanis; from Afghanistan and the tribal areas, FATA, the war theatre was now shifting to their country, with Robert Gates, the secretary of defence, and Richard Holbrooke, the special envoy for Pakistan and Afghanistan, threatening a hot pursuit of al Qaeda 'wherever found'.

Within two weeks of Obama's Af-Pak policy announcement, Pakistan experienced a dramatic surge in violence; from Waziristan to Peshawar to Lahore to Islamabad and Chakwal, dozens of people perished, either in suicide attacks or in drone strikes. The primary target of the suicide bombers were either police or paramilitary forces while the drone-fired Hellfire missiles targeted al Qaeda operatives in hiding in various pockets of FATA.

The battle between the US-led coalition forces including those of Pakistan and the radical militants led by Al Qaeda seemed to have put Pakistan on fire. Statistics on the spiral of violence was mind-boggling. In the first six months of 2009, militants staged at least thirty-seven suicide attacks and carried out another 225 bombings and ambushes, killing close to 600 people. The deadliest of these suicide attacks took place on 27 March at a mosque in the tribal Khyber agency; as close to 200 people began offering Friday prayers, the bomber pulled the trigger of the suicide jacket, leaving behind a trail of death and destruction with about eighty-five casualties.

On 30 March, terrorists raided and seized a Police Training Academy on the outskirts of Lahore, the capital of Punjab province; the siege ended through a commando operation that lasted about eight hours, with twelve casualties including four terrorists. Earlier in the month, on 3 March, an equally dramatic commando-style attack in the heart of Lahore had left the entire security establishment stunned, and badly bruised; shortly after nine in the morning, about a dozen heavily armed young attackers ambushed the convoy of vehicles carrying the Sri Lankan cricket team members to the Gadaffi stadium. Most players escaped unhurt. As the escort police engaged the attackers, the driver sped the bus away from the scene and rushed into the stadium. All terrorists managed to flee after killing about ten policemen, and injuring many. One of the umpires was seriously injured as a bullet pierced through his lungs.

The brazen incident left everybody baffled and awestruck over the massive security lapse, particularly when the Sri Lankan cricketers had volunteered to play in Pakistan after the Australian and New Zealand teams had cancelled their visits in view of the precarious security situation.

Local police was still grappling with the aftermath of the attack on Sri Lankan cricketers, when terrorists struck at the Police Academy in Lahore. A day later, Baitullah Mehsud himself came on phone and stunned many in and outside the country by owning responsibility for the commando raid and the ensuing bloody siege on the police academy.

'We did it as a retaliation for US missile strikes off drones inside the Pakistani territory,' said Mehsud, the first such admission he made himself. But he did not stop there. 'Soon we will launch an attack in Washington that will amaze everyone in the world,' Mehsud said in an interview with the US-funded Dewa Radio and also identified the White House as one of the targets.

'He sounded unrepentant and pretty cool,' the journalist Alamgir Bhittani told me of his conversation with the diminutive Mehsud on 31 March. 'He was cutting jokes, offered me blessings and vowed to kill more.' Bhittani told the *Herald*, 'I thought I was talking to a man to whom life and death don't matter at all.'

Only a week before the Lahore attack, the US had announced a USD 5 million bounty on Mehsud's head, describing him as a clear threat to American interests in the region. This way, the US administration finally addressed a long-standing concern that figured in many meetings between the military officials in particular; Pakistani authorities have for long been suspicious of Baitullah Mehsud's connections with 'external forces' and had openly expressed their surprise over why the US drones never targeted Mehsud.

Mehsud has certainly inflicted losses on Pakistani security forces, the police and the paramilitary being his special targets; since 2006 Mehsud and allies have killed close to 3000 policemen and paramilitary security personnel. It is also suggested that secrecy at these institutions is still extremely compromised, and Al Qaeda supporters, or those inspired by them, continue to leak crucial information, enabling militants to target key installations. Operations against Baitullah Mehsud and his strongholds are now under way denoting perhaps a change of heart in Islamabad.

In early April, another wave of suicide strikes shocked Pakistanis. On 4 April a suicide bomber drove his vehicle into a group of civilians on the side of the road in Miranshah, North Waziristan, killing eight people, including schoolchildren. The same evening, a suicide bomber struck in the posh F-7 neighbourhood of Islamabad, killing eight paramilitary security officers assigned to guard foreign diplomats and affluent residents. As if not enough, another bomber blew himself up at the entrance to a crowded Shiite mosque in Chakwal, south of the capital on 5 April, leaving at least twenty-six people dead. Chakwal, a town that has historically had strong ties to the Pakistan army, had thus far been one of the most peaceful towns near the famous Salt Range, where salt mines count among the largest in the world. The same day, Hakeemullah Mehsud claimed responsibility for the suicide strikes in Islamabad and Chakwal.

Hakeemullah, based in the Orakzai agency south-west of Peshawar, said the Islamabad bombing had been in retaliation for an attack against him by a pilotless American aircraft on 1 April, which had killed at least ten people.

Hakeemullah Mehsud also promised two bombings a week within Pakistan in what he called 'revenge' against Pakistan for the American missile strikes, which not only stirred controversies at the top diplomatic level but also stoked anti-American sentiment.

Between 14 January 2006 and 8 April 2009, CIA-operated Predators and drones conducted about sixty-one cross-border strikes. Only ten of these hit their actual targets, killing some fourteen Al Qaeda leaders but they also took lives of over 700 innocent Pakistani civilians. Just the two drone attacks in January and October 2006 killed 100 civilians, while three strikes in 2007 resulted in the death of seventy Pakistani civilians. Most of these attacks were based either on flawed intelligence or result of delayed information and action, which resulted in the deaths of non-combatants.

'There exists a big gap on the issue of drone attacks which impinge on our sovereignty,' foreign minister Shah Mehmood Qureshi told media at the ministry of foreign affairs on 7 April, as a displeased Richard Holbrooke and Admiral Mike Mullen, chairman joint chiefs of staff, looked on. Moments before this press stake-out, officials told me later, the US visitors had exchanged words that were certainly not pleasant.

Drone Attacks between 2006 and 2009

Year	No. of Attacks	Civilians Killed	Al-Qaeda Dead
2006	2	98	0
2007	3	66	0
2008	36	385	12
2009	14	152	2

Resentment over the US drone strikes and growing differences over how to handle militancy notwithstanding, the course of events, particularly since the first major Al Qaeda–military standoff at Kaloosha, South Waziristan, in March 2004, left little doubt that forces that had taken birth and sheltered in FATA for years had turned on their own mentor, Pakistani security forces.

Taliban/Al Qaeda: Anti-US–NATO or Anti-Pakistan?

Although, for several months, the Pakistan army had been ranting about its successes in the Bajaur agency, on 10 April, Maulvi Faqir Mohammad, the TTP chief in the agency, sprung a surprise on the authorities by declaring enforcement of sharia in his area. In a 40-minute speech he delivered through his illegal FM radio channel, Mohammad barred women from leaving homes without a male relative. He also asked men not to shave beards and warned people against accepting financial assistance from a government income support scheme launched in the name of former prime minister Benazir Bhutto for vulnerable families. The TTP leader vowed his group would strictly enforce the Islamic laws in the region.

In order to ensure transparency and effectiveness of the scheme, the government is distributing money among housewives but Faqir Mohammad misconstrued it as an 'attempt to mislead simple women of the tribal region'. Preparation of lists of people supporting the Benazir Income Support Programme and non-governmental organizations is already under way, Mohammad told awestruck listeners in Bajaur.

The brazen pronouncement, coupled with the Taliban ascendancy in neighbouring Swat valley, demonstrated how the tentacles of militants were fast spreading all around, with the military and civilian authorities practically looking on silently, perhaps hoping a miracle might help turn the situation around.

Meanwhile, the situation in Bajaur, Mohmand and the Waziristan region remained explosive because militants sensed the increasing American pressure on the border region, manifest in the drone attacks. A statement by a US army officer explained why the Taliban militants increasingly view and treat both the Pakistan army and the US–NATO troops based on the other side of the Durand Line as their common enemy.

As the militancy raged in various parts of FATA and Taliban stalked the streets of Swat, Pakistan's national legislature—National Assembly—recommended that the President sign (13 April 2009) the Nizame Adl Regulation. President Asif Ali Zardari signed the Regulation within hours of the recommendation by the Parliament and thus sanctified the agreement that had been signed on 16 February between the provincial government and Maulana Sufi Mohammad, the elderly leader of the Tehreek-e-

Nifaze Shariate Mohammadi (TNSM). This agreement had provided for the enforcement of the Islamic justice system—Nizame Adl, a demand that had been resonating in the region since the mid 1990s.

Most civil society organizations as well as foreign governments had opposed the deal as 'a surrender to militants'. This also explained why Zardari was reluctant to put his stamp of approval on it. In Washington, a White House spokesman, Robert Gibbs, went public in criticizing the Nizame Adl Regulation as 'against human rights and democracy'. 'Solutions involving security in Pakistan don't include less democracy and less human rights. The signing of that denoting strict Islamic law in Swat valley goes against both these principles,' Gibbs said (AFP, 14 April). Yet the provincial government insisted the deal must be honoured to bring peace back to Swat and protect human lives. TTP militants, too, made similar demands and threatened to return to violence if the President did not approve the regulation.

Volatile conditions in Peshawar, the provincial capital, Swat—once considered the second most developed in the province because of its tourist attraction—and in most of FATA not only traumatized the non-combatants, but also forced an unprecedented exodus of people from the affected areas; unabated fighting between the militants and security forces, spate of suicide and sniper attacks not only compelled businesses and educational institutions to shut down but also displaced over a million people from Bajaur, South Waziristan, North Waziristan, Kurram, Mohmand agencies and Swat—all looking for safety. Those who could not continued to live at the whims of the militants and the mercy of the security forces. By mid 2009 the army had moved into Swat to end the reign of terror by the TTP leader Maulana Fazlullah.

An ascendant Taliban movement, their damning Islamic propaganda—wrapped in religious ideology and loaded with innuendos against the existing symbols of state, government institutions such as the police and security forces—were all signs that the terror born in FATA was fast on the move.

The ever growing Indian presence in Afghanistan—the building of roads, its two consulates in two cities close to Pakistan, the telecommunication facilities its satellites offer to Afghanistan and involvement in infrastructure projects—makes Pakistan believe it is being encircled by a tripodal Indo-Afghan-American alliance.

Pakistani intelligentsia as well as the establishment believe Washington must get India to back off in Afghanistan if it wants Islamabad to think away from its eastern border with India.

'But to build this trust Pakistan needs to change its threat perception, which is right now focused on India and needs to be refocused on the western border where the Taliban and Al Qaeda activists operate. This starts, frankly—all of this in Pakistan begins with them embracing the idea that the biggest threat to their country's very existence is the internal extremist threat rather than the threat to their east,' General David Petraeus, commander, US Central Command, told a US Senate hearing on the new strategy for Afghanistan in early April 2009.

The American advice to Pakistan would have made sense under normal circumstances but it is not likely to evoke interest within the Pakistani establishment given the current low intensity insurgency that this country faces, and the nature of its complicated relationship with India.

Recapturing FATA from the clutches of extremist militants, and preventing more lands and towns from drifting into Taliban violence and Al-Qaedaization necessitates a comprehensive, multi-pronged response by members of the international coalition against terrorism—an endeavour whose success hinges on mutual trust and sincerity and not mutual suspicion and mistrust.

As of 2009, the writing on the wall was clear; the Godzilla, born out of the anti-Soviet jihad, funded by the American CIA and executed by Pakistan's might ISI, had meanwhile multiplied and thrown up scores of smaller godzillas all around. They are now threatening the very existence of the country that had midwived their creation.

For years, Pakistani agencies abetted in indoctrinating, motivating and training jihadi cadres for export in the neighbourhood—to Jammu and Kashmir and Afghanistan. But since the turn of events since 9/11 in 2001, many of the godzillas went their own way, some, inspired by Al Qaeda, also co-opting suicide bombing into their 'jihad'.

These human bombs, originally designed and nurtured to destroy enemies of Islam and Pakistan, have meanwhile started exploding themselves inside their own country, killing their fellow Muslims—civilians and military alike. The terror that was planned and nurtured in FATA is now knocking at our own doors.

Appendix 1
FATA: The Background

In September 2005 during a visit to Miranshah, the administrative headquarters of North Waziristan, I came across the news of a bomb blast near an electricity distribution facility owned by Pakistan's state-owned electricity and water resource development organization. The impact of the blast disabled the transformer, plunging Mirali village into darkness. A day later, the villagers received an order from the political agent (PA), the administrative head of the area, to hand over the person responsible for the blast or face a penalty of Rs 5 million (approximately USD 65,000).

'No need to panic,' said my host, Mehfoozullah. 'We will negotiate it downwards with the authorities,' he said, explaining that every tribe maintains a so-called 'national fund' to meet such contingencies. All members of the tribe—businessmen, farmers, transporters and shopkeepers—contribute a certain fraction of their income to the national fund to take care of such 'crises'. Mefoozullah later told me the tribe paid just about a fifth of what the PA had demanded.

In a similar incident a couple of years ago, a day before the NWFP governor was to inaugurate a new telephone exchange in Mirali, unknown attackers blew up the main phone line distribution boxes, thereby sabotaging the programme. Outraged, the PA called for the elders of the tribe, demanding the perpetrators be produced, or the tribe would face a fine of Rs 15 million. After several rounds of negotiations, the PA agreed to bring the penalty down to a million rupees.

Mirali has been a hotbed of militancy and militants since early 2002, when the retreating Taliban and Al Qaeda began to take refuge there. Dozens of US missile attacks and scores of Pakistan army operations in Mirali also bore out the view that radical Islamists had gathered in this small town. The situation in FATA today is also a result of its unique history, administrative structure and culture.

History

The Federally Administered Tribal Areas (FATA) of Pakistan are spread over an area of 27,220 kilometres, which constitutes 3.5 per cent of Pakistan's landmass. It runs in a narrow belt along the 2430-kilometre Pak-Afghan border, popularly known as the Durand Line, named after Sir Mortimer Durand, who surveyed and established it during 1890–94.[1] Although part of Pakistan, the FATA region functions as a semi-autonomous area, run under special laws designed and implemented by the British in 1901. FATA served as the buffer between the British Empire and Russian-influenced Afghanistan. The system of governance established by the British in the early twentieth century continues to operate in tandem with the jirga (assembly of tribal elders) that determines the law and its execution when necessary.

The 1998 national census puts the FATA population at 3.2 million (the current estimate is 3.5 million), that is, less than 2.5 per cent of Pakistan's total population. Official statistics notwithstanding, the literacy rate is known to be dismally low because of the region's poor education facilities. The socio-economic infrastructure is also extremely deficient with inadequate medical cover, insufficient water and few roads. Less than 10 per cent of the land area is cultivable.[2] Most people live off smuggling 'custom-free' goods from

Afghanistan into Pakistan, car theft rackets, drug trafficking from Afghanistan and the illegal sale of locally made weapons.

Geographically, FATA runs north to south, forming a wedge between Afghanistan and the settled areas of the NWFP. As many as sixty Pashtoon tribes inhabit the FATA lands. The numbers rise above 400 if all sub-clans are counted. The largest and most influential tribes are the Afridis, Bangash, Daurs, Mehsuds, Mohmands, Orakzais, Safis, Shinwaris, Tarklanis, Turis, Utmankhels, Ahmadzai Wazirs (South Waziristan) and Utmanzai Wazirs (North Waziristan).

The Durand Line, which divided Pashtoon tribes between British India and Afghanistan in 1893, has always been viewed with resentment by the Pashtoons. After Pakistan's emergence in 1947, this line became a major source of tension between Pakistan and Afghanistan.[3]

Despite being a legal-geographical part of Pakistan under Article 247 of the Constitution, the FATA region remains in the clutches of an entrenched political administration, which, in association with 35,000-odd tribal elders called maliks, perpetuates a system that sometimes requires Pakistani nationals to seek permission to visit these areas. The rules for the media and non-Pakistanis are even more stringent.

The alliance of bureaucrats and the maliks opposes any attempt to reform the legal-administrative structure. The existing set of laws called Frontier Crimes Regulation (FCR) gives the office of the political agent (PA) not only great power, but also funds that are not auditable or extremely difficult to audit. Moreover, the maliks, too, enjoy a privileged status within the tribal society which they are loath to relinquish.

Laws

The Frontier Crimes Regulation is a complex body of laws which comprises six chapters, sixty-four sections and three schedules, the FCR 40 being the most notorious. This talks of collective responsibility and allows the PA to punish any tribe or sub-tribe if he deems fit. This means if someone damages government property in Area A, the PA can punish people from Area B on mere suspicion and impose heavy penalties. If a crime takes place in area C, the tribe living in the area is responsible for redemption, even though rivals might be responsible for the act.[4]

FCR 40 empowers the political administration to jail anyone for three years without assigning a reason. The PA and his subordinates can arrest members of any tribe who are 'accused of the breach of peace or for the purpose of maintaining good behaviour to execute a bond' (sections 40, 41), failing which the accused or male members of his tribe can be imprisoned for up to three years (sections 43, 44) without any right of appeal in any civil or criminal court (section 48). The term of imprisonment can be extended if the magistrate (who is the PA) is of the opinion that it should be extended further (section 45).

Frequently this section is invoked when the PAs arrest people who raise their voice against their authority. The PA has to essentially conduct business with the border tribes on behalf of the central government of Pakistan. However, under the FCR the PA, usually a civil servant, acts as a prosecutor, investigator and judge in dealing with crimes. He nominates members of a council of elders, locally known as jirga (section 8), to inquire into a dispute. However, the findings of the council of elders are not binding and the PA can reject the jirga's recommendations. Nobody can question him nor can his acts be challenged in any civil or criminal court (section 10, 60).

Sections 20 and 21 allow an entire tribe that is considered hostile or unfriendly to be jailed, their property seized or confiscated or both, and even allows their houses to be demolished (section 33, 34). Fines can be imposed and recovered from the whole tribe that an accused person belongs to (section 22); if a tribe is held to be guilty of conniving at crimes, the money that its members earn from government schemes or jobs can be forfeited under section 26.

These sections are called Territorial Responsibility (see below), implying that every person of a tribe is responsible for any crime that takes place in the territory of the tribe.

Additionally, tribesmen living within eight kilometres of the border of the district cannot undertake any construction without permission; moreover, if on military grounds a village or habitation is found dangerous, it has to be removed. An infamous clause directs that no hujra can be constructed or used as such without the approval of the PA. The hujra is central to Pashtoon culture— it is a social meeting place, usually in front of the house, with an opening to the main street. Residents of the area usually get together in hujras to watch TV, listen to the radio, help resolve conflicts and discuss the issues of the day.

Under clause 40, the PA can ask any member of the tribe to provide security, if he determines this would prevent murder or sedition. If a person fails to do so or the PA finds the securities inadequate, the targeted person may be imprisoned for three years. Such a period of imprisonment can be extended to a total of six years. And the PA also decides if the imprisonment is to be simple or rigorous. These provisions continue even though they are in violation of the Constitution of Pakistan (articles 8–28) and the Universal Declaration of Human Rights (UDHR).

The PA is thus the 'pivot of the entire administrative set-up of the tribal areas', says Khalid Aziz, an analyst who had held the position in the early years of his career. 'The PA controls, governs and rules the areas with the help of the FCR. The PA administers justice in accordance with local and tribal customs. He avoids interfering with domestic affairs of the tribes who are regulated by an unwritten "code of honour" which the tribesmen guard fiercely.'

Rule 40 of the FCR empowers the PA or the assistant political agent (APA) to force a person to execute a three-year bond, with or without sureties, for good behaviour. The objective of such bonds, which can be revived after three years, is said to be to maintain peace and to prevent warring parties from violence. Offenders can be arrested any time, either on suspicion or on the basis of information provided to the authorities by paid informers, usually from within the community. Granting bail against personal or third-party bonds and awarding punishment including up to three years of jail without assigning a reason is within the purview of the PA or his deputy. The informers are paid handsome amounts from the PA's secret funds, depending upon the nature and circumstances of the case. The bail bond is confiscated to the state and the bail amount realized from the culprit in case the terms of bond are violated.

The jirgas of local elders and maliks can intervene to the extent they can plead for the convict to be forgiven. Sometimes the jirga also invokes the tribal tradition of 'Nanewati' to pre-empt the conviction of an individual wanted by the authorities. Nanewati is the practice where, in the presence of the tribal elders, the wanted person simply appears before the PA, pleads guilty and also asks for forgiveness.

There is no appeal against any decision, order, decree or sentence passed by the PA or the APA. Though the final review of such orders and sentences rests with an FCR Appellate Tribunal, few cases make it to the tribunals. Appeals against decisions by the PA or his deputies can take years before the tribunal gives a verdict.

The Law and Order Department for FATA was created in 2006. According to the FATA website (www.fata.gov.pk) its functions include '. . . [to] establish writ of the government, ensure security and protection of tribesmen, readdress grievances of the people, framing rules for Khassadars/Levies, ensuring a poppy-free FATA, administrating justice through courts, ensuring availability and control of essential commodities, livestock etc to the tribesmen, dealing with emergencies/natural calamities . . .'

FATA elects members to the federal legislature through adult franchise. The system of devolution introduced elsewhere in the country in 2001 by means of provincial Local Government Ordinances (LGOs) has not been extended to the tribal areas. A separate LGO for FATA has been drafted and is awaiting promulgation. A system of partial local-level governance does, however, operate through councils in the tribal agencies and the six Frontier Regions (FRs). Elected councillors are involved in various aspects of development planning and decision making.

Security Apparatus

A number of law enforcement agencies currently operate in the tribal areas. Led by the officers of the Pakistan army, the Frontier Corps (FC) is the principal force responsible for law and order in FATA and is required to man the border between Afghanistan and Pakistan. Every agency has at least one FC comprising a minimum of five wings known either as Scouts or Rifles—for example, the Bajaur Scouts or Mohmand Rifles. The FC chief, usually a major general from the Pakistan army, is called the inspector general. Another law enforcement agency in FATA is the Frontier Constabulary; its officers are from the police and the ranks are filled by tribesmen or personnel from the settled districts of NWFP. The Frontier Constabulary is required to man the border between FATA and the settled districts of NWFP—the Frontier Regions.

Along with the military-led Frontier Corps and the police-led Frontier Constabulary, various militias, usually known as Khassadars drawn from local tribes, are responsible for the administrative control in the region. In fact the Khassadars form the first tier of security inside the tribal areas. The institution of Khassadari, introduced by a former Afghan king, Nadir Shah Durrani, in 1849 for the border regions, ensures the good conduct of the tribes and imposes on them the obligation of allowing the safe passage of ordinary travellers and government officials through their tribal lands. The British strengthened this system when they came into the tribal areas after the boundary alignment with Afghanistan in 1893. Now this system operates all over FATA.

The distribution of the Khassadar jobs is the hereditary prerogative of the tribal chief. Members of the Khassadar force draw salaries from the tribal chief, who gets the money from the federal government in proportion to the area his tribe controls. The Khassadars must bring in their own weapons.

The Levies Force is another law-enforcement agency in FATA. Levies are essentially government jobs with pensions, and the policing of their respective area is their primary responsibility. The government provides salaries and service rifles to the Levies and they can be replaced by selection.

Origins of Security Forces Specific to FATA

The first militia in the Indian subcontinent was the Turi Militia, which was raised out of the Turi tribe of Kurram agency in 1892 by Captain C.M. Dallas. The Turi Militia eventually became Kurram Militia in later years. Subsequently many militias were raised in different areas and the local tribes enrolled as soldiers.[5] The main objective of raising local militias was to remove the army from these regions where maintaining control was becoming increasingly difficult for the British. They devised the militia and Scouts system which functioned with the help of local officials and elders to deal with the continuing resistance to the British presence while maintaining law and order and providing employment to local youth. These militias were also established to ensure effective central control over these unruly areas with their rugged, inhospitable terrain. The officers, however, were from the central armed forces, while the sepoys and the non-commissioned ranks were mainly drawn from local tribesmen. Some of the famous militia corps created by the British exist even today. This system formed the basis of the modern day Frontier Corps, Levies and Frontier Constabulary.

Social System

As FATA is predominantly Pashtoon, the social system is based on the Pashtoon code of conduct, which has a unique character based on long-standing Pashtoon tribal traditions or principles.

Nikat: One of the main pillars of the tribal system, nikat essentially denotes the resources that the government pays to a tribe. This payment depends on the area that is controlled by that particular tribe. These shares were originally determined by British rulers in the early 1900s and remained unchanged, making the current rates of nikats for certain tribes unrealistic or even absurd. Until 2005 even government development funds were distributed in proportion to benchmarks set nearly a century earlier.

Moajib: Subsidies and goodwill allowances payable to certain privileged people within tribes. Usually, heads of tribes receive the moajib but the sums involved are negligible as these rates have not been revised for many decades. Moajib guarantees the continuous allegiance of the tribe to the state. During the Mughal and Durrani period these subsidies were paid in lieu of right of way through various passes. The British followed this rule in every new area brought under their control.

Maliki/Lungi Allowance: Maliki allowance is hereditary, that is, transferable to the next generation. It can range from Rs 2000 (USD 25) to Rs 34,600 (USD 433) a year. Maliks are usually nominated by the President. Malik Faridullah, a former MP from the Shakai valley in South Waziristan, who was gunned down by unknown militants in June 2005 for alleged collaboration with the government, was the highest paid malik, with an annual government allowance of Rs 34,600. Second to him was General Jamaldar Khan of the Orakzai agency, who until his death had received Rs 34,000 (USD 425) a year. His son, former minister G.G. Jamal, now receives this money.

This allowance keeps the holders of this title on the right side of the political administration and in the loop regarding important decisions about their communities or their areas.

Next to the maliks are the lungi-holders, usually nominated by the governor. They can be called the second-tier tribal leadership, drawing small amounts, sometimes as low as five rupees. The maximum payment for a lungi-holder would not be more than a couple of thousand, and is handed over by the political agent. The latter terminates the lungi title upon the death of its holder, and can pass this on to any of the deceased's relatives he chooses.

Collective Tribal Responsibility

The principle of collective tribal territorial responsibility is enshrined in the customs and usages prevailing in the tribal areas. Under this system, even if a crime originates elsewhere, the section of the tribe on whose soil the crime is committed is held accountable and answerable to the government. Political agents use (and very often abuse) this system to impose heavy penalties on tribes for 'failing to guard government assets and installations in their areas'.

Khassadari/Protective Responsibility: The Khassadar or Levies forces ensure good conduct of the tribes for safe passage through their country and are thus known as 'protective tribal responsibility'.

Easement Rights: Under the Durand Agreement, the same tribes living on either side of the Pakistan–Afghanistan border are allowed free ingress into one another's areas. No immigration restrictions can be imposed on the long and porous border but it gives an added sensitivity to the border, because militants take cover of the easement rights by crossing the border using fake permits that show them to be members of the divided tribes.

At least 40,000 Afghans, Pakistanis and tribesmen cross the border daily from Torkham, some fifty kilometres west of Peshawar. Torkham is located in the Khyber agency, connecting with Afghanistan's Ningarhar province. The other important international border crossing is Chaman in Qilla Abdullah in the north-west of Balochistan, which connects it with Kandahar province in Afghanistan. The crossing at Chaman was in the news when Pakistani officials attempted to impose restrictions on the cross-border movement through a new biometrics system. The Afghans rejected it as did the tribes living across the Durand Line. In fact combatant groups and individuals have exploited the Easement

Rights Regulation to sneak in and out of the tribal areas to plan raids, for training or shelter from the time of the CIA–ISI-led anti-Soviet-Russian jihad in the 1980s.

Against the backdrop of the widespread resentment against the FCR, demands by tribesmen to have the FCR replaced or amended are growing. Over a decade ago, in January 1995, I attended several meetings that the then political agent of Khyber agency, Amjad Ali Khan, held with tribesmen from the agency at his office in Peshawar. The demand that resonated the most was the tribesmen's desire to be rid of the FCR. The PA tried to deflect the demands by playing on the conservatism of those present. 'Would you like to see the corrupt Pakistani police desecrate your homes, would you like them to intrude into your private homes the way they do all over Pakistan?'

The meetings were being held to counter Maulana Sufi Mohammad's Tehreek-e-Nifaze Shariate Mohammadi (TNSM) which at the time had galvanized tens of thousands of people across the Malakand division of NWFP. Their most disturbing demand revolved around Islamic sharia. Interestingly, however, the specific demand for sharia has not featured very high in tribal jirgas of FATA elders. In the vacuum caused by the absence of a legal justice system and the tribals' powerlessness to challenge decisions by the PA or his subordinates, non-state actors—the likes of Sufi Mohammad, Mangal Bagh Afridi and Baitullah Mehsud—could stir public emotion and exploit the yearning for justice for their own objectives.

The main reason for the popularity of successive Islamist movements in the FATA also stems from the draconian system of FCR. If the hundreds of conversations I have had with dozens of tribal friends and common people were any indicator, the search for a justice system and the craving for equal citizenship have come to be synonymous with sharia. Inaction by successive governments and the perennial state of conflict in which the FATA region has found itself since the early 1980s.

A grand tribal jirga held in Peshawar on 14 June 2007 representing various tribes drawn from all the seven agencies demanded a separate legislature for the FATA to enable the people to chalk out policies that are more in sync with their culture and traditions rather than an import from Islamabad.

Other demands made at the conclusion of the jirga asked for good governance and socio-economic justice, for instance, jobs in the FATA secretariat, the introduction of a system of local governance in FATA, the extension of Islamic financial assistance (the Zakat Act), setting up utility stores, the resolution of disputes on Pak-Afghan border through peaceful means, and the inclusion of tribal elders, intellectuals and parliamentarians in the proposed Pak-Afghan peace jirga that was held in August 2007 for the first time. Several such meetings organized by the government and political parties separately voiced more or less similar demands.

Perhaps because of this, Prime Minister Yousuf Gilani, in his maiden address to the nation in March 2008, announced the good news that the FCR would be abolished. While this pleased and surprised many, many others were shocked because Gilani offered no alternative to the FCR. Gilani's detractors, including several bureaucrats and maliks, believed that abolishing the FCR overnight might create a vacuum and result in chaos.

The announcement, however, never became a reality and the prime minister did not mention it again. Since then all that has happened is attempts by the federal law ministry to prepare draft proposals that amend and not repeal the FCR. The amendments are likely to give tribesmen a right to appeal against the decisions of the PA. The amendments might not do away with the collective responsibility clause but might restrict its scope. The government is finding it hard to completely replace the FCR with the normal laws of Pakistan in FATA because of stiff opposition from strong pressure groups like the civil bureaucracy and the maliks, who have lost political power, and the attendant privileges, to the militants since the launch of the war again terrorism in October 2001.

Appendix 2
Militant Leaders in FATA

TTP Leaders

Name	Father's name	Tribe	Village	Known facts
Baitullah Mehsud	Muhammad Haroon	Baromi Khail Mehsud	Dawa toyi Ladha, S. Waziristan	Held to be among the most dangerous in FATA; known to be a diabetic
Qari Hussain Mehsud	Muhammad Ilyas	Eshangi Mehsud	Kotkai Sarogha, S. Waziristan	Master of TTP suicide squad
Noor Said		Kakari	Khysorha Tarza, S. Waziristan	Leader of local Taliban
Mufti Niamatullah				Commander; affiliated with Baitullah Mehsud
Maulvi Shamim		Shamankhel	Langerkoot Laddha, S. Waziristan	Local commander; runs a madrassa
Hakeemullah Mehsud		Ashangi	Kotkai Sara Rogha	Responsible for TTP operations in Khyber, Mohmand and Orakzai agencies
Asmatullah Shaheen				Aide to Baitullah Mehsud

Name	Father's name	Tribe	Village	Known facts
Shah Faisal Barki			Saam in Kanigoram, S. Waziristan	
Mulla Asmatullah			Tank	A self-proclaimed Taliban leader
Khan Gul Bhittani		Bhittani	Bubbakhel, S. Waziristan	Notorious as criminal but calls himself a Taliban leader
Wali-ur-Rehman				A key deputy of Baitullah Mehsud

Non-TTP Leaders

Name	Father's name	Tribe	Village	Known facts
Mulla Nazir	Abdul Salam	Kakakhel Wazir	Zayri Noor Wana, S. Waziristan	Fought against Uzbek militants in areas near Wana
Khanan Wazir				Supported Mulla Nazir against Uzbeks; was killed by Uzbeks in June 2008
Haji Omar	Paiendai	Yargulkhel Ahmedzai Wazir	Kaloosha Barmal, S. Waziristan	Cousin and successor to Nek Mohammad; sided with Uzbek militants
Haji Sharif	Paiendai	Yargulkhel Ahmedzai Wazir	Kaloosha Barmal, S. Waziristan	Brother of Haji Omar; backed Mulla Nazir
Noorul Islam	Paiendai	Yargulkhel Ahmedzai Wazir	Kaloosha Barmal, S. Waziristan	Another brother of Haji Omar; supported Uzbek militants

Name	Father's name	Tribe	Village	Known facts
Zawal Khan		Zillikhel Wazir	Khanghi	A supporter of Uzbek militants
Maulvi Abdul Aziz		Yargulkhel Wazir	Ghwakha, S. Waziristan	A cousin of Haji Sharif
Maulvi Abbas		Malik Khel Wazir	Kaloosha, S. Waziristan	A supporter of Haji Sharif
Maulvi Javed Karmazkhel		Ahmedzai Wazir		Supported Uzbeks and local militants in March–April 2007
Mittha Khan				Fought alongside Mulla Nazir
Muhammad Wali alias Malang	Gul Nawaz	Gangi Khel Wazir	Sra Khawra Barmal, S. Waziristan	
Halee-mullah		Tojikhel Ahmedzai Wazir		A member of the Mulla Nazir-led shura
Ghulam Khan		Ahmedzai Wazir		Sided with Uzbek militants during clashes with locals

Militants in North Waziristan

Name	Father's name	Tribe	Village	Known facts
Maulana Sadiq Noor		Hamzoni Daur	Khati-Kelay, Miranshah	Believed to be housing a number of foreigners in his compound
Maulvi Abdul Khaliq		Daur	Miranshah city	Mulla in a mosque; fond of delivering speeches against Musharraf, Bush
Haji Gul Bahadur		Madakhel Wazir	Tati Madakhel Miranshah	Made alliance with close-to-govt Mulla Nazir to isolate Baitullah Mehsud

Name	Father's name	Tribe	Village	Known facts
Sangeen Khan Zadran		Jadran (Afghani)	Khost	
Maulvi Saifullah		Kabelkhel Wazir	Saifali Kabulkhel, Mirali	
Maulana Siddique Darpakhel			Darpakhel	Prominent militant leader
Haleem Khan				A militant who has links with Arabs, Uzbeks etc.; involved in target killing
Abu Okash/ Abu Kashif		Iraqi	Has influence in Mirali and Miranshah	Injured in aerial bombardment in 2007
Khalifa Sirajuddin Haqqani	Jalaluddin Haqqani	Afghani	Danda Darpakhel Miranshah	

Militants in Bajaur Agency

Name	Father's name	Village	Known facts
Maulvi Sufi Mohammad		Kumbar (Bajaur)/ Maidan (Dir)	Founder of defunct TNSM
Maulvi Faqir Mohammad		Chenagai Bala, Damadola	A TNSM leader
Maulana Fazlullah	Beladar	Imam Deri	Son-in-law of Maulvi Sufi Mohammad; deputy of Baitullah Mehsud in Malakand and Swat
Maulana Saifullah			Ameer (head) of TNSM in Malakand

Militants in Khyber Agency

Name	Father's name	Village	Known facts
Mufti Munir Shakir		Originally belongs to Kurram agency or Karak	Founder of Lashkar-e-Islam; arrested and sentenced to indefinite jail
Mangal Bagh Afridi			Successor to Mufti Munir Shakir to lead LI
Pir Saifurehman		Khyber agency	Founder of Ansarul Islam
Haji Naamdar		Influence is restricted to Bara Kamberkhel tribe in Khyber agency	Founded Amar bil Maroof wa Nahi Analmunkir, inspired by Mulla Omar; shot dead on 13 August 2008
Mehbubul Haq		Tirah valley	Successor to Pir Saifurehman; keeps a very low profile
Maulana Hazrat Nabi		Landikotal	Prayer leader; organized local Taliban
Farmanullah		Landikotal	Brother of Maulana Hazrat Nabi; spokesman of local Taliban

Militants in Mohmand Agency

Name	Father's name	Village	Known facts
Abdul Wali Raghib alias Umar Khalid	Haji Sahib	Kared, Lukro	Formerly a journalist; affiliated with Harkatul Mujahideen
Sangeen Khan Kandahari			Abducted 10 FC men, but later released them
Abu Nauman Sangari or Dr Assad Sangari			TTP strongman in Mohmand agency

Militants in Orakzai Agency

Name	Father's name	Village	Known facts
Hakeemullah Mehsud			One of Baitullah Mehsud's important commanders, operating in Khyber and Mohmand too
Maulana Mohammad Nabi Orakzai			Local TTP representative; also responsible for TTP affairs in Kurram agency
Islam Gul and Hassamuddin			Local Taliban operatives
Maulana Fazal Saeed			Local TTP operative in lower and central Kurram area

Appendix 3
Militant Organizations
in Pakistan

Organization	Founders/ Current heads	Outlook
Harkatul Mujahideen (HM)	Maulana Fazlurrehman Khalil Farooq Kashmiri	Deobandi Sunni school of thought; emerged as Harkatul Ansar in 1980s to fight the Soviet Union in Afghanistan; strongly supported Sipahe Sahaba move against Shiite community; moved to Kashmir in 1989
Jaish-e-Mohammad	Maulana Masood Azhar	Deobandi Sunni militant organization, a break-away from HM; launched in early 2000 with the goal of liberating Kashmir
Tehreekul Irfan	Maulana Abdullah Shah Mazhar	Successor to Jaish; launched after ban on militant organizations in January 2002
Lashkar-e-Taiba (LeT); renamed Jamatud Dawa (JuD) after ban in January 2002; JuD claims it has nothing to do with Lashkar any more	Hafiz Mohammad Saeed (ex-head and founder)	Salafi Sunni school of thought; draws spiritual inspiration from Saudi Arabia and was the armed wing of Pakistan-based religious organization Markaz-al-Daawatul Ershad; ideologically closer to Al Qaeda, and created in late 1980s in Afghanistan; it is one of the three largest and best-trained groups fighting in Kashmir against India

Organization	Founders/ Current heads	Outlook
Sipahe Sahaba Pakistan (SSP)	Haq Nawaz Jhangvi (founder) Maulana Azam Tariq (successor)	Rabidly anti-Shia outfit, founded in 1984; espoused the goal of restoration of Khilafat; countered by Shia organization Sipahe Mohammad
Lashkar-e- Jhangvi	Riaz Basra, killed in police encounter in 2002	Rabidly anti-Shia outfit, founded in late 1980s by Riaz Basra, who was also formerly associated with HM and SSP; he believed in using force to further Maulana Haq Nawaz Jhangvi's mission

Overview of FATA Militant Outfits

Organization	Founders/ Current heads	Outlook
Tehreek-e- Taliban Pakistan (TTP) South Waziristan	Baitullah Mehsud	Trans-agency outfit, wedded to anti-Americanism and determined to enforce sharia; also pursuing the goal of driving foreigners out of Afghanistan
Tehreek-e- Taliban Pakistan (TTP) Bajaur agency	Maulvi Faqir Muhammad; also deputy to Baitullah Mehsud	Enforcement of sharia; drew spiritual inspiration from Baitullah Mehsud
Tehreek-e- Taliban Pakistan (TTP) Orakzai, Khyber and Kurram agencies	Hakeemullah Mehsud, emerging successor- apparent to Baitullah Mehsud; responsible for three agencies bordering Peshawar	Enforcement of sharia; drew spiritual inspiration from Baitullah Mehsud
Tehreek-e- Taliban Pakistan (TTP) Swat	Maulvi Fazlullah, also deputy to Baitullah Mehsud	Enforcement of sharia; drew spiritual inspiration from Baitullah Mehsud

Organization	Founders/ Current heads	Outlook
Tehreek-e-Taliban Mohmand (TTM)	Omar Khalid, also deputy to Baitullah Mehsud	Wanted Mulla Omar-style of sharia justice through sharia court which would dispense justice according to the group's interpretation of Islamic law
Tehreek-e-Taliban Pakistan (TT) South Waziristan	Mulla Nazir	Formed tribal lashkar and mounted a vicious campaign against foreign militants, predominantly of Uzbek origins around Wana
Tehreek-e-Nifaze Shariate Mohammadi (TNSM)	Sufi Muhammad	Deobandi Sunni school of thought; its goal is enforcement of Islamic sharia and it is also opposed to the presence of foreign troops in Afghanistan
Lashkar-e-Islam	Mufti Munir Shakir (founder) Mangal Bagh Afridi (current head)	Deobandi Sunni school of thought, close to the Egyptian Ikhwanul Muslimoon and Jamaate Islami (India and Pakistan)
Ansarul Islam	Pir Saifurrehman (founder) Mehbubul Haq (successor)	Deobandi Sunni school of thought
Amar bil Maroof wa Nahi Analmunkir	Haji Naamdar (founder) Maulvi Gul Niaz	Deobandi Sunni school of thought; inspired by the Afghan Taliban supreme leader Mulla Omar, Naamdar espoused enforcement of Islamic sharia in Pakistan

Notes

Prologue

1. As told to the author in June 2004 during interviews with Mohammad Noor Wazir and several other Wana residents.
2. As told to the author in an interview with an ex-militiaman at Shakai, who eventually moved out of Waziristan in search of security and employment.

Chapter 1: Why Pakistan's Tribal Areas Fell to Al Qaeda

1. Cohen, Stephen P., *The Idea of Pakistan*, Brookings Institution Press, 2004.
2. Todd, Paul, and Jonathan Bloch, *Global Intelligence: The World's Secret Services Today*, Zed Books, 2003.

Chapter 2: Tribal Lands: Cauldron of Militancy

1. CRSS interviews with Waziristani tribesmen who occasionally shuttle between Peshawar and their hometowns.
2. Gul, Imtiaz, www.thefridaytimes.com, 9–15 September 2005.
3. Rana, Muhammad Amir, analysis in South Asianet, Pakistan Institute of Peace Studies, August 2006.
4. *Daily Times*, 26 January 2007.
5. Also see Tables of Militant Leaders in FATA and Militant Organization in Pakistan.

6. Rana, Muhammad Amir, *Daily Times*, 12 April 2003.
7. *Daily Times*, 4 August 2007.
8. CRSS interviews with locals in Wana.
9. CRSS interviews during the FATA survey, April/May 2008.
10. Gul, Imtiaz, *The Unholy Nexus: Pak-Afghan Relations under the Taliban*, Vanguard Books, 2002.
11. The profiles of the seven agencies are based on Hassan Abbas, 'Profiles of Pakistan's Seven Tribal Agencies', *Global Terrorism Analysis*, Volume 4, Issue 20, October 2006.

Chapter 3: Al Qaeda's Extensions in FATA: South and North Waziristan

1. Rana, M. Amir, *A to Z of Jihadi Organizations in Pakistan*, Mashal Books, 2004, p. 190.
2. Also see Taliban in Orakzai Agency.
3. Interview with a FATA journalist who met Baitullah Mehsud on 24 May 2008.
4. Personal interviews at Peshawar. For security reasons, the journalist cannot be identified.
5. Personal interview at Peshawar.
6. Author's interview at Peshawar, 28 July 2008.
7. *Nation*, 26 July 2008.
8. Press briefing near Wana, South Waziristan, 1 April 2007.
9. CRSS interview at Rawalpindi, 10 April 2008.
10. Speech at National University of Defence, 12 April 2007.
11. CRSS interviews.
12. *Friday Times*, April 2007.
13. *Dawn*, 29 March 2007.
14. *Dawn*, 12 April 2007.
15. CRSS interviews.
16. CRSS interviews.
17. Author's interview at Peshawar, 27 July 2008.
18. Voice of America, Urdu and Pashto broadcasts, 6 August 2008.
19. NNI news agency, 22 July 2007.
20. *Dawn*, 7 May 2007.
21. *New York Times*, 17 June 2008.

Chapter 4: Khyber and Bajaur Agencies

1. *Pulse*, 23 November 2007.
2. Author's interviews with intelligence and security officials at Torkham, 3 May 2008.
3. Associated Press, 21 May 2008.
4. CRSS interview at Hayatabad Market, Peshawar, May 2008.
5. *Friday Times*, 31 March 2006.
6. Sources in Bara, and *Daily Times*, 20 May 2007.
7. Author's interviews with senior intelligence officials responsible for FATA, May 2008.
8. Interviews with officials and locals in Peshawar.
9. *Daily Times*, 4 May 2008.
10. *News*, 3 May 2008.
11. I. Kukikhel, a resident of Jamrud in interview for CRSS.
12. *Daily Times*, 4 May 2008.
13. Author's article in the weekly *Pulse*, 1 August 2008.
14. Interview at Peshawar, 20 July 2008.
15. Ahmed, Khaled, www.thefridaytimes.com.
16. *Daily Times*, 4 May 2008.
17. Media/Online news agency reports, 24 May 2008.
18. *Dawn*, 7 May 2007.
19. NNI news agency, 5 May 2008.
20. CRSS interview.
21. *Daily Times*, 29 July 2008.
22. *Daily Times*, 29 July 2008.
23. Associated Press, 14 January 2006.
24. *New York Times*, 15 January 2006.
25. Gul, Imtiaz/Jason Burke, *Observer*, 15 January 2006.
26. ABC-News, 30 October 2006.
27. Gul, Imtiaz, *Telegraph*, 9 November 2006.
28. *Washington Post*, 12 November 2006.

Chapter 5: Mohmand, Kurram, Orakzai Agencies and Swat

1. CRSS interview with intelligence official, Peshawar.
2. CRSS interviews in Ghalanai.

3. *News*, 27 May 2008.
4. *News*, 27 May 2008.
5. Geo TV, 27 May 2008.
6. Interviews/views obtained through Ghalanai based contacts, 24/25 July 2008.
7. Telephone interview on 29 July.
8. *Daily Times*, 24 July 2008.
9. Discussion took place during a meeting at Peshawar, 20 July.
10. *Aaj*, 27 July 2008.
11. CRSS source in Ghalanai, 3 August 2008.
12. CRSS report from Ghalanai.
13. *Dawn*, *Daily Times*, 27 May 2008.
14. Compiled from various sources including *Aaj*.
15. Author's interview at Rawalpindi, 25 July 2008.
16. Peshawar newspapers, APP reports, 26/27 July 2008.
17. BBC Urdu broadcast, 27 July 2008.
18. *News*, 10 May, Online news agency, 9 May 2008.
19. CRSS source interview.
20. Gul, Imtiaz, *Pulse*, 1 November 2007.
21. *Daily Times*, 29 July 2008.
22. Author's meeting with the official at Peshawar, December 2006.
23. *News*, 28 July 2008.
24. Online news agency, 5 August 2008.
25. Based on CRSS discussions with Swat residents.

Chapter 6: Al Qaeda and Foreign Militants in FATA: Uzbeks and Arabs

1. *News*, 21 July 2008.
2. *News*, 21 July 2008.
3. *News*, 5 June 2008. The CRSS has also secured the telephone conversation of Mudassir where he admits to having killed Khanan.
4. *News*, 5 June 2008.
5. *New York Times*, 30 April 2008.
6. Gul, Imtiaz: *The Unholy Nexus: Pak-Afghan Relations under the Taliban*, Vanguard Books, 2002; and Mir, Amir, *The True Face of Jehadis: Inside Pakistan's Network of Terror*, Roli Books, 2006.
7. Jane's Intelligence Report, June 2001.

8. Jane's Intelligence Report, October 1999.
9. Reuters, 31 July 2008.
10. *Daily Times*, 19 July 2008.

Chapter 7: Al Qaeda Brings Suicide Bombings to Pakistan

1. *News*, 1 June 2008.
2. *Guardian*, 20 May 2008.
3. *Dawn*, 20 May 2008.
4. CBSNews.com, 20 May 2008.
5. *Ilhaq, Aaj*, 4 November 2008.
6. Geo TV, 22 July 2008.
7. NBC News Online, 28 March 2007.
8. NBC News Online, 28 March 2007.
9. http://www.longwarjournal.org report on 13 November 2006.
10. Based on the author's interview with his friend from Miranshah who had interviewed the would-be suicide bomber in Peshawar in February 2008.
11. Khaled Ahmed in his review of the book *Dying to Kill: The Allure of Suicide Terror* by Mia Bloom, Columbia University Press, 2007.
12. Author's interview at Dera Ismail Khan, December 2007.
13. Rahimullah Yusufzai in *News*, 5 August 2007.
14. Rahimullah Yusufzai in *News*, 5 August 2007.
15. *Washington Times*, 25 July 2008.

Chaper 9: Profiles of Militants

1. Masood, Talat, *Daily Times*, 9 May 2008.
2. From interviews with a group of journalists who met Mehsud at Kotkai, 24 May 2008.
3. NNI news agency, BBC Online, Samaa TV, 24 May 2008.
4. *Time*, 28 April 2008.
5. Online news agency, May 2008.
6. *Daily Times*, May 2008.
7. Accounts of members of the journalists' group that met Mehsud and his colleagues in May 2008.
8. *News*, 25 August 2007.
9. NNI news agency, 17 July 2007.

10. *Daily Times*, 4 May 2008.
11. Urdu daily *Jang*, 19 July 2007.
12. Author's meetings with the officials in Peshawar.
13. *Daily Times*, 3 May 2008.
14. *Daily Times*, 3 May 2008.
15. *Daily Times*, 3 May 2008.
16. Interview with Mohmand journalist Mukarran Khan, June 2008.
17. *Daily Times*, 24 July 2008.
18. *News*, 6 June 2008.

Chapter 10: The ISI Factor

1. *New York Times*, 30 July 2008.
2. Interview with ABC-News, 1 August 2008.
3. Press release ISPR, 28 July 2008.
4. *New York Times*, 30 July 2008.
5. Interviews with Pakistan army officials in Rawalpindi, January 2008.
6. *Los Angeles Times*, 30 July 2008.
7. *New York Times*, 1 August 2008.
8. Author's interview at Rawalpindi, 1 August 2008.
9. *News*, 5 August 2008.
10. Author's meeting with Azizuddin in Kabul, June 2008.
11. Author's interview with ISPR head General Athar Abbas.
12. The CRSS survey of seven tribal agencies was based on personal interviews, in which 950 people of different ages were asked about their views on Taliban, sharia, education and on the presence of foreigners.
13. News agency AFP, 16 June.
14. CRSS interview, 16 June 2008.
15. STRATFOR, 22 April 2007.
16. Council on Foreign Relations, 10 October 2006.
17. NBC interview in late September 2006.
18. *India Express*, 16 September 2003.
19. Todd, Paul and Jonathan Bloch, *Global Intelligence: The Worlds Secret Services Today*, Zed Books, 2003.
20. *New York Times*, 21 July 2008.
21. Amir, Mohammad, *A to Z of Jihadi Organizations in Pakistan*, Mashal Books, 2004.

22. CRSS interview at Peshawar, 13 June 2008.
23. CRSS interview, May 2008.
24. *News*, 29 July 2008.
25. Gul, Imtiaz, *The Unholy Nexus: Pak-Afghan Relations under the Taliban*, Vanguard Books, 2002.
26. Human Rights Watch annual report, 2002.
27. Author's interviews in Kabul, Kandahar and Islamabad with diplomats who served in Afghanistan between 1995 and 2002.
28. Author's interviews with a militant at Muzaffarabad, capital of Pakistani Kashmir.
29. Interview with a Kashmiri militant leader, who quoted his officer friend as narrating this incident, Islamabad, June 2003.
30. Bruce Riedel Paper on Kargil, April 2000.
31. Author's interviews with Kashmiri leaders in Muzaffarabad, Rawalpindi and Islamabad in 2002/2003.
32. Tim McGirk in *Time*, 6 May 2002, Vol. 159, No. 17.
33. Author's interview in Islamabad, January 2004.
34. DIA Assessment, 24 September 1999.
35. *Friday Times*, 26 January 2001.
36. Author's interview with Ansar Abassi at Islamabad, 1 August 2008.
37. *Friday Times*, 1 August 2008.

Chapter 11: Who Funds Militancy in FATA?

1. Author's interview with Shams Mohmand and a few others in Peshawar after their visit to Mehsud.
2. Author's interview with a Mehsud friend at Dera Ismail Khan, June 2008.
3. General Kayani's meeting with a select group of journalists at his residence in Rawalpindi, 12 July 2008.
4. Briefing at the General Headquarters, November 2007.
5. Khattak, Iqbal, *Daily Times*, 30 May 2008.
6. US government official website, March 2008.
7. Ghani's interview with Voice of America, 2 August 2008.
8. *Dawn*, 31 May 2008.
9. *Dawn*, 31 May 2008.
10. Author's interview at Peshawar, December 2007.
11. Author's interview at Islamabad, July 2008.

12. Author's interview at Islamabad, 7 August 2008.
13. Author's interview at Kabul, April 2005.
14. Peshawar meeting after the visit, early June 2008.
15. 31 July 2008.
16. Author's interviews at Peshawar between February and July 2008.
17. *News*, 31 May 2008.
18. Author's interview with a senior FATA secretariat official at Peshawar, 5 August 2008.

Appendix 1
FATA: The Background

1. FATA Secretariat documents.
2. FATA Development Strategy, FATA secretariat.
3. Khalid, Aziz, 'Reasons of Failure', article for the Regional Institute of Policy Research, Peshawar, 2006.
4. Khalid, Aziz, 'Tribal Areas of Pakistan, Challenges and Responses', paper for the Regional Institute of Policy Research, Peshwar, September 2005.
5. Shah, S. Iftikhar Hussain, *Some Major Pukhtoon Tribes along the Pak-Afghan Border*, Areas Study Centre, 2000.
   (NOTE: Much of the information in this Appendix also comes from official briefs prepared for successive governors and presidents.)

Acknowledgements

Much of the content used in the book comes from my own experience—from first-hand information on the tribal areas I gathered through scores of interviews during trips that I made to the area, as well as several visits to Afghanistan made since 1988. I have also drawn on over three hundred articles that I wrote for the Pakistani weekly *Friday Times*, for the Peshawar daily the *Frontier Post* and the national daily the *News* on the subject. I have used material from my book *The Unholy Nexus: Pak-Afghan Relations under the Taliban* (Vanguard Books, 2002) and several papers on the subject. My work between 1988 and 2006 for the German Press Agency dpa and for Deutsche Welle Radio, Germany also helped me tremendously in allowing me to make friends and acquaintances in the tribal areas on both sides of the Durand Line as well as in Pakistan, all of whom were valuable sources of information.

I must acknowledge that for reference and research while compiling this book, I drew on the following published works:

* *Some Major Pukhtoon Tribes along the Pak-Afghan Border*, S. Iftikhar Hussain, Areas Study Centre, Peshawar, 2000.
* *The True Face of Jehadis: Inside Pakistan's Network of Terror*, Amir Mir, Roli Books, Lahore, 2006.
* *A to Z of Jihadi Organizations in Pakistan*, Muhammad Amir Rana, Mashal Books, Lahore, 2004.
* *Tribal Areas of Pakistan: Challenges and Responses*, edited by Pervaiz Iqbal Cheema, Islamabad Policy Research Institute, Islamabad, 2005.

Finally, a survey the Centre for Research and Security Studies (CRSS), Islamabad conducted in all the seven tribal agencies of FATA also provided extremely valuable information and insights about the area and its people. The CRSS, a think tank based in Islamabad, has permitted me to use the results of the FATA survey in this book.

I would like to thank my publishers, Penguin Books India, especially Jaishree Ram Mohan and Ranjana Sengupta.

My heartiest thanks go to a number of very good friends—journalists, retired and serving army officers and intelligence officials—who have been very helpful in this compilation, particularly those who provided valuable input on the subject but who would not like to be named for obvious reasons.

I am also indebted to my friends Dr Farrukh Saleem and Mubashir Akram, and especially to Aarish Khan, whose critical review provided extremely useful help in correcting and fine-tuning the contents of the book.

My special thanks to Alamgir Bhittani, Ehsanullah, Noor Mohammad Wazir, Shaukat Khattak and Sailab Mehsud who served as a compass on the basics of FATA and kept correcting me where I erred.

I must also thank Hafeez Khan, whose meticulously collected FATA Press Review kept the contents of the book as updated as possible.

I also owe a debt of gratitude to Mohammad Anwar Durrani, who on behalf of the CRSS risked his life and toured some of the most risky areas inside FATA and helped to conduct the survey for the centre.

Thanks also go to all friends within the Inter-Services Public Relations (ISPR), the Pakistani armed forces' media wing, who always extended support and enabled me to visit some of the remotest and embattled areas inside FATA ever since I began reporting from out of Islamabad in 1988.

I also owe thanks to the following:

Khalid Aziz, ex-Chief Secretary (North West Frontier Province); Shamim Shahid, Peshawar; Ehsanullah Dawar, Mirali; Manzoor Khan Wazir, Wana; Mehfoozullah, Miranshah; Noor Mohammad

Wazir; Khan Zaman Dawar; Malik Azhar Khan, Wana; Noor Ahmed Wazir, Wana; Shahjehan Khan, Swat; Gen. (Rtd) Ali Mohammad Jan Orakzai (ex-Governor, North West Frontier Province) and Owais Ghani (Governor, North West Frontier Province).

Index

Abassi, Ansar, 229
Abbas, Brigadier Ali, 136, 176
Abbas, Major General Athar, 86, 108, 203, 206, 250
Abbas, Maulvi, 1, 3, 10, 181–82
abductions and kidnappings for ransom, 45, 46, 71, 99, 100, 178, 233, 239–40, 251
Abdullah, Malik Inayat, 5
Adil, Peer, 58
Afghanistan, 37–38, 40, 45, 58–59, 62, 67, 84, 91, 97, 100, 113, 116, 126, 130, 133, 135, 139, 167, 186–87, 199, 203, 211, 218, 220, 222–23, 235–38, 259, 262; foreign occupation, 191; role of ISI, 23, 25, 31, 227; role of India, 243; infiltration to and from, 28, 29; intelligence, 63, 234; jihad. *See* jihad; mujahideen. *See* mujahideen; Pakistan army in, 26–27, 32, 36; Soviet invasion, 19–21, 74, 122, 156, 200;— pullout, 25, 42, 209, 215; stipend to ethnic tribal elders, 5; suicide bombings, 144, 148;

Sunni sectarian militants, 105; Taliban. *See* Taliban; Trade and Development Cell (ATDC), 219; Transit Trade Agreement, 19; US-led coalition forces, 18, 25, 26, 28, 30–31, 39, 43, 44, 52, 53, 74–75, 122, 124–25, 129, 145, 152, 177, 188, 195, 201–02, 206, 209–10, 239, 254, 261. *See also* NATO; US hands-off policy, 200; war, 28, 50, 215
Afridi tribes, Afridis, 47, 73, 255
Afridi, Hameedullah Jan, 239, 252
Afridi, Mangal Bagh, 52, 72, 73, 77, 80, 189–90, 263
Ahmad, Abu (alias Amir Butt), 127
Ahmed, Mulla Nazir, 42–43, 50, 52, 55–58, 64–66, 125, 128, 129, 132, 178–79, 180, 181, 182, 183, 185, 249–50; Uzbek fallout, 58–63
Ahmadzai Wazir tribe, 9, 10, 12, 13, 26, 45, 50, 56, 127, 178–80, 181, 182, 183, 255
Ahmed, General Mahmood, 227
Ahmed, Khaled, 89, 148